MUDDYING THE WATERS

DISSIDENT FEMINISMS
Piya Chatterjee, Editor

*A list of books in the series appears
at the end of this book.*

MUDDYING THE WATERS

COAUTHORING FEMINISMS ACROSS SCHOLARSHIP AND ACTIVISM

RICHA NAGAR

University of Illinois Press
Urbana, Chicago, and Springfield

This book builds on coauthored work in English and
Hindi with "Farah Ali," Sangtin Writers, members of
Sangtin Kisaan Mazdoor Sangathan, Susan Geiger,
and Tarun Kumar

Library of Congress Cataloging-in-Publication Data
Nagar, Richa.
Muddying the waters: coauthoring feminisms across
scholarship and activism / Richa Nagar. pages cm.
— (Dissident feminisms)
Includes bibliographical references and index. ISBN
978-0-252-03879-2 (hardback)
ISBN 978-0-252-08035-7 (paper)
ISBN 978-0-252-09675-4 (ebook)
1. Women's studies. 2. Feminist theory.
3. Feminism. I. Title.
HQ1180.N34   2014
305.4201—dc23   2014014563

To Baba, Maa, and Medha

Contents

Acknowledgments

This book emerged from a decision to not translate certain stories about struggles of sangtins that I felt I was expected to deliver in translation. The process of enacting that resistance has become as heavy—and light—as life itself. Heavy by its indebtedness to every person and every encounter that has helped to shape what I write or share here. And light in that it assumes the inevitability of all the gaps and mistakes that make life; errors that one can merely hope to identify but never aspire to "fix."

Muddying the Waters is about dreams and labor that are shaped by relationships and encounters, and that demand faith in endless and seemingly impossible border crossings. It is about the *zubaans* or tongues that one inherits or embraces as well as those to which one's access is foreclosed, and about that which can or cannot be expressed in available languages. Above all, this book is about sustaining journeys that require hope when hope seems unattainable. The work of sustaining such journeys is itself an intense "coauthorship," albeit one that, by its very nature, makes it impossible to recognize all of one's coauthors. *Muddying the Waters*, too, is enabled by the labor, insights, and sacrifices of countless people whose journeys have intersected with my own—sometimes deliberately and sometimes by sheer accident. In acknowledging some of those people by name here, I am surely missing the names of many others without whom this book would not exist in its current form. I hope that my unnamed acquaintances, friends, critics, and coauthors will forgive me for my failure to name them.

The journeys that have informed and created this book were often undertaken with the help of the institutional and financial support I have received while at the University of Minnesota, first as a graduate student between 1989 and 1995 and subsequently as a faculty member since 1997. Parts of this book have emerged from my doctoral research in Dar es Salaam between 1991 and 1995. Funding for this work included a fellowship from the MacArthur Program (1989–95), a Davis Fellowship from the Department of Geography (1992–93), and a graduate school fellowship (1993–94), all at the University of Minnesota, as well as a grant from the National Science Foundation (SES-9205409). Support from the University of Minnesota that has helped to advance and sustain my work as a faculty member includes research funds, course releases, and a Scholar of the College Award (2008–11) granted by the College of Liberal Arts and support in the form of a McKnight Land-Grant Professorship (2000–2002), a McKnight Presidential Fellowship (2002–5), two grants-in-aid (1998, 2003), two sabbatical supplements (2003–4, 2013–14), and a single-semester leave. I have also benefitted from residential fellowships that allowed me to spend the academic year 2005–6 at the Center for Advanced Study in the Behavioral Sciences (CASBS) at Stanford University and parts of the academic year 2011–12 at the Jawaharlal Nehru Institute for Advanced Study (JNIAS) in New Delhi. A Mellon Faculty Exchange award from the Interdisciplinary Center for the Study of Global Change (ICGC) at Minnesota and the University of the Western Cape (South Africa) allowed me to conclude this project at the UWC Centre for Humanities Research in 2013. I thank James Parente for his support of my work during his time as associate dean for faculty and dean of the College of Liberal Arts (CLA) at the University of Minnesota. I am indebted to Raymond (Bud) Duvall for the many ways in which he has engaged and enabled my work over the years in his multiple roles as a teacher, colleague, critic, reader, and interim dean of CLA at Minnesota.

Susan Geiger's scholarship, and her passion for the places she made a commitment to, profoundly influenced the research I undertook in Tanzania and my approach to academia. Although it has been two decades since I was in Dar es Salaam, Fatma Alloo has never given up on me. Her friendship enriched my time in Dar and helped to shape several pieces of my research. I remain grateful to Muhsin Alidina, "Francis Fernandes," Jasu Damji, Parin Jaffer, Sujata Jaffer, Razia Janmohammed, Julie Mohammed, Damji Rathod, Sarla Rathod, Abdul Sheriff, Issa Shivji, Razia Tejani, and Nizar Visram for sharing valuable insights with me during my fieldwork in Dar es Salaam between 1991 and 1993.

The unflinching intellectual support and generosity of many scholars, colleagues, and thinkers at various critical junctures have proved essential for the growth of my own vision and scholarship, and for the arguments I make here. Lila Abu-Lughod, Ruth Fincher, Louise Fortmann, Jim Glassman, Gillian Hart, Sangeeta Kamat, Cindi Katz, Helga Leitner, Chandra Talpade Mohanty, Linda Peake, Geraldine Pratt, Laura Pulido, Abdi Samatar, Naomi Scheman, Eric Sheppard, and Shruti Tambe have been sources of intellectual inspiration and strength. The interest and encouragement of Jacqui Alexander, Ayşe Gül

Altınay, Nebahat Akkoç, Ron Aminzade, Amrita Basu, Aksu Bora, Urvashi Butalia, Piya Chatterjee, Anil Chaudhari, Arundhati Dhuru, Dwijendra Nath Guru, Krishna Kumar, Ashok Maheshwari, Biju Mathew, M J Maynes, Alok Mehta, Kalyani Menon-Sen, Sudha Nagavarappu, Sophie Oldfield, Philip Porter, Rachel Silvey, Shankar Singh, Ashwini Tambe, Ganesh Visputay, and Joel Wainwright has invigorated my alliance work and writing with Sangtin Kisaan Mazdoor Sangathan (SKMS).

This work also has been enlivened by the critical and creative engagement of G. Arunima, Ebru Nihan Celkan, David Edmunds, Alondra Espejel, Iman Ghazalla, Patricia Hayes, Dorothy Hoffman, Salma Ismail, Premesh Lalu, Maggi Wai Han Leung, Anu Mandavilli, Eli Meyerhoff, Saraswati Raju, Ciraj Rassool, Sharmila Rege, Alvaro Reyes, Martina Rieker, Mallarika Sinha Roy, Anagha Tambe, Mary Thomas, Ilknur Ustun, Ronald Wesso, and Alison Wylie. Shukriya, also, to members of Aalochana in Pune; Ayizi Kitap and Insan Hakları Ortak Platformu (IHOP) in Ankara; the KAMER women throughout Turkey; the Church Land Programme in Pietermaritzburg; the Mazdoor Kisaan Shakti Sangathan in Devdoongri; and the Pangea World Theater and the (short-lived) Parakh Theater group in Minneapolis.

In my home department of Gender, Women, and Sexuality Studies at Minnesota, I have been enriched by many lively conversations with Jigna Desai. Jigna's insightful engagement with several translated segments of *Ek Aur Neemsaar* in 2010–11 proved crucial for the ways in which I have come to share SKMS's stories in this book. Zenzele Isoke, Naomi Scheman, Edén Torres, and Jacquelyn Zita have engaged my work and energized me with their own committed and inspired labor in multiple sites of knowledge making. Amy Kaminsky, Regina Kunzel, Susan Craddock, and Jigna Desai have also extended valuable support in their role as previous and current department chairs.

Comments from Mazhar Al-Zo'by, Koni Benson, Antonádia Borges, Sharad Chari, Patricia Connolly, Diane Detournay, Aniruddha Dutta, Vinay Gidwani, Ketaki Jaywant, Diyah Larasati, Desiree Lewis, Maria Mendez Gutierrez, Himadeep Muppidi, Sophie Oldfield, Quynh Pham, Elaine Salo, Naomi Scheman, Sofia Shank, Ajay Skaria, and Marion Werner have allowed me to refine several thoughts and arguments that I present in this book. An "Authors Meet Critics" session on *Playing with Fire* organized by Geraldine Pratt and sponsored by *Social and Cultural Geography* at the 2007 Association of American Geographers meetings proved pivotal for the writing that Richa Singh, Surbala, and I undertook with one another, and with saathis of SKMS. I acknowledge the generative influence of the panelists at that session: Sharad Chari, Gillian Hart, Rupal Oza, Geraldine Pratt, Matt Sparke, and Anant Maringanti.

Shukriya to Katyayani for allowing me to include and translate her poem, "Samajh"; to Mukesh Bhargava for permitting me to include and translate part of his poem, "Global Dunia"; and to Raza Mir for translating my poem, "Dar es Salaam ke Naam." I thank Özlem Aslan, Nadia Hassan, Omme Rahemtullah-Salma, Nishant Upadhyay, and Begüm Uzun for a stimulating interview that they carried out with me in Toronto in February 2011 for the Turkish online journal, *Kültür ve Siyasette Feminist Yaklaşımlar*. This conversation triggered thoughts that subsequently crystallized into some of the arguments presented here. Students in my Transnational Feminist Theories and Feminist Theory and Methods courses in fall 2012 became the first readers for what I have come to share in *Muddying the Waters*. Without their generosity and imagination, I may not have been able to become "radically vulnerable" in the ways that I have.

Elakshi Kumar became involved in this book project in the last months of its making and left an indelible imprint on its ultimate form. In addition to providing incisive comments on the manuscript and making brilliant suggestions on how to "assemble" the journeys and encounters described in the book, he revised translations of two of my poems from Hindi into English and helped steer us toward a final book title. Through all of this, Elakshi instilled a new collaborative creativity in this work, for which I remain grateful. I also appreciate the valuable partnership of my copyeditor, Deborah Oliver, whose queries and suggestions allowed me to undertake revisions that have improved the book.

Piya Chatterjee and Larin McLaughlin have been critical fellow travelers throughout the making of *Muddying the Waters*. They have allowed me to imagine freely, and they have been there to work through every idea that raised a question mark or seemed "impractical." I am indebted to Piya for allowing me to integrate into chapter 1 the letters that I wrote to her as part of our exchange following the 2010 National Women's Studies Association Meetings in Denver. And I thank Larin for never letting rules become a barrier in attempting new border crossings.

The intense back-and-forths between many worlds on an almost daily basis bring their share of both joys and challenges. In many difficult and happy moments, Subir Banerjee, Margalit Chu, Divya Karan, Helga Leitner, Sophie Oldfield, Thitiya Phaobtong, Abdi Samatar, Simona Sawhney, Eric Sheppard, Ajay Skaria, T Steele, Amanda Lock Swarr, and Shiney Varghese have provided political camaraderie, companionship, and a home and family.

My debt to the Sangtin Writers—Reshma Ansari, Anupamlata, Vibha Bajpayee, Ramsheela, Richa Singh, Shashi Vaishya, Shashibala, and Surbala—to Amma (Shiv Kumari Singh), and to saathis of SKMS cannot be expressed in words. In particular, Anil, Banwari, Bitoli, Jagannath, Jamuna, Kailasha Amma, Kamala, Kusuma, Manohar, Meena, Mukesh Bhargava, Prakash, Radhapyari, Rajendra, Ram Kishore, Rambeti, Reena, Roshanlal, Saraswati Amma, Sarvesh, Shammu, Sri Kishan, Suneeta, Surendra, Tama, and Ved Prakash have been *hamsafars* and teachers. Together, we have learned and revised our definitions of hopes and mistakes, of success and failure, and of what makes life meaning-ful. These lessons have been particularly poignant in light of the tragic murder of Maya, whose spirit will always remain alive among us, reminding us of the long-term evolution of solidarities and struggles, and of the terrible violence that some are subjected to as a price for dreaming and living differently.

I could not have sustained the journeys across worlds without the undy-ing inspiration and energy of Sharad-Purnima, my Babuji and Maa. Babuji's boundless creativity, courage, and intellectual generosity supported by Maa's tireless enthusiasm and extremely hard labor has nourished the visions that have originated not only in Lucknow, but also in Sitapur, Mumbai, Dar es Salaam, and Minneapolis–St. Paul. Babuji pushed me to learn the Gujarati alphabet in 1979 and to begin typing in Devnagari in 2002, skills that have forever changed the meanings and possibilities of border crossings for me. Deeksha Nagar is always there to help me in every imaginable way, to fill the gaps in my memory, and to point out unexplored openings in our shared and unshared paths. The interbraided autobiographical writing in Hindi and English that she and I em-barked on in 2007 for a project that we tentatively called "Baa, Baba, Munni" has significantly informed the first chapter of *Muddying the Waters*. I thank Eric Baker for always reminding me how impoverished scholarship would be without dedicated librarians. And I am grateful to Narendra Kumar Verma, Rinki Awasthi, and Kamal Bajpayee for ensuring that the geographical distances between Lucknow, Sitapur, and Minneapolis–Saint Paul never became hurdles in multilingual creative production. Richa Singh, my *namarashi*, has been a *sakhi* and a *setu*, enabling some of the most difficult reflections and translations that I have attempted through our collective work in SKMS.

Without Sanchit Baba, David Faust, Tarun Kumar, and Medha Faust-Nagar, I would have not learned to grapple with the possibilities and contradictions of love, vulnerability, and border crossings in ways that I have. Baba's death in 1996 has not changed the countless ways in which he lives inside me every day. David has been a saathi in some of my most difficult and rewarding journeys over the last twenty-five years. He has been my honest critic and my most reliable reader, and co-parenting with him—including across oceans and time zones—has helped me grow more in life than anything else. In the last ten years, Tarun has pushed me to explore the implications of inserting one's body in whatever one creates; his eye has allowed me to see life's complexities and colors from angles that I had not previously known. Last but not least, Medha's love and poetry, and her wisdom and sacrifices, help me find words when none seem to be available.

. . .

The ideas that became the chapters of this book have been presented since 2007 at a number of forums in various stages of their evolution, and were enriched by the conversations that they sparked. These venues include the Centre for Humanities Research and the Department of Geography at the University of the Western Cape, Cape Town; the Centre for Indian Studies in Africa at the University of Witwatersrand, Johannesburg; the Department of Gender Studies at Indiana University, Bloomington; the Humanities Institute at the State University of New York, Buffalo; the Department of Geography at the University of Wisconsin, Madison; the Gender and Women's Studies Program at the University of Illinois, Chicago; the Department of Geography at the University of Arizona, Tucson; the Jan Monk Gender, Place, and Culture lecture at the 2012 Annual Meetings of the Association of American Geographers; the Gender Forum and the President's Annual Book Event at the Sabancı University, Istanbul; a lecture at the University of Ankara hosted by Ayizi Kitap and IHOP; the Departments of Geography and Gender, Women, and Sexuality Studies at the University of Minnesota, Twin Cities; the Departments of Geography, Women's Studies, and South Asian Studies and the Simpson Center for the Humanities at the University of Washington, Seattle; the Women's Studies Programme and the Jawaharlal Nehru Institute for Advanced Study at the Jawaharlal Nehru University, New Delhi; University College at Utrecht University; the Department of Geography at the University of Kentucky, Lexington; the Department of Geography at the University of North Carolina, Chapel Hill; the Savitribai Phule Women's Studies Centre and the Department of Sociology at the University of Pune; the Department of Development Studies, Geography, and Planning, and the Women and Gender Studies Institute at the University of Toronto; the Department of Geography at the University of Cambridge; the Ethnographies of Activism Conference at the London School of Economics and Political Science; the Women's and Gender Studies Department at Syracuse University; the Department of Women's Studies at the Chinese University of Hong Kong; the Crossing Borders Conference at the University of Iowa; the 2007 Atwood Lecture at Clark University; the Departments of Geography, Asian American Studies, and South Asian Studies at the University of California, Berkeley; the Departments of Women's Studies and Geography at the Ohio State University; and the African Gender Institute at the University of Cape Town.

Each chapter of *Muddying the Waters* draws, in varying measures, on previously published work in English and Hindi. These are listed below.

Introducing *Muddying the Waters*:
Richa Nagar and Richa Singh (with Surbala Vaish and Reena Pande), *Ek Aur Neemsaar: Sangtin Atmamanthan aur Andolan* (New Delhi: Rajkamal Prakashan, 2012).

Sangtin Writers (Reena, Richa Nagar, Richa Singh, Surbala), "Solidarity, Self-critique, and Survival: Sangtin's Struggles with Fieldwork," in *The Global and the Intimate: Feminism in Our Time*, edited by Geraldine Pratt and Victoria Rosner, 289–304 (New York: Columbia University Press, 2011).

Chapter 1:
Richa Nagar and Tarun Kumar, "Theater of Hopes," in "Fictional Worlds: A Review Section Symposium on the Influences of the Imagined," edited by Mary Thomas and Christian Abrahamsson, special issue, *Environment and Planning D: Society and Space* 20, no. 3 (2011): 54–55.

Richa Nagar and Richa Singh, "Churnings of a Movement: Sangtins' Diary," *South Asian Popular Culture* 8, no. 1 (2010): 17–30.

Richa Nagar, "Local and Global," in *Approaches to Human Geography*, edited by Stuart Aitken and Gill Valentine, 211–17 (Thousand Oaks, Calif.: Sage, 2006).

Richa Nagar, "Dar es Salaam ke Naam" and "Sofia," *Vagarth* 95 (June 2003): 92–93.

Chapter 2:
Richa Nagar, "Exploring Methodological Borderlands through Oral Narratives," in *Thresholds in Feminist Geography*, edited by J. P. Jones III, H.J. Nast, and S.M. Roberts, 203–24 (Lanham, Md.: Rowman & Littlefield, 1997).

Chapter 3:
Richa Nagar and Susan Geiger, "Reflexivity and Positionality in Feminist Fieldwork Revisited," in *Politics and Practice in Economic Geography*, edited by Adam Tickell, Eric Sheppard, Jamie Peck, and Trevor Barnes, 267–78 (London: Sage, 2007).

Richa Nagar, "Footloose Researchers, 'Traveling' Theories and the Politics of Transnational Feminist Praxis," *Gender, Place and Culture* 9, no. 2 (2002): 179–86.

Richa Nagar, "Languages of Collaboration," in *Feminisms in Geography: Rethinking Space, Place, and Knowledges*, edited by Pamela Moss and Karen Falconer Al-Hindi, 120–29 (Lanham, Md.: Rowman & Littlefield, 2008).

Chapter 4:
Richa Nagar in consultation with Farah Ali and Sangtin women's collective, Sitapur, Uttar Pradesh, "Collaboration across Borders: Moving Beyond Positionality," *Singapore Journal of Tropical Geography* 24, no. 3 (2003): 356–72.

Chapter 5:
Richa Singh and Richa Nagar, "In the Aftermath of Critique: The Journey after *Sangtin Yatra*," in *Colonial and Postcolonial Geographies of India*, edited by Saraswati Raju, Satish Kumar, and Stuart Corbridge, 298–319 (London: Sage, 2006).

Richa Nagar and Richa Singh (with Surbala Vaish and Reena Pande), *Ek Aur Neemsaar: Sangtin Atmamanthan aur Andolan* (New Delhi: Rajkamal Prakashan, 2012).

Richa Nagar and Richa Singh, "Churnings of a Movement: Sangtins' Diary," *South Asian Popular Culture* 8, no. 1 (2010): 17–30.

Chapter 6:
Richa Nagar, "Storytelling and Co-authorship in Feminist Alliance Work: Reflections from a Journey," *Gender, Place and Culture* 20, no. 1 (2013): 1–18.

Richa Nagar and Richa Singh (with Surbala Vaish and Reena Pande), *Ek Aur Neemsaar: Sangtin Atmamanthan aur Andolan* (New Delhi: Rajkamal Prakashan, 2012).

Richa Nagar, translator and commentator, "*Aag Lagi Hai Jangal Ma (The Jungle Is Burning)*: Confronting State Corruption and Rural (Under)development through Feminist Theatre," in *Gender, Space and Resistance: Women's Theatre in India*, edited by Anita Singh, 569–88 (New Delhi: DK Printworld, 2013).

Unless otherwise noted, I conducted all the interviews cited in this book.

"Dar es Salaam ke Naam" was translated into English by Raza Mir for *South Asian Magazine for Action and Reflection* (winter/spring 2001): 19. All other translations presented in this book from Awadhi, Gujarati, Hindi/Urdu, and Kiswahili into English are mine, unless otherwise noted.

Explanations of acronyms and of Awadhi, Gujarati, Hindi/Urdu, and Kiswahili words are provided in the glossary. Occasionally, words and sentences have been deliberately left untranslated.

Some community publications referenced in chapter 2 are no longer available, and therefore it has not been possible to cite page numbers from those publications.

The authors of *Playing with Fire* (PWF) were identified as "Sangtin Writers" in the Indian edition (Zubaan Books, 2006) and as "Sangtin Writers and Richa Nagar" in the U.S. edition (University of Minnesota Press, 2006). In *Muddying the Waters*, the authors of PWF are referred to as "Sangtin Writers."

MUDDYING THE WATERS

Introducing
Muddying the Waters

Coauthoring Feminisms across Scholarship and Activism

I can formalize responsibility in the following way: It is that all action is undertaken in response to a call . . . that cannot be grasped as such. Response here involves not only "respond to," as in "give an answer to," but also the related situations of "answering to," as in being responsible for a name (this brings up the question of the relationship between being responsible for/to ourselves and for/to others); of being answerable for . . . It is also, when it is possible for the other to be face-to-face, the task and lesson of attending to her response so that it can draw forth one's own.

—Gaytri Chakravorty Spivak, "Responsibility"

The notion of "solidarity" that still pervades much of the Left in the U.S. . . . dresses itself in the radical rhetoric of the latest rebellion in the "darker nations" while carefully maintaining political action at a distance from our own daily lives, thus producing a political subject (the solidarity provider) that more closely resembles a spectator or voyeur (to the suffering of others) than a participant or active agent, while simultaneously working to reduce the solidarity recipient to a mere object. . . . At both ends of this relationship, the process of solidarity ensures that subjects and political action never meet; in this way it serves to make change an *a priori* impossibility . . . [and] urges us to participate in its perverse logic by accepting the narrative that power tells us about itself: that those who could make change don't need it and those who need change can't make it. To the extent that human solidarity has a future, this logic and practice do not!

—El Kilombo Intergaláctico, *Beyond Resistance Everything*

> The intellectual basis for the demand to decolonize the academy
> has been eroded by skeptical, postmodern philosophies that
> have called into question the founding terms such as humanism,
> identity, progress, truth, and liberation. Postmodernism . . . [has
> opened] up new ways to diagnose the causes of oppression and
> to critique domination, but it has also resulted, particularly in the
> humanities, in a demoralization and confusion about what unites
> our diverse constituencies, what language we can use to make
> demands, and what vision we are working toward, just as it has
> called into question the ability to invoke any "we" here at all. I
> believe we need today to re-invoke that "we" that would include all
> groups targeted by identity based forms of oppression.
> —Linda Martín Alcoff, "An Epistemology for the Next Revolution"

Muddying the Waters is about ever-evolving journeys that confront and embrace the messiness of solidarity and responsibility. In describing and analyzing these journeys—frequently through stories, encounters, and anecdotes—this book aims to both separate and intimately link the question of scholarship with that of political action. These chapters—based on essays written between 1994 and 2013, often with coauthors, collectives, co-artists, and comrades—engage this relationship without claiming the label of activist scholarship, and without invoking categories such as transnational, postcolonial, or women-of-color feminisms as pure bodies of thought that can help us sort through the challenges posed by these journeys. Far from providing a methodological engagement with questions such as "how to" undertake transnational feminist studies or alliance work across the borders of academia and activism, then, this book places question marks on the utility and logic of neat positions and categories. I underscore the necessity of muddying theories and genres so that we can continue to embrace risks of solidarities that might fail and of translations that might refuse to speak adequately.

When academic engagements become locked into pure theoretical positions and loyalties, the possibility or impossibility of solidarity and responsibility is already pronounced, sometimes through their dismissal or celebration as self-contained categories such as "deconstructivist theory," "postmodernism," or "activist scholarship." Consequently, the journeys in and through which the complexities of solidarity and responsibility are felt, known (however, partially), and struggled with, either get relegated to methodological appendices of critical ethnographies or articles on "action" research, or they are dismissed a priori as invalid or unworthy of academic discussion.[1] Such segregated conversations also serve to reinforce the problematic division between "abstract thinking" and "concrete doing."

A related problem arises when the lenses that academics deploy to address questions of epistemic hierarchies betray the logic and investments emanating from our own locations. Structural asymmetries grant metropolitan researchers access to more resources, richer rewards, and control over the means of widespread dissemination of knowledge. This material hierarchy can result in a taken-for-granted epistemic hierarchy in which metropolitan knowledges are privileged as "sophisticated" and where nonmetropolitan knowledges are perceived as "raw data" or stories that need to be framed and put into perspective by the formally certified intellectual. Critical scholars have long recognized the need to provide an ongoing critique of these co-constitutive hierarchies, and have grappled with ways in which we can name, interrogate, and unlearn our privileged analytical frameworks. More frequently, however, one encounters a wholesale dismissal, or a radical reinterpretation, of "other" knowledges on the terms of the supposedly more evolved paradigms. At the same time, metropolitan assumptions of privileged understandings are often deflated in encounters with nonmetropolitan subjects or interlocutors who may neither acknowledge nor respect this hierarchy and who may be disdainful or critical of metropolitan academics, their misplaced priorities, or their inadequate frameworks.

These politics of language, location, engagement, and epistemic hierarchies raise several questions: Can notions such as solidarity and responsibility, trust and hope, vulnerability and reflexivity serve a useful purpose in ethically navigating the forms of epistemic violence in which metropolitan academics are, and will always remain, complicit? Is it possible to ethically navigate this terrain without lumping different kinds of epistemologies and knowledges into simple categories where one is regarded as inherently superior to the others, or where all are deemed as commensurable, and therefore, legible, transparent, and comparable to one another? Can such ethics be articulated in ways that do not foreclose an intermingling of stories, truths, and affects, on the one hand, and commitments to scholarly objectivity, on the other?[2]

While some scholars have approached these questions through concepts such as sustainable epistemologies (Scheman 2012), others have framed their arguments in terms of the sites from where scholarship should emerge (Mohanty 2003, Mama 2009, Alexander and Mohanty 2010), as well as the need to question the separation of methodology from theory (Bennett 2008, Nagar and Swarr 2010). For example, Naomi Scheman's inquiry into the responsibility of the public university underscores the importance of the social contracts that are contingent to research and discovery, teaching and learning, and outreach and public service of the university, and that necessarily involve those who are subject to or vulnerable to the work of the university (Scheman 2012). Bennett, in comparison, frames the dilemmas facing Africa-based feminist research by refusing to draw a line between theory as a way of approaching realities and experiences, and research methodologies as the "how" of engaging with those realities and experiences and of making alternatives possible when injustices emerge (Bennett 2008, 3).

For a growing number of university-based intellectuals, "activist scholarship" (Sudbury and Okazawa-Rey 2009a) and "ethnographies of activism" (Chari and Donner 2010) have become important rubrics for working through the above-mentioned questions of location, engagement, and responsibility. Critical of the tendency to separate activism from scholarship, Sudbury and Okazawa-Rey "argue for activist scholarship as a model of active engagement between the academy and movements for social justice" and commit themselves to making "activist scholarship possible as a viable mode of intellectual inquiry and pedagogical praxis"(Sudbury and Okazawa-Rey 2009b, 3). In examining innovative and participatory research methodologies developed by activist scholars in partnership with social movements, however, they also remain alert to "the danger of producing an idealized vision of collaborative or anti-oppressive research, recognizing that even research with emancipatory intentions is inevitably troubled by unequal power relations" and "ethical and political complicities and contradictions" (Sudbury and Okazawa-Rey 2009b, 3).

Some politically engaged scholars, in contrast to Sudbury and Okazawa-Rey, fear that the creation of a more permanent institutional space for activist scholarship might displace the model of objective, value-free inquiry. For instance, Kamala Visweswaran provides the example of Hindu nationalist groups who were active in the school textbook controversy in California to remind us of the multiple meanings of "politics" and "activism" and of the dangers of automatically elevating political engagement to a higher platform. She argues that there are times when it may be as important to uphold the model of objective inquiry as it is to recognize that fellow activists may not share the same goals or political sensitivities (Visweswaran 2011). She argues that

> activist scholarship or social science must too often presume agreement on what constitutes the political in order to place "action" on the agenda. And yet what constitutes the "political" is radically contingent upon time and place . . . This is all the more reason not to let an a priori understanding of something called "activism" or "politics" unreflexively shape scholarship. Now, more than ever, we need a commitment to thinking the political through its multiple guises. . . . To do so, I would argue that it is often productive to separate—but not detach—the question of scholarship from political action. (Visweswaran 2011, 77)

While we may argue whether or not it is truly possible to separate scholarship from political action without "detaching" the two, it is worth grappling with the ways in which we might attend to the radical contingencies of time and place while also resisting simplistic assumptions about shared political sensitivities or agendas. Susan Geiger and I have proposed what we call "situated solidarities" as a way to facilitate this grappling (see chapter 3). In attending to the specificities of geographical, socioeconomic, and institutional locations of those who enter into intellectual and political partnerships, and to the particular combination of processes, events, and struggles underway in those locations, situated solidarities resonate with Chela Sandoval's "differential consciousness," Carole Boyce Davies's "critical relationality," Sara Ahmed's "ethical encounters," and Jodi Dean's "reflective solidarity" (Sandoval 2000, Davies 1994, Ahmed 2000, Dean 1998).[3]

Sandoval's conceptualization of "U.S. third world feminisms" necessitates differential consciousness as a mode of theoretical engagement that is flexible and tactical in its analysis and intervention based on context and climate (Sandoval 2000, 41). Davies similarly underscores relational and deeply contextual negotiation, articulation, and interrogation of a variety of resistant and multiply linked discourses. As an "inherently migratory" epistemology, her notion of critical relationality "asserts the specificity of the other," but "moves beyond singularity or sameness to varied interactions, transgressions and articulations" (Davies 1994, 41). This fluidity allows for an "anti-definitional" analytical space in which multiple theoretical positions interact relationally in one's critical consciousness to create "complexly-integrated and relational theoretics" that allow for "possibilities of alliances which recognize specificities and differences" (Davies 1994, 41).[4] In an analogous vein, Ahmed calls for deconstructing "stranger fetishism" by working toward an ethics of encounter. These ethics require opening up the encounter in order to learn—without an expectation of fully accessing—a stranger's thick histories and complex positionings in time and space, as well as their connections to other places and times that enable such a meeting. This articulation is reminiscent of Jodi Dean's vision of "reflective solidarity" that envisions feminist solidarity as rooted in two moments—"that of opposition to those who would exclude or oppress another and that of our mutual recognition of each other's specificity" (Dean 1998, 4).

Muddying the Waters resonates with and extends these and similar understandings by laboring through the concepts and promises of radical vulnerability and love, reflexivity and risk, translation and coauthorship as mutually constitutive and interdependent in knowledge making and alliance work. In these journeys of the "I" and the "we," defined by situated solidarities, the possibilities of alliances are inseparable from a deep commitment to critique that is grounded in the historical, geographical, and political contingencies of a given struggle. These are journeys enabled by trust with the ever-present possibility of distrust and epistemic violence; journeys of hope that must continuously recognize hopelessness and fears; and journeys that insist on crossing borders even as each person on the journey learns of borders that they cannot cross—

either because it is impossible to cross them, or because it does not make sense to invest dreams and sweat in those border crossings.

In a way, *Muddying the Waters* can be seen as an academic memoir, a self-conscious attempt on my part to become radically vulnerable, even as I share knowledge and truths that become possible only through coauthorship with many others. I turn the gaze upon myself as a researcher, writer, and cultural worker who has wrestled with critiques of identity and meanings and possibilities of authorship and politics through academic projects. These projects have been undertaken across places as far removed from each other as the classrooms of the University of Minnesota, the streets and neighborhoods of Dar es Salaam, and the villages of Sitapur district in Uttar Pradesh. Places, and the languages in and through which those places become alive or are rendered invisible or powerless in academic engagement, become significant "characters" in this story of my academic journey as the chapters grapple with the politics of taking on research sites and making expert knowledges, as well as the politics of leaving places alone when one cannot adequately grapple with one's responsibility to those sites of knowledge making.[5]

Wounded Truths / Troubled Fields: Considering Stories, Solidarity, Suspicion, and Hope through Sangtins' Diary

EXCERPTS FROM A COAUTHORED DIARY 1:
THE BOATMAN AND THE PUNDIT

Once upon a time a learned man who considered himself highly accomplished climbed on a boat. The simple boatman respectfully welcomed him. As the boat started sailing, the pundit asked the boatman, "Hey, do you know anything about capitalism?"

The boatman folded his hands, "I am an illiterate man, sir. How would I know about capitalism?"

"What's the point of living in such darkness? You have wasted twenty-five percent of your life," the learned man pronounced as he tossed some pan-masala in his mouth.

As the boat sailed further, the pundit was once again taken by an urge to establish his intellectual authority—"So, you are a laborer. I am sure you have heard of Marxism!"

"Where would I learn about that, Sahab? I have no clue what Marxism is."

"What a pity. You have ruined fifty percent of your life . . . But you must be married. Don't tell me you haven't heard of feminism."

When the boatman expressed his ignorance of feminism, too, the pundit declared seventy-five percent of the boatman's life wasted. Before the boatman could respond to this declaration, the boat began to sink in mid-stream. The boat-man said to the scholar, "Punditji, you know everything. Now, swim."

But alas, the pundit had not learned to swim.

"Punditji, I have merely wasted seventy-five percent of my life, but you are just about to lose all of yours!" Saying this, the boatman quickly swam across the river. The scholar drowned.

This story is often told by the members of Sangtin Kisaan Mazdoor Sangathan (SKMS) in the villages of the Sitapur District.[6] And the story is often followed by the question: "Why didn't the boatman try to save the scholar?" If the scholar had not incessantly mocked the boatman and belittled his knowledge and exis-tence, there is a good chance that the boatman would have extended his hand to save the scholar and perhaps the knowledges and lives of both the men could have been saved.

If we agreed that each one of us is part pundit and part boatperson, there would be very little to hold in place the wall that separates intellectuals from the authors of everyday lives and struggles. Unfortunately, however, our world is inflicted with a system in which the gaps between the pundit and the boatperson work to reinforce differences of caste, class, gender, race, and place. Who be-comes the subject of knowledge and who is designated as the pundit to produce, legitimate, and disseminate that knowledge? And what are the implications of this inequality? Raising these questions in the context of the politics of rural develop-ment and women's empowerment, nine sangtins began a journey as writers in Sitapur district of India in 2002, a journey that first acquired the form of the book *Sangtin Yatra* and subsequently evolved into Sangtin Kisaan Mazdoor Sangathan (SKMS), a movement that now comprises several thousand workers and peasants, both women and men, over 90 percent of whom are dalit.

Grappling with the nuances of class, caste, gender, and communal differences in relation to Development, this journey is, on the one hand, committed to secur-ing livelihoods and the right to information and to ensuring water supply to a dry irrigation channel for the saathis or members of SKMS. On the other hand, in linking the issue of socioeconomic disempowerment of the poor with their intel-lectual disempowerment, this journey poses the question of who determines target populations, issues, and activities for projects of empowerment, and how? Who keeps the accounts of these activities and for whom? And how do the coordinators of these projects, in becoming the "experts" on the disempowered, contribute to maintaining the status quo? As saathis go through their own soul searchings on these issues, we also explore ways in which connections between intellectual labor and grassroots organizing can be deepened, and how the realities of sociopolitical and intellectual hierarchies, as well as the very definitions of who and what consti-tutes the margins, can be complicated and transformed.

EXCERPTS FROM A COAUTHORED DIARY 2:
RETHINKING "HERE" AND "THERE"

Richa Singh's U.S. Diary
Syracuse, 6 April 2007

For two women traveling from what some would call the third world of the third world, this is Surbala's and my eleventh day in the USA. Surbala, Richa [Nagar] and I were supposed to leave Syracuse University and reach Minneapolis today but we couldn't. The gathering that some of our supporters had planned in Minneapolis was canceled. Northwest Airlines stopped twelve passengers from boarding the overbooked flight today, and the three of us were part of that group. And then began Richa Nagar's four-hour-long fight with the representatives of the Northwest Airlines—a fight in which Surbala and I could not participate verbally because we did not speak English. It was a fight in which no one screamed with anger but where an extremely tense argument with clenched jaws and hostile glances went on forever. I remembered many *dharnas*. This was also a *dharna*. A "civilized" *dharna* in a land of so-called civilized people. The three of us remained solid in our protest. But I could not help thinking: "What would have happened if only Surbala and I had been traveling today?" Everything that happened today broke my confidence to travel alone in America. The long, hard journey from Delhi to Minneapolis began to seem easier. . . . The humiliation that we lived today has sharpened my perspective.

In a world defined by casteism, I come from the category of discriminating castes; I have never been subjected to the humiliation that a dalit experiences, and even with my lower-class background I have enjoyed the benefits of my caste privilege without desiring them—sometimes in the form of an "admiration" for my determination to fight and sometimes as compliments for my "shrewdness" or "cleverness." I had known that race discrimination exists, but now I am seeing and feeling it. I am beginning to recognize the expressions of those eyes, which sometimes seem to be struggling to come out of their temptation to discriminate, and at others, seem trapped in the confidence of their assumed superiority. I keep realizing the ways in which Surbala's and my racial difference makes us weak here. . . . The ways in which it invites others to insult us. . . . It's not simply a matter of our color—it's the matter of our color that is intensely differentiated by its class, its language, its clothing, its walk, its smile. . . . This discrimination is more dangerous than caste discrimination because it is one that begins with the eyes. It is not that the pain of caste discrimination is any less than this. But racial discrimination seems so quick and so dangerous—just like the automatic doors of this country—they open and shut with a speed that leaves us stunned. At least for us, this speed is terrifying.

Between late March and early May of 2007, Richa Singh and Surbala crossed multiple borders between Satnapur, Sitapur, Lucknow, Delhi, Amsterdam, and Minneapolis so that they could spend five weeks in the United States participating in a series of academic and activist forums that focused on discussions of the Sangtin Writers' book, *Playing with Fire*, and the movement building that emerged from our Hindi book, *Sangtin Yatra*. This border crossing into the United States post-9/11 was one of the hardest trips that either Richa Singh or Surbala had ever taken anywhere. It inflicted humiliations and silences that they had not encountered before. And it produced tensions and tears among three sangtins, whose audiences, despite best intentions, could not escape the desire to judge who among us was the "most authentic" sangtin. The nonstop turbulence throughout this trip led us to reflect, argue, analyze, and travel across many borders in ways that we found generative for the future of our alliance. For example, the three full-time organizers—Richa Singh, Surbala, and Reena—who were working mainly with dalit women and men to build SKMS in the villages of Sitapur in 2005–6, came from the sawarn castes, and this reality became an important focal point of the collective critical reflexive work of SKMS around caste and gender. Richa Singh's and Surbala's stark confrontation with racism in the United States helped to deepen this reflexivity by triggering an embodied awareness of race and caste in ways that none of us had approached before. We noted how languages of race arbitrarily draw on signifiers of difference, and how language, clothing, moving, laughing, and talking become markers of racial otherness. On the one hand, we appreciated how our different environments construct racism and casteism. On the other hand, the process of jointly inhabiting and experiencing particular spaces and places in the United States heightened our awareness of how power operates in those contexts with which we took our intimacy for granted.[7]

In her diary, Richa Singh wrestles with her experience of racism through her knowledge of caste. As a lower-class member of one of "the discriminating castes" she grapples anew with the implications of caste-based politics as she tries to make sense of her hitherto unknown experience of racialized exclusion and othering. She feels that racial discrimination is worse than caste-based discrimination, even as the stories retold by saathis of SKMS make the trauma of casteism unforgettable for her or anyone else associated with SKMS. This is a point to which Surbala, Richa Singh, and I return again and again throughout Surbala's and Richa's stay in the United States. Rethinking and articulating the dreams and struggles of SKMS while breathing and moving in the sociopolitical spaces of the United States reshape our understandings of race and caste, of belonging and citizenship, of borders and border crossings. These spaces also make us acutely aware of how "progressive" North American audiences judge our authenticity as members of a collective. Whose experiences of marginalization are definitive, after all? Who should be authorized to speak about those experiences to whom, and when? Who is the true representative of an alliance? This phase of our journey also raises questions about intimate structures of power, about how we understand the politics of speech, representation, solidarity, and agenda setting in a movement. Grappling with this and similar questions becomes part and parcel of our commitment to trouble the dominant meanings of the "field" and of seeing our "heres" and "theres" as intertwined. This self-conscious collective process inspires a search for new "truths" that have evolved since the writing of the *Sangtin Yatra*—the truths of lives and relationships that have come to define SKMS.

EXCERPTS FROM A COAUTHORED DIARY 3:
GHOONGHATS AND WITHDRAWALS

In a restaurant in Delhi, a friend from SKMS and I are in a discussion with two feminist scholars. The SKMS saathi shares that, despite repeated efforts to end segregation between women and men in the monthly meetings of the SKMS, quite a few women cover their faces with *ghoonghats* and choose to sit separately from the men.

This narration immediately draws a sharp response. Our Delhi friends question the SKMS member's desire to see women out of the *ghoonghats*. Why and for whom is segregation a problem? they ask her.

The SKMS member is taken aback, not because the questions surprise her but because she is known to pose precisely such questions before others whom she deems guilty of simplistic assumptions about rural women's oppressions. Since I know the SKMS member well, I can sense that she made the comment about the *ghoonghats* in the hope of initiating a more complex discussion about the dilemmas of organizing women and men in the current phase of SKMS's struggles. However, the reaction that her comment triggered silences her. She withdraws.

I want to prove to the other two academics that SKMS's engagement with feminism is more nuanced than what they have assumed. I give the example of a starkly opposite scenario—the theater workshop of SKMS where seven men and five women shared the space of a room for five days and nights and where the intimacy of the process led to incidents that could shock those who make quick assumptions about the "oppression" faced by rural women of Uttar Pradesh. I tell them about Radhapyari who, on the third day of the rehearsals, refused to enact a scene of domestic conflict with Sri Kishan and stated flatly, "I can't put my heart into this role. The person who is assigned the role of my husband reminds me of my father-in-law." The faces of the men listening to Radhapyari turned red. A woman in the group asked, "So whom do you want?" "Manohar," said Radhapyari. Blushing, Manohar entered the scene and Sri Kishan quietly exited.

This second story fascinates our friends; they find it far more interesting than the "*ghoonghat* story" and urge us to write about it. But the SKMS member barely listens. She has checked out from the conversation by this time.

Retelling Encounters, Making Knowledges: A Praxis without Guarantees

In imagining feminist polyvocal testimonies as "cross border (reading) alliances," Patricia Connolly-Shaffer deploys the idea of "truth telling as tale telling," a phrase that can also be used to describe my representation of the above excerpts from a coauthored diary that offers glimpses of SKMS's attempts to formulate its vision of solidarity and alliance work. If stories are experience-based accounts, then it is helpful to consider Connolly-Shaffer's conceptualization of stories as the medium through which fragmented truth claims subtly emerge and get interwoven and reworked to gain a kind of epistemic wholeness. Rather than providing ready-made solutions or unproblematized truth claims, then, storytelling becomes a "deliberative" exercise in which "hesitations and contradictions are rhetorically employed to comment on the limits of memory to convey social knowledge" (Connolly-Shaffer 2012, 20).

In the context of the journeys and border crossings embraced in this book, storytelling is enabled through what Hanan Sabea calls "encounters and conversations." Sabea critiques the taken for granted and "catch-all" nature of the term *transnational* and expresses concern about the ease and facility with which the idea of the transnational circulates and thus naturalizes its critical analytical potential. As a possible "cleansing practice" that can impart some utility to the term, she includes encounters and conversations that take shape "from particular locations and positions, while simultaneously attempting to traverse compartmentalized and already packaged forms of knowledge" (Sabea 2008, 16). Noting how several of these encounters are products of the shifting locations from which we practice and produce knowledge, Sabea reminds us of Walter Mignolo's articulation of "conversation as research method." By conversations, Mignolo does not mean "statements that can be recorded, transcribed and used as documents." Instead, he cites the most influential conversations as "people's comments in passing, about an event, a book, an idea, a person. These are documents that cannot be transcribed, knowledge that comes and goes, but remains with you and introduces changes in a given argument" (Mignolo 2000, xi).

As an entry point into imagining and practicing radical vulnerability, the excerpts from the coauthored diary suggest how conversations can enable or stifle arguments and hopes for dialogue and alliance. They also offer an opportunity to extend and complicate discussions on the politics of location, authenticity, trust, and relevance in cross-border engagements and alliance work, a subject that has triggered passionate discussion for at least two decades. More recently, Mama reframes this problem in terms of the manner in which politics of location and positionality limit the ability of "visiting and expatriate researchers [who] can hardly ever develop the intellectual, political, and practical connections and everyday knowledge that local activist scholars accumulate and develop through many years of work and involvement" (Mama 2009, 63). Arguing that the "global feminist" literature is often not intimate enough to be useful to women engaged in struggles on the ground, and that "the grand theories put forward by Western-based academics are for the most part too general and removed to inform local strategy," she argues for "creating and building relationships of solidarity and service" that, despite their challenges, can "enable outside researchers to overcome some of these limitations" (Mama 2009, 63). Activism, for Mama requires locally based feminist work, and "it seems we have a long way to go in developing intellectual solidarities that work against the global systemic political-economic inequalities that frame our work, regardless of our intentions" (Mama 2009, 64).

While I am sympathetic to Mama's concerns about the need to recognize the knowledge that can only become possible through a deep engagement with the local, the earlier excerpts from a coauthored diary suggest a need to seriously complicate the frequently invoked division between "inside" and "outside" researchers as well as the accompanying binaries of global (as general or research-driven) and local (as grounded or activist) in order to realize the possibilities of alliance work. A categorizing of investments and abilities of researchers or activists in ways that render some as more authentic or involved than others by virtue of their location or "origins" can be dangerous. A commitment to cultivate radical vulnerability through situated solidarities demands that we grapple with the material and symbolic politics of our locations and imagine how researchers might play a role in evolving ethics and methodologies that seek to build dialogues across locations. On the one hand, those who wish to enter into difficult long-term dialogues can do so only if the conditions of dialogue allow them to interrogate, and to express suspicion of, one another. On the other hand, the expression of suspicion and interrogation must happen in ways that enhance—rather than foreclose—sensitive negotiations of experiences and interpretations, for it is precisely in these negotiations that possibilities for shared yearning and dreaming reside.

My retelling of the above tales here (and of similar tales throughout this book), then, is an invitation to explore ways of building trust and accountability by becoming radically vulnerable. If mistakes and complicities with violence

necessarily accompany our actions, memories, desires, and locations as representers, then our methodologies must allow all the members of an alliance to
become vulnerable before one another about these mistakes and complicities,
while also recognizing that our ability to grasp or know these can only be partial and provisional. Only then can we feel brave enough to voice suspicion of
each other's desires and interpretations without fearing that such expressions
might stifle hopes for alliance work. This kind of vulnerability cannot rely on
traditional notions of transparency and accountability in its logic because it is
grounded in bonds emerging from multifaceted relationships and trust, in hopes
and dreams, in affect.[8] However, as Dia Da Costa reminds us, this grounded-
ness cannot slip into a celebration of affect as an innocent space that is "not yet
usurped" by dominant ideologies and practices; instead, affect connotes "the
visceral sense of social structures, ideologies, histories, policies and bodies that
constructs their ongoing vitality, intensity and resonance in social life."[9]

In a way, the ethics and methodologies of encounters, anecdotes, conversations, and storytelling that I am invoking through radical vulnerability strive to
achieve, in the realm of research praxis, a politics of indeterminacy, or a politics
without guarantees.[10] If the academy is not the only site of knowledge making,
then an opening up of the horizon of theorizing must begin with a recognition
that academic knowledges might be enriched through creative conversations
with knowledges that evolve in sites of struggle that seem distant to the academy,
including knowledges that are "vernacularized" or remarginalized through their
contradictory instrumentalization and incorporation in globalized identities,
discourses, and projects (see Dutta 2013). Such an intellectual project also requires us to appreciate that knowledge claims—and truth claims—from "other"
locations are often invoked in the form of stories, and to pay attention to how
we might be listening to, or ignoring, these stories and the knowledge or truth
claims that they make or imply, and with what results.

At the same time, an engagement with stories is itself a politics of negotiation.
Poststructuralist and postmodernist feminist scholars have long underscored
the necessity of grappling with discursive contexts and histories of experience,
rather than considering experience to be the constitutive core of discourse (see
Butler 1990, Scott 1991). This insight is fundamental to any responsible engagement with stories. In reflecting on the possibilities of political theater through
alliance work, Sofia Shank and I argue that deployment of concepts such as
"subalternity" and "transexperience" by social scientists often betrays a desire
to demonstrate embodiment or "real experience"—sometimes in a celebratory
multicultural mode, and at other times in a more self-reflexive vein, about the
marginalization of particular kinds of bodies or lives (Shank and Nagar 2013).
We point out that stories can neither reveal the experiences of those they are
inspired by, nor can they be imagined as being contained by predefined "subal-

tern" or "trans" identities. Rather, the responsibility and labor of telling stories involves a series of delicate negotiations through which one must underscore the impossibility of ever accessing "lived experiences" and where one's engagements with who is speaking, who is referenced, and who is listening can become legible only when contextualized within the multiple and shifting social relations in which they are embedded (Shank and Nagar 2013, 106). Only then can one hope to represent structures of violence without reducing them to accessible narratives that reenact the very violence that "we" seek to confront.

A politics without guarantees, then, is rooted in a praxis of radical vulnerability that is committed to opening up spaces for negotiation by always returning us to the ethics of how and why one comes to a story and to its variable tellings and retellings. The telling of stories must continuously resist a desire to reveal the essential or authentic experience of the subject; instead, every act of storytelling must confront ways in which power circulates and constructs the relationalities within and across various social groups. This struggle happens as much through what is narrated as it does through the gaps and silences, and through that which remains obscured or unavailable within narrative. On the one hand, such praxis unavoidably struggles to decenter the authors and to complicate the meanings of authorship and coauthorship by forging conversations among seemingly disparate sites, languages, texts, and arguments, while simultaneously analyzing the ways in which power functions to make these mutually illegible or invisible. On the other hand, such praxis creates texts in and through which coauthors from multiple locations can negotiate subalternity and theorize power by strategically staging truths and stories about their evolving encounters and struggles. Such multilocational coauthorship by a political alliance requires that the authors try to retain a certain amount of control over their intellectual and theoretical production and over the ways in which their texts and stories—as well as their circulation and consumption—can be interpreted as part of the politics of knowledge production. At the same time, this exercise of rethinking and complicating the politics of knowledge making remains undergirded by the inevitable contradiction posed by the centrality of the professional researcher in enabling this decentering of the authors and readers.

Radical Vulnerability, Reflexivity, and Coauthorship: Outline of a Journey

As processes of growing and becoming, journeys convey evolution without closures and yield important insights into what is possible. Journeys are about risks that we must take in making choices. And journeys are also about the price we must pay for making mistakes. The six chapters in this book, then, can be described collectively as a journey in which I have sought to grapple with politics and ethics of research, and with methods and languages of collaboration in the context of feminist engagement across north-south borders. Starting from my historical and ethnographic research on the spatial politics of race, class, caste, religion, and gender in postcolonial Dar es Salaam (Tanzania) and traversing the complex terrain of possibilities and limitations of alliance work with (but not limited to) the SKMS, these chapters follow a loose chronology to highlight the central theoretical and political questions that have accompanied my explorations of different forms of feminist engagement to grapple with questions of location, power, translation, and representation. I underscore the necessity and inevitability of becoming radically vulnerable in and through critically self-reflexive collaborations, translations, and coauthorship. These co-constitutive and ever evolving labors and processes lie at the heart of struggles to produce knowledges that can travel meaningfully and responsibly within, between, and across worlds.

The first chapter, "Translated Fragments, Fragmented Translations," draws attention to the ways in which a commitment to radical vulnerability can enable and enrich politically engaged alliance work, and the particular ways in which affect and trust empower translations across borders. If becoming radically vulnerable requires all the members of an alliance to open ourselves—intellectually and emotionally—to critique in ways that can allow us to be interrogated and assessed by one another, then how might one begin to write such praxis? I share excerpts of letters, conversations, poems, and narratives from contexts that might seem disjointed and disparate on the surface but that tell stories—of encounters, events, and relationships—that have enabled the arguments I have made in the rest of this book. These fragments also point to the intense entanglements between autobiography and politics and seek to initiate a discussion on feminist praxis that commits itself to learning and unlearning by inserting one's body—individually and collectively—in the process of knowledge making and the generative challenges that such insertion poses for imagining storytelling and engagement across socioeconomic, geographical, and institutional borders. Even as they underscore the importance of resisting closures in feminist engagement with questions of translation, representation, and solidarity, the fragments remain rooted in the specific sociospatial and institutional contexts and locations (in the United States, Tanzania, and India) in and through which my concerns for theorizations of praxis have evolved over the last two decades. In particular, the question of language and place is tightly interwoven with my engagements with politics and praxis of knowledge production—the languages that enable or foreclose the making of certain kinds of knowledge about specific places and people; the languages in which knowledges are (or are not) allowed to travel to particular spaces and communities, and the intended and unintended effects of the ways in which knowledges and their translations travel in often unforeseen ways and directions.

Three additional things are worth noting about "Translated Fragments, Fragmented Translations": First, the splitting of the text into two columns interrupts the usual expectations around conventions of genre, temporality or chronology, and coherence, while implicating the reader in the making of knowledge through the physical act of reading itself. The reader can choose which fragment to pursue and for how long, and how to give it meaning in relation to other fragments. Second, rather than describing and reflecting upon my positionality as an author, the fragments I have chosen to share here make me an object of study and scrutiny. This sharing, I hope, can serve as an invitation to explore new imaginaries through which critical scholarship can render and animate the researcher's own making and unmaking of the research process as well as the pasts and presents with which that research is always entangled. Finally, in "Translated Fragments" and throughout *Muddying the Waters*, I highlight how the labor and praxis of translation constitute the core of engaged research. At the same time, my choice to leave some words and concepts as untranslated is deliberate, a simple reminder of the impossibility of ever achieving fully accessible translations.

Students sometimes ask whether I have encountered resistance in making the choices that I have in the academy. There are certainly stories to tell. For example, I could talk about the time when an editor at a university press told me to take the manuscript of *Playing with Fire* to the university printing services, which would dutifully print whatever the authors requested. This was when I insisted that the names of nine authors needed to be on the cover and that no epigraphs from the original Hindi book, *Sangtin Yatra*, could be shortened or modified in the English translation. Or I could talk about all those times when students who have been attracted to the kind of work I do have been instructed to stay away from the naive approaches to academic engagement that my work exemplifies. However, even without these stories, the sequence and the timing of publication of ideas can itself generate insights about the politics and possibilities of knowledge production, and about the interpretive communities that enable us to make and circulate certain kinds of knowledge in a given time and place.

Chapters 2 to 4 sketch an intellectual journey that I began with my research on South Asian communities in postcolonial Dar es Salaam. The arguments are molded by an unfolding process of my own understandings of the issues and how these translated into specific forms of engagement as I learned to navigate and rework the rules and expectations of the U.S. academic establishment. Although I think differently about some of these arguments now, revising them substantially would interrupt the stories they tell about my own intellectual history and disciplinary locations and relocations, and about my journeys between and across worlds, communities, and political projects and commitments. Together, these three chapters suggest that the kind of radical vulnerability that I argue for in chapter 1 goes hand in hand with a critical self-reflexivity that is attuned to our institutional and geopolitical positions; such reflexivity constitutes the core of situated solidarities that enable engaged intellectual work across divergent and unequal locations.

The second chapter, "Dar es Salaam: Making Peace with an Abandoned 'Field,'" is based mainly on an essay (Nagar 1997) that emerged from my doctoral dissertation (Nagar 1995). This essay has been used by researchers as an example of "how to" undertake the challenge of understanding and interrogating one's own multilayered positionality in critical feminist ethnographic research, and the manner in which such exercise can allow us to grapple with the complex politics of intersectional difference in the context of fieldwork. The piece discusses the manner in which my own gendered, racialized, and communally marked body was read by different Tanzanian Asian communities in various social sites in the city of Dar es Salaam and how these encounters shaped the knowledge I was able to produce about Asian communal politics in that city in the early 1990s.

The second part of chapter 2 turns to questions of reciprocity, power, trust, and ethical engagement in research relationships by focusing on examples of two life historians who participated in my study. The first was Frances (pseudonym), a Goan taxi driver with strong views about gender and race, and the second was Nargis (also an alias), a divorced Shiite feminist professional who had returned to Dar es Salaam from London to fight a property case on behalf of her father. To offer an example of the kind of feminist "ethno-geography" that this self-reflexive methodological exploration helped me create, the chapter ends with a sidebar drawn from excerpts from an unpublished chapter of my dissertation that focuses on the politics of languages and mother tongues in Dar es Salaam. This chapter underscores that a complex self-reflexivity that is attuned to time, place, and sociopolitical and cultural specificities must accompany any feminist engagement with questions of power and difference. However, my involvement as an academic researcher with Dar es Salaam and my need to subsequently distance myself from that research site became inseparable from my struggles with the practice of self-reflexivity in feminist research, a point that I introduce here and develop variously in the subsequent two chapters.

Chapter 3, "Reflexivity, Positionality, and Languages of Collaboration in Feminist Fieldwork," owes its origins to a project that Susan Geiger and I undertook between 1997 and 2000. Originally titled "Reflexivity, Positionality, and Identity in Feminist Fieldwork: Beyond the Impasse," this project addressed an impasse that, Susan and I posited, emanated from narrow discussions of identity and positionality in interdisciplinary feminist fieldwork, as well as a growing anxiety among feminist scholars based in the northern academy about engaging with subaltern subjects in "the field." Our argument for the need to radically rethink why and how we engage in self-reflexivity in order to allow politically transformative agendas to emerge encountered resistance in feminist scholarly circles in the late 1990s. Two leading feminist journals rejected our manuscript without reviewing it, even as the arguments that Susan and I had begun to explore continued to gain prominence in my own intellectual journey. This prominence found expression in the writing I undertook after Susan's death, which forms the basis for what appear as parts 2 and 3 of chapter 3. In "Footloose Researchers" (first published in *Gender, Place and Culture*, or *GPC*, in 2002), I revisited the key arguments that Geiger and I made about the nature of this impasse by analyzing three feminist responses that I received in 2000 to my manuscript "Mujhe Jawab Do (Answer Me!)." Thanks to Lynn Staeheli and Linda Peake, the editors of *GPC* at the time, the conversations around the writing of "Mujhe Jawab Do" and "Footloose Researchers" became part of a self-reflexive project for feminist geography and for the journal itself, and found expression in a special issue of *GPC* in which Lynn and I coedited a section titled "Feminists Talking across Worlds" (Staeheli and Nagar 2002). The last section of chapter 3, based on a chapter written in 2005–6 at a time of hope in the aftermath of the battles won by the authors of *Sangtin Yatra*, elaborates on threads of earlier discussion on reflexivity and location, with specific reference to the politics of language and collaboration.

"Reflexivity, Positionality, and Languages of Collaboration in Feminist Field-work" begins with a re-presentation of the original argument that Susan and I made in our 2000 essay. We argue that, despite the proliferation of self-reflexivity in feminist ethnographic research, much feminist scholarship has tended to avoid some of the most vexing political questions in transnational feminist praxis: Who are we writing for, how, and why? What does it mean to coproduce relevant knowledge across geographical, institutional, or cultural borders? How do we interrogate the structure of the academy and the constraints and values embedded therein, as well as our desire and ability (or lack thereof) to challenge and reshape those structures and values? We posit that effective participation in border crossings necessitates a processual approach to reflexivity and positionality, combined with an acute awareness of the place-based nature of our intellectual praxis. Such praxis commits itself to building situated solidarities that can grapple with the larger interconnections produced by internationalization of economies and labor forces while challenging the colonialist prioritizing of the West. These solidarities must be simultaneously attentive to the ways in which our ability to evoke the global in relation to the local, to configure the specific nature of our alliances and commitments, and to participate in social change are significantly shaped by our geographical, temporal, and socio-institutional locations, and by the processes, events, and struggles unfolding in those locations.

Part 2 of chapter 3 elaborates on some of the problems discussed in the previous section by highlighting the manner in which narrow academic engagements with reflexivity fail to account for the ways in which identities form, shift, and reconstruct themselves in and through the processes and encounters that constitute fieldwork. The section ends with a brief meditation on what might count as theory in feminist research that seeks to speak responsibly to audiences and colleagues located in starkly different locations, an argument that I continue to modify and refine in later chapters with the evolution of my own journey in multiple locations across the sites of academia, NGOs, social movements, and community theater.

In part 3 of chapter 3, I argue that an ongoing political praxis of language and translation resides at the core of any struggle that seeks to decolonize and reconfigure the agendas, mechanics, and purposes of knowledge production, a point to which I return in the last chapter of the book. This preliminary discussion links struggles in the realm of cultural and identity politics with those about the inclusiveness or exclusiveness of sites from which knowledge and norms of expertise and professionalism are produced. It also suggests that formulation of political ideas, intellectual concepts, and languages of collaboration in a collective with open membership is a constantly evolving process. It is only by nurturing this dynamism that we can appreciate knowledge as being produced in both place and time, drawing on diverse sources of experience and expertise, in ways that the "fields" created by the academy, NGOs, and social movements can become means, rather than ends.

Chapter 4, "Representation, Accountability, and Collaborative Border Crossings: Moving Beyond Positionality," is a revised version of an article originally written between 2002 and 2003 in consultation with Farah Ali (an alias) and what we then called the Sangtin Samooh, or Sangtin women's collective, of Sitapur District in India. The original essay, invited for a special conference on postcolonial geographies at the National University of Singapore, evolved in close relationship with aforementioned struggles around how and why to "do" reflexivity. It advances the discussion in the previous chapter by summarizing how considerations about collaborative spaces in postcolonial feminist and geographical analyses have often hinged on questions of positionality, reflexivity, and identity, largely in relation to the politics of representation. Such approaches, especially in fieldwork-based feminist research, have translated into a kind of reflexivity that mainly focuses on examining the identities of the individual researchers rather than on the ways in which those identities intersect with institutional, geopolitical, and material specificities of their positionality. I then take this discussion forward by arguing for a postcolonial and transnational feminist praxis that focuses on (a) conceptualizing and implementing collaborative efforts that insist on crossing difficult borders; (b) the sites, strategies, and skills deployed to produce such collaborations; and (c) the specific processes through which such collaborations might find their form, content, and meaning. To ground this discussion, I draw on two collaborative initiatives that I undertook in Uttar Pradesh—the first with "Farah Ali," a Muslim woman who shared her life story with me in the aftermath of 9/11 with an explicit aim of reentering the United States with her daughter, and the second with members of the Mahila Samakhya Programme in Sitapur (MSS), who were beginning to imagine the future of the organization, Sangtin. Chapter 4 ends with a poem, first written in Hindi and subsequently translated into English, in which I confront the limits of critique that we undertake as academics. At the same time, the process of writing and sharing the poem with women I had built close relationships with in MSS and Sangtin constituted, for me, important moments of learning how some forms of articulation travel and resonate more effectively across borders than others, and that embracing radical vulnerability as a mode of being and trusting, analyzing and building together has much to do with making this resonance possible. It was this belief in the possibility of coexisting resonances, furthermore, that led me to retain the poem in the final version of this essay despite criticism by two feminist geographers attending the conference in Singapore, who argued that the poem performed emotional manipulation in ways that contradicted my own critique of critical geographers' predominant modes of engaging the question of representation.

The last two chapters of *Muddying the Waters* focus on the coauthorship that emerges from collaborative praxis: How might we approach the idea of coauthorship when critical engagement seeks to complicate the sites of knowledge making as well as the dominant ideas about what counts as valid knowledge? Even as these chapters resist, even foreclose, the possibility of anything resembling a typology or "tool kit" for practicing coauthorship, they provide insights into the labor and challenges of stepping into long-term journeys with co-learners and co-teachers across sociopolitical, geographical, linguistic, and institutional borders.

Chapter 5, "Traveling and Crossing, Dreaming and Becoming: Journeys after *Sangtin Yatra*," is based on writing that I undertook with members of SKMS in Hindi and English between 2004 and 2012, as well as on my own reflections (shared with various academic and nonacademic audiences) on that writing. These include an invited essay coauthored with Richa Singh (Singh and Nagar 2006) and translated excerpts from SKMS's Hindi book, *Ek Aur Neemsaar* (Nagar and Singh et al. 2012). The chapter traces the beginnings of the creative journey with sangtins that led to the making of *Sangtin Yatra* and analyzes the political battles that emerged from this yatra in multiple sites. In simultaneously documenting and critically examining the manner in which shared dreams and commitments evolve and fail in an alliance, it raises questions about professionalization, expertise, aspirations, and knowledge making in the context of movement building. It also engages the politics of language by weaving together multiple genres, writing styles, and idioms to tell the stories of SKMS after the publication of the books *Sangtin Yatra* and *Playing with Fire* and in its growth as a movement. At the same time, the chapter questions and complicates a romantic desire to seek lasting "sisterhood" or solidarity through alliance work. In highlighting the key moments in a collective journey, the reflections focus on the analytical frameworks and forms of knowledge that have emerged, as well as the dialogues triggered by our collaboration in multiple institutional sites—academic presses, NGOs, activist collectives, donor agencies, solidarity networks—and discussions of curriculum and structures of basic and primary education at the national level. Academic theories, reflexive activism, and critical pedagogy become interwoven and extended as members of the collective work in multiple sites to democratize hierarchical structures of knowledge production—and to rethink the meanings of the political—through collaborative praxis.

The final chapter ties together the insights gained from a twelve-year journey, chiefly with members of SKMS, in a loose and open-ended articulation of "Four Truths of Storytelling and Coauthorship in Feminist Alliance Work." For those who work in alliances across borders, coauthoring stories can become a powerful tool to mobilize experience in order to write against relations of power that produce violence, and to imagine and enact contextually grounded visions and ethics of social change. Such work demands that we not only grapple with the complexities of identity, representation, and political imagination, but also rethink the assumptions and possibilities associated with engagement, expertise, and the very ideas of storytelling and authorship. Drawing on partnerships with sangtins and others, I reflect on the labor process, assumptions, possibilities, and risks associated with coauthorship as a medium for mobilizing intellectual spaces in which stories from multiple locations in an alliance can speak with one another and evolve into more nuanced critical interventions that destabilize dominant discourses and methodologies. Chapter 6 ends with the last scene of a play in Hindi and Awadhi that I coauthored with members and supporters of SKMS, *Aag Lagi Hai Jangal Ma* (The Forest Is Burning), in 2010. Even as this scene articulates the ways in which rural lives and livelihoods are relentlessly violated by structures of power and by our own complicities with those structures, it calls for continuing to place our hopes in fighting, dreaming, writing, and singing together.

The four truths underline the forever-entangled nature of theory, story, and strategy in coauthoring struggles through a praxis of radical vulnerability. The truth claims that are articulated in and through struggle are part of knowledge as movement. They cannot be foreshadowed or captured in a schema or model;

they can only emerge from processes, from relationships, and from encounters and conversations; and they can only be identified and retold through anecdotes that are often slippery, indeterminate, subjective, and inseparable from the context in which they are experienced, felt, or uttered. Thus, there cannot be any universal truths or anecdotes that can be verified, falsified, or repeated—only an invitation to come up with more truths rooted in more journeys and relationships that must continuously unfold.

In Muddying the Waters, I retell tales in order to learn from the partial truths they have to offer. Is it possible to grapple seriously with questions of epistemic violence without giving up a belief in politically engaged scholarship? Can immersing ourselves in translations of struggles across multiple institutional, sociocultural, linguistic, and theoretical borders through a praxis of radical vulnerability make the processes and products of our labor simultaneously accountable to multiple interpretive communities? In wrestling with such questions throughout the book, I am deeply aware that many of those who have made it possible for me to craft my arguments here will remain distant from this book for myriad reasons. At the same time, I hope that these arguments will trigger conversations in and beyond the spaces of U.S. research universities among students, readers, and colleagues in Lucknow, Pune, New Delhi, Istanbul, Diyarbakir, Cape Town, and Pietermaritzburg; in organizations and struggles I have worked and learned with, made mistakes with, and celebrated victories with; among critics and interlocutors who might be suspicious of my claims as well as among those who think that there is a legitimate and useful place for this pursuit. What I offer here is a blending of genres, concerns, and meditations that may speak more to one audience than the other at a given time, but then switch to a more direct conversation with a specific audience. And through all of this, my objective remains simple: to nourish difficult collaborations, alliance-work, and coauthorship across borders—even if they seem impossible to undertake or sustain at times—so that we can continue to hope for sociopolitical and epistemic justice within, despite, and beyond our institutions and locations.

1. Translated Fragments, Fragmented Translations

हिरन हुए हम।	We became deer.
वन चरे समझ–बूझ के साथ।	Grazed forests intelligently.
यात्रायें योजना बनाकर कीं।	Undertook journeys after careful planning.
युद्ध रणकौशल से लड़े।	Fought wars with martial perfection.
चीज़ों को जानने में	Applied all our attentiveness
पूरी समझदारी बरती	in understanding issues
और तमाम नासमझियां बचाये रखीं	and set aside countless carelessnesses
प्यार के विरल,	for the rare,
अल्पकालिक,	momentary,
अप्रत्याशित	unexpected
क्षणों के लिये।	moments of love.
	—Katyayani, "Samajh"

If the politics of alliance making are about making oneself radically vulnerable through trust and critical reflexivity, if they require us to open ourselves to being interrogated and assessed by those to whom we must be accountable, then such politics are also about acknowledging, recognizing, and sharing our most tender and fragile moments, our memories and mistakes in moments of translation, in moments of love. For, it is in the acknowledgment, recognition, and sharing of these moments, memories, and mistakes that we live our trust and faith, and where we often encounter our deepest courage and insights. It is also in these fragile, aching moments that we come to appreciate alliance work as constituted by fragments of journeys—some fully lived, and others abandoned at different stages . . . interrupted passages through which the co-travelers recognize the power of becoming radically vulnerable together. These fragmented journeys are marked as much by opening ourselves up to the risks of becoming wounded, as they are marked by silences and withdrawals, and by returning to forgive and to love—again and again.

In this section, I share excerpts of letters, conversations, poems, and two previously published essays titled "Local and Global" and "Theater of Hopes" from contexts that might seem disjointed on the surface but tell stories that have enabled the arguments I have made in the rest of this book.[1]

Patches and Quilts / Betrayals and Bonds

It was in November 2010 that I met Piya Chatterjee for the second time (our first meeting was a brief encounter at a gathering hosted by a colleague in Minnesota almost a decade earlier), at a panel that she co-organized with Amanda Swarr for the Annual Conference of the National Women's Studies Association in Denver. There, in one of the very last panels on the final day of the conference, we heard each other speak, were moved by the stories and connections that we could hear and sense, but had no immediate openings (time or space) to explore. Later, in a phone conversation, we decided to continue the process of sharing and discussing through letters. Fragments of these letters, alongside excerpts from essays, journals, and poems—some untouched and some revised since they were first written or published—have found their way into this chapter, for they have allowed me to become radically vulnerable through dialogue with a colleague who is grappling with similar entanglements of power, knowledge, and their possibilities and impossibilities.[2]

Dear Piya,

It's 3:11 am on the morning of Dec 23rd and I have finally come to terms with the reality that there will be no ideal moment in which I can begin and end this first letter to you. Words will spill only when I selfishly steal time for this writing from difficult memos and emergency emails on faculty matters; from reading promotion and tenure files in Minnesota while remotely organizing a theater workshop in Uttar Pradesh; from trying to grapple

Local and Global

Rumor has it that Kothhi Sah ji, the grand eighteenth-century house where I grew up in the old city of Lucknow—and where the warrior Begum Hazrat Mahal took shelter at the time of the Indian revolt against the British—was constructed from building materials stolen from the Asaf-ud-daula Imambara. My grandfather, who was to become an eminent Hindi novelist by the time of my birth in the late 1960s, started renting this *kothhi* located in the historic neighborhood of Chowk for 100 rupees in 1958. It was in this *kothhi*; in the narrow, bustling lanes surrounding the *kothhi*; and in the manner in which the rest of the world related to those lanes and the *kothhi* that my first and most intensely felt encounters with geographies of difference, inequality, and social injustices happened.

My childhood memories are filled with times spent with cousins, neighbors, and domestic workers and their children in the big and small courtyards; in the winding, narrow stairwells; and in the secret little doorways and tunnels that linked many of the old houses and tightly compressed lanes of Chowk. Chowk, by the way, was considered as the only real tourist attraction of Lucknow, because it was here that the past glory of Shi'i Nawabs nurtured not only the Lakhnavi Urdu and culture of modesty, finesse, and hospitality, but also the craftsmanship of the local Sunni and Hindu artisans, and the practices of Khattry business families who hired and exploited them.

Inside the spaces of the *kothhi*—at once imposing, stifling, and nurturing—I came to admire my grandfather's genius and his popularity among people of all classes. And with the gravity of complaints from Ta-run in Mumbai, my father in Lucknow, and my daughter in Saint Paul that I don't make enough time for the promises that I have made to them; from the temptation to fix the five-month-old leak in my kitchen ceiling so that I do not have to live in David's basement for the rest of this dark long Minnesota winter.[3]

It all sounds so dramatic (living in starkly different worlds at the same time imbues life with a permanently dramatic quality, doesn't it?), but this writing seems too critical and fragile to postpone or bury under other seemingly urgent worries. After our phone conversation earlier this month, I feel as though I have stumbled on a new ocean of thoughts and memories to work through. I sense an urge to process struggles in my seemingly fragmented journeys as a political, intellectual, and creative being. I feel a need to share stories about feminisms and feminists, about solidarities and betrayals that I haven't dared to repeat for fear of them being misunderstood. I want to share hard truths without worrying about the possibility that they might rebound when they reach the other side. For me our commitment to talk through letters is a simple act of trust that inspires me to relive and remember, to connect and weave in words so many important pieces of life—and death—that I have not allowed to belong together for myriad reasons.

But along with this urge I also hear echoes of the poem by Adrienne Rich that you shared with me:

When my dreams showed signs
of becoming
politically correct
no unruly images
escaping beyond border

in the same spaces, I watched my mother being shunned by the family because of her parents' poverty. I learned how child labor became transformed into a lifetime of bonded labor through the stories of Baba, who raised me and my sister. I was taught what my socio-spatial and behavioral limits were as the oldest girl in the joint family.[9] And I saw my young and dynamic father battling an aggressive muscular dystrophy that gradually imprisoned his body but could never stifle his soaring creativity. Immediately outside the *kothhi*, I met *bhangi* women and men who inhabited the other side of our residential lane, and who came with their baskets every day to collect the filth from our homes and non-flush latrines.[10] In the covered alley beside the *kothhi*, I knew girls of my own age who cooked, ate, and slept with their families with only an eighteenth-century arch over their heads. These were girls who never got a chance to go to school or to use a "real" toilet; whose growing, barely clothed bodies filled their mothers' hearts with fears; and who were married off and had babies by the time I reached college.

When I was seven, my mother—who had by then become an assistant teacher of Hindi in a primary school—rebelled in a startling way. In a family that prided itself in serving Hindi literature and theater, and where "English schools" were considered both elitist and beyond financial reach, she demanded that her daughters be sent to an Angrezi school and announced that she would spend her earnings to help with the fees. Her victory resulted in my admission in 1976 (followed by my sister's in 1979) to La Martiniere, a school founded by a French general that is known as much for

when walking in the street I found my
themes cut out for me
knew what I would not report
for fear of enemies' usage
then I began to wonder.[4]

Like everything else that we struggle
with, this letter writing is also about learning our responsibility as translators, as quilt
makers who struggle to patch together that
which we want to translate with that which
should not or cannot be translated.

But how do we make decisions about
what to narrate and what to swallow?

How do we learn to let free those unruly
images escaping beyond border without
fearing that they might empower our enemies?

How do we facilitate what Spivak
terms as "love between the original and its
shadow, a love that permits fraying"?[5]

How do we decide which stitch to use
for which patch while helping each other
to appreciate the broad contours of our
stitches—our bittersweet relationships with
English, Bangla, Hindi, Urdu, Awadhi,
Gujarati, Kiswahili? Some stitches I learned
very long ago from my mother and aunts
and neighbors, from the women who visited my grandmother every afternoon, and
from the teachers in La Martiniere Girls'
School, who dismissed pretty much everything I learned in my home and neighborhood. The remaining stitches I worked
out by myself as I recognized the value of
discontinuity and dissonance, and grappled
with the violence that a desire for harmony
often inflicts on the very worlds that are
in uncomfortable, even frayed, conversations between the original and the shadow,
between all that tears us apart in our many
homes and worlds.

its high-quality education as for the historical role its boys played in fighting against
Indians and helping to restore British power
during the Revolt of 1857. In retrospect,
the journey to La Martiniere—barely two
miles away from Kothhi Sah ji—was at once
a traumatic and an enabling journey that
changed the course of my future life.

From Chowk to La Martiniere

When I arrived in La Martiniere, I became
silent. The people, sounds, and sensations
that throbbed in the veins of Chowk were far
removed from this world. I was surrounded
by Anglo-Indian teachers, administrators,
and boarders; and by daughters of bureau-
crats, professionals, military officers, local
legislators, and business families, who were
raised in the modern "residential colonies"
of Lucknow in nuclear families, who often
spoke English comfortably, and who chat-
ted about travels, films, novels, and parties
that I had never heard of. To many of them,
Chowk was a "backward Muslim interior"
where everyone wore *chikan* fabrics, chewed
beetle leaves, flew kites, and visited cour-
tesans. I tried hard not to feel embarrassed
of belonging to Chowk or of coming from a
joint family that did not own a car or house,
and the most sophisticated members of
which could speak only broken English. I
searched for words and points of connection as I traversed back and forth on cycle
rickshaws between Chowk and La Martiniere. For the next nine years, I struggled
to muster the tools to translate the pieces
from one world of my childhood and early
adolescence to another.

My later years in La Martiniere were
not as difficult as the initial ones, however—partly because my sister and I had

• • •

It is a hot humid afternoon in August 2010. A team of fifteen saathis, women and men, from the Pisawan block of Sitapur have been working with Tarun, Kamal, Shivam, and me almost around the clock for the last several days to create a play that can encapsulate and advance the struggles of SKMS. Working on creating a script, that is predominantly in Hindi (with some songs and occasional phrases in Awadhi) and memorizing the lines that only four out of eleven actors are in a position to read, has been far from easy. The team is sleep-deprived, soaked in sweat, and still going strong. But the long power outage is becoming trying. We break for lunch. Rajendra has been cooking lovingly for us—he has made *khichdi*. This is not like the *khichdi* with equal proportions of rice and *dal* that I often cook myself or consume at Richa Singh's home right here in Sitapur. This is a big vessel of rice mixed with less than a cup of *dal*, and it is served with mustard oil, salt, and *hari mirch* on the side. As I eat this *khichdi*, I realize that I won't eat my next meal with the group later that night because Richa Singh and I plan to work at her home on our book about the Sangathan while the team continues its rehearsals in the office. I worry about the absence of flesh on the bodies of so many saathis who are sitting around me. I recall how so many of them are perpetually running a mild fever that has never been diagnosed. I know that saathis will eat *khichdi* again for their next meal, maybe with some watery *aaloo-tamatar ki sabzi*. Richa's mother will probably cook roti, *aloo-pyaz ki sabzi*, and *bhindi* tonight, and there should also be some left over *gulgula* from this morning.

co-devised several survival strategies; partly because I began to find solace in Hindi creative writing; and partly because I had earned a reputation as a so-called pundit of things non-English. It was toward the end of the La Martiniere days that I also discovered Ms. McClure. Raised in Burma, Ms. McClure disapproved of two things: her husband's cigarettes and girls who "stitched like *mochis*" (shoe-makers) in her sewing class.[11] But she loved stories by Rudyard Kipling and geography textbooks by Goh Cheng Leong. Even with her weakness for Monsoon-Asia-type regional geography, Ms. McClure effectively communicated to us that everything in our world happens in space and place, and one can never escape geography. Although Ms. McClure never said it in so many words, somehow her adoration of geography convinced me that it was possible for geographers to move between many worlds without compromising their passion for any of them. I think it was while listening to one of Ms. McClure's lectures in 1983 that I decided to become a geographer. Three years later, this decision was to become a second battle point in my family.

The Aborted Journey to Allahabad

The desire for geography led me to pursue my bachelor's degree at Avadh College, where I studied anthropology, geography, and English literature, but at the master's level geography was nonexistent in Lucknow. No one in my entire *kunba* had ever heard of sending a daughter away to study something as inconspicuous as geography! A hundred relatives interrogated my father: "Where will you find the means to put her in a hostel?" If I had been selected for a

What is the appropriate label for this momentary solidarity of stomachs in which I am participating? A joke? A ritual? A way for middle-class members and supporters of the Sangathan to deal with their own burdens?

Bitoli comes and sits near me as we eat that same *khichdi*; she talks about this and that, and then abruptly stops and asks me how old I am. I say forty-one. Richa Singh chimes in with her familiar laughter, "And guess what? I am older than her by more than a year!" Bitoli does not smile. She mentions her bony arms and shriveling skin, her disappearing teeth, her sunken eyes, and suddenly the loud, ringing voice of Bitoli that I feel thudding in my own chest rehearsal after rehearsal seems very soft and sad:

"I must be younger than both of you. Do you see a single white hair? Yet, I look older than everyone else here. You know why? Because poor become much older much sooner. Poverty means living a short and hard life."

Eight years ago, during the writing of *Sangtin Yatra*, we talked about the importance of every saathi of the Sangathan eating the same food when we were together so that we could begin to break the walls of untouchability that prevented some sawarn saathis from eating food prepared by the dalit saathis. The Sangathan succeeded in achieving this goal. But how does this Sangathan—or any Sangathan—prepare itself to honestly confront Bitoli's truth without risking its own survival?

. . .

On a warm summer night in Lucknow, my six-year-old body is wrapped around Baa's on her cot, and its loose coir weave is al-

medical or engineering program, it would have been worthwhile to beg or borrow, but that was not the case: "What wonders will she accomplish with a master's in geography? Work for the Geological Survey of India?" And then, there was the larger question lurking behind these minor anxieties: "What if she does something that disgraces the family?"

In some ways, perhaps, my father shared bits of all of these fears but deep inside he also believed in his children. He decided that since the government of India had decided to give me a merit scholarship of 150 rupees per month to pursue higher studies, I should be allowed to go Allahabad, four hours by train from Lucknow, to get my master's degree in geography.

But a year of intense student activism led to the academic year 1986–87 being declared a "zero session" at the University of Allahabad. As I devoured Bangla and Russian classics (in translation) and waited in vain for classes to start, my father convinced me that this was a good time to develop my creative faculties. I worked for educational television, received lessons in writing and directing children's plays, transcribed life-history interviews with theater activists, and reviewed Kathak dance performances for the local dailies. Hindi literary writing continued to pull me as I began to publish short stories and poems in magazines such as *Dharmyug* and *Sarika*. I also became the unofficial personal assistant of my grandfather, who was then fighting glaucoma and diabetes. I took dictation as he narrated his last novel, answered his mail, accompanied him to seminars in Lucknow and Delhi, and escorted him to Bombay when the well-known filmmaker Shyam most touching the ground of the enormous *aangan* of Kothhi Sah ji. With my right leg on her hip and my arm over her side, I snuggle close to Baa's beautiful, comforting body and ask her hesitatingly, "Baa, can I go to Nani's house with Maa and Bhaiyya?"

Baa stiffens. Her hand on my back seems hard and cold. She says sternly, "Bhaiyya is glued to your mother. She is still nursing that two-year-old *doond*. Let them go. You and Babli will stay here with me.[6] Your Nani's house has no running water or electricity. You will be without a fan in this heat for a month. There isn't even a toilet in that broken, clay house. '*Itli garmi maa bilbilai jasho tyan. Agla waras joyun jashe!*"

Maa never got Baa's permission to take me to her parents' house where she grew up. It was the symbol of everything shameful. Filth. Poverty. Possible disease. While Bhaiyya went year after year with Maa to Mathura and thoroughly enjoyed each one of his trips to Nani's, my first—and last—visit to that house was in 1980. Babli and I had gone with Baa to spend our summer vacation with our grandfather, who was then living in a guest house in Mathura to work on his historical novel, *Khanjan Nayan*. The three of us stayed in Dadaji's room for a month, and Nani invited all of us for lunch to her house one day. Once in that prohibited place, my sister and I convinced Baa to let us stay with Nani for a night. That is probably the only time I got away with accomplishing something that was against Baa's wish without being punished later.

Baa loved me so much she could die for me. But the day after she died in 1985, I was crying with anger. Not only had she gone away, she had also stolen my relationship with my mother forever.

Benegal invited him to discuss one of his novels for a film project.

The month-long trip to Bombay with my grandfather impacted me deeply. It exposed me to a vibrant political and artistic atmosphere and to the excitement of being in a big city, and it triggered in me a desire to step outside of Uttar Pradesh. I decided against going to Allahabad when studies resumed there and applied instead to the universities of Bombay and Poona. With student political activity delaying the start of the academic year in Bombay this time, I found myself starting a new life in the Savitribai Phule Hostel in Pune in August 1987.

From Pune to Minneapolis

University of Poona was a subsidized state university and boasted one of India's best geography departments. Of the large number of students who came to pursue geography at Poona, almost eighty percent were Marathi-speaking men from middle-to-lower-class farming families from the adjoining districts. Of the small minority who were educated in English, four students in 1987–89 were from the Pune metropolitan region, and two (including me) were from the capital cities of Manipur and Uttar Pradesh. The composition of our regional, class, and educational backgrounds made the linguistic medium of instruction an interesting challenge for instructors and students alike. Nevertheless, the department succeeded in giving its students a two-year immersion in all key subfields: geomorphology, climatology, human geography, economic geography, cartography, and research methods. Although everything we covered in these areas was dominated by the work of British, U.S., and German geographers, the department did a good job of introducing

. . .

Angrezi ka imtihan. Aur toofani barish. I
can no longer tell the difference between
the two—the thunderstorm that is drench-
ing Baba and me as he holds his huge black
umbrella over our heads, and the deluge of
tears that is falling down my face as I try to
memorize the "words and meanings" that I
will be tested on in my English class.

The Chowk branch of City Montessori
School is close to home, and Baba walks me
and my cousin there every morning, then
picks us up at the end of the day. Baba frequently hangs out to chat with the *chapra-
sis, ayahs,* teachers, and other parents, and
he often returns during recess with our tif-
fins. Baba has never gone to school, but he
can sign his own name. He has dealt with
white policemen, military officials, and
lawyers in Agra during the colonial period.
He is not afraid of anyone, not even of big
literary people like Dadaji or of people who
speak fluent English, like Phuaji. Baba believes that teachers and parents who don't
know how to treat children with sensitivity
are butchers, and I always trust Baba because he instinctively understands everything that matters, everything that makes
me happy or sad, scared or adventurous.

I shake with fear as I tell Baba that I am
going to fail the test. That I can't memorize
a thing. That I am scared of my teacher,
who will either scream at me or make fun
of my mistakes before the whole class.

Baba feels helpless, "I wish I could help
you, Bhaiyya. *Hanuman-ji sab raksha ka-
renge. . . . Jai Hanuman gyan gun saagar, jai
Bajrangbali, todenge dushman ki nali."* Baba
recites his one-verse-long version of *Hanuman Chalisa* to protect me from the terror of
the test and the wrath of the teacher.

us to geographers working in Maharashtra—
Dikshit, Diddee, Sawant, and Arunachalam.

Ironically, however, all this geography
remained untouched by larger political issues that had captured the imagination of
students on campus: the furor over Rushdie's *Satanic Verses* and the murder of *sati*
Roop Kanwar in Rajasthan. Terms such
as Marxism, feminism, political economy,
imperialism, and even colonialism never
became part of our classroom discussions.
Our training remained faithfully entrenched
within positivist, Malthusian, and neoclas-
sical paradigms no matter what specialty
we chose during our last semester in the
program. For me, all these sociopolitical
influences remained confined to the extracurricular realm, and I did not imagine that
they could become part of geography—until
I came to the University of Minnesota.

Minnesota was the most unbelievable
accident of my life. Three factors facilitated
this accident: First, Dr. Jayamala Diddee,
my mentor, urged me to contact Joseph
Schwartzberg because he had authored
An Historical Atlas of South Asia. Second,
several of my friends in the Savitribai Phule
hostel decided to take the TOEFL and GRE
so they could apply to graduate programs
in the United States, and I decided to embrace the challenge of these tests, as well.
Third, I did not look for Minnesota on the
world map until after I got a MacArthur Fellowship to study geography there.

From Minneapolis to Dar es Salaam

The trip from Delhi to Minneapolis on 31
August 1989 was the most difficult trip I
have ever taken anywhere. The joint household had split, my family had been in the
grip of some serious illnesses and economic
hardships, and my presence was needed in

Suddenly Baba guides me outside the school building, and we are standing in the petrol station adjoining the school. He stops a car in which two suited men are sitting and begs them to help this terrorized child. One of the men helps me inside the car and I sit in the middle of the two men (who smell like cigarettes) as they decipher my word-meaning assignment, which is soaking wet by this time. They ask me the meaning of each word, correct a pronunciation here and there, and then assure me that I have nothing to worry about because I know everything. Baba touches their feet with gratitude, "You both are very kind, Sahab. You have saved this child from big trouble today."

When I first started making sense of my world, I believed that Baba was Baa's brother. I gradually learned that he joined the family as a teenager the year my father was born. He began as a "dispatch boy" for a small newspaper called *Chakallas* that Dadaji published for a few years in Lucknow, and he gradually became a member of the family. It was not until 1993 that Baba shared with me that he was a child laborer who had fled his home because his mother was forced to remarry. It was not until Baba died that I heard some people in my extended family refer to him as a "servant." And it was only after he had gone that I fully realized the terms on which he had been allowed to live and die for my family.

Baa could steal my mother, but she could not steal my Baba. My relationships with Maa and Baba were intimacies of poverty in a family that had enormous cultural wealth. As I struggle to define all that I lost with Maa and all that I found with Baba, I feel as if Baba and Maa were always competing for my sister's and my love and Baba

Lucknow. Although I received nothing but complete support for my decision to go to the United States, the circumstances in which I left made me feel guilty and fearful.

But exciting things were in store for me. The MacArthur Program had just begun to generate tremendous opportunities as a community of international and U.S. students came together with a dynamic group of left-leaning faculty at Minnesota to create new interdisciplinary agendas. I was particularly drawn to the conversations happening among the African Studies scholars in the MacArthur Program, as well as the energetic discussions on oral histories, personal narratives, and popular memory that had animated the work of a large group of feminist scholars at Minnesota. At the same time, postcolonial approaches had started stirring exciting critical conversations about feminisms and the projects of ethnography.

The energy created by the MacArthur Program was nourished by the Geography Department, which encouraged me to grow theoretically and methodologically in the directions that were drawing me. I decided to do my doctoral research among the South Asian communities in Tanzania, under the support and advice of six inspiring mentors. Philip Porter and Susan Geiger, my co-advisors, taught me the importance of telling stories in academia—without losing a sense of responsibility and commitment to either the people I was studying or the issues I wished to confront and struggle for. Eric Sheppard and Helga Leitner exposed me to the most exciting ideas in social and economic geography and cultivated the spaces where their students could come together to expand their own—as well as geography's— horizons. Ron Aminzade and Prabhakara Jha made me attentive to temporality and

Photo 1. Maa. Lucknow, 1981.
(Courtesy: Sharad Nagar)

Photo 2. Baba. Lucknow, 1990.
(Courtesy: Sharad Nagar)

always won on that front because Baa let him win. Maa won our brother, Pracheta.

भाष्वती के नाम

एक भीगी उदास अमरीकी शाम को
रात की बारिश की टपर–टपर में
तुम्हारे लफ़्ज़
पता नहीं क्यों
मेरे छिले से दिल पर
मरहम बन कर फैल गये
और याद दिला गये
बाबा की उंगलियों की
जो बचपन में कोई गहरा ज़ख़्म
हो जाने पर
रात भर दर्द को सोखने में लगी रहती थीं...
बाबा की आंखों की
जिन्हें नींद से झपकते
कभी देखा नहीं

वो बाबा जो हमारे सबसे क़रीब थे
जिन्हें खुश करने के लिये हम उनके सामने
अपनी माँ की ख़ामियां गिनाते थे...
वो बाबा जो हमारे इतने सगे थे कि
उनके मरने के बाद ही हमने जाना
कि हमारे कुनबे के लिये वह
बस एक मामूली नौकर थे
और ईमानदारी से देखा जाये तो एक ऐसा
बंधुआ मज़दूर
जिसके आगे पीछे कोई नहीं था...

तो बस, पता नहीं क्यों
अचानक तुम्हारे लफ़्ज़...
नानी की कहानी...
शहज़ादी और जिन्न
मन को कुरेद कर
कुछ ऐसे पसर गये मेरे भीतर
जैसे मेरे बाबा की उंगलियों पर
अरसे से बिछा मरहम।

FOR BHASHWATI

On a sad, wet Amreeki evening
in the pitter-patter of the night rain
On a whim of their own
your words
spread on my bruised heart, like *maraham*
reminding me of Baba's fingers

postcoloniality, and pushed me to grapple with the meanings and possibilities of interdisciplinarity.

After having been immersed in race politics in the United States and developing a strong identity as a woman of color, confronting the racialized realities of East Africa in a physical way was jarring. As a woman from India who had arrived in Dar es Salaam (Dar) via the United States and who didn't easily fit the stereotypical category of a local *muhindi*, I was sometimes treated as an honorary *mzungu*. But soon I found myself negotiating and actively exploring other layers of politics as well—class, caste, religion, language, neighborhoods, as well as those of sexual practices and privileges—in a Tanzania that was shifting from being Nyerere's dream to a thoroughly liberalized multiparty democracy. The worlds that I had moved between—from Chowk and La Martiniere to Poona and Minneapolis, as well as my ancestral links to the Gujarati language—gave me the tools and passion to analyze the complexities of gender, race, class, and community in the everyday spaces and identities of South Asian immigrants in Dar. And all this happened right as the Babri Masjid was being razed in Ayodhya next to my hometown, and the effects of the Bhartiya Janata Party's rise in India could be felt as strongly among the upper-caste Hindus in Dar as Ayatollah Khomeini's preachings could be heard in the Khoja Shia Ithna Asheri Jamaat. All these interwoven processes became the subject matter of my dissertation, as well as a string of nine articles and book chapters that followed between 1995 and 2000.

that worked tirelessly all night long to
    absorb my pain
from all those deep childhood wounds
of Baba's eyes
which I never saw heavy with sleep
of Baba who was dearest to us
for whose amusement
we would recount the faults and failings of
    our mother
of Baba who was so closely kindred to us
that only after he was gone did we figure
    out
that he was just an ordinary servant for
    our *kunba*
to be honest, a bonded laborer
who had no one else before or after him.

So, I don't know why suddenly
your words
that story Nani told
the princess and the *jinn*
penetrated my heart
and spread in ways
that reminded me of
the *maraham* ever present
on my Baba's fingers.[7]

दार अस्सलाम के नाम

टीसों और मुस्कानों के साथ
याद आता है
शहर–ए–दार अस्सलाम
जिसकी हवायें, आवाज़ें, खुशबू और घाव
मेरे जिस्मोजान में
ठीक उसी तरह बस गये हैं
जैसे शाम–ए–अवध की सांसे

लेकिन
शहर–ए–दार अस्सलाम
जब तुम याद आते हो
पता नहीं क्यों
दर्द का गुबार समेटे नहीं सिमटता
क्या इसलिये कि मेरा खून और रंगत
उन लोगों से ज़्यादा मिलते हैं
जिन्होंने तुम्हारा खून चूसा है?
टुकड़ा–टुकड़ा होकर जिनके ज़मीर
बिखर गये हैं दुनिया भर में?

From Geography to Women's Studies

In 1995, I began my first tenure-track job in the Department of Geography at the University of Colorado in Boulder. To put it in Minnesotan English, Boulder was "different." And I do not mean simply its physical geography. Both interdisciplinarity and engagement with transnational politics were difficult to carry out at Colorado at that time, especially in the face of overt hostility that was frequently expressed against faculty who happened to have a combination of specific traits (relatively young, radical women of color who mentioned U.S. imperialism in their undergraduate lectures, for example). However, I did find wonderful colleagues to learn from and grow with. Don Mitchell, Lynn Staeheli, Tony Bebbington, and Tom Perreault in geography and Michiko Hase, Kamala Kempadoo, and Alison Jaggar in women's studies, in particular, gave sustenance to mind and soul. David Barsamian of Alternative Radio became a source of political nourishment, while Amy Goodman did some of that work through the radio waves every morning.

But the massive shift in institutional culture and context that Boulder brought in my life sparked questions that went beyond Boulder. As I moved from being an adopted "daughter" of Dar to becoming an assistant professor at Colorado, I found myself caught between intellectual, political, and personal commitments I had made in three continents. In strategic terms, I learned to respond to the administration's message of "publish or perish." But I was troubled by the realization that the only things that counted were those that could be discussed or consumed within Western academic circles. There was hardly any institutional

या फिर उनसे
जो चाहकर भी तुम्हारे न हो सके
क्योंकि उन्हें
अपनी चाहत दिखाने का
अपनी तवारीख़ अपने लफ़्ज़ों में लिखने का
मौक़ा ही नहीं मिला?

FOR DAR ES SALAAM

With pangs of pain and smiles
I remember
The city of Dar es salaam
Whose breezes, sounds, smells, and
     wounds
Surround my being
Like the breath of those evenings in
     Awadh.
But Dear Dar es Salaam
When your memory hits my heart
Why do I feel this excruciating pain?
Is it because my blood and color seem
Closer to those who have sucked your
     blood?
The splinters of whose conscience have
     scattered across the globe?
Or perhaps to those
Who could not be yours despite their
     intense desire
Because they never got an opportunity
To show you their love, or
To write their destinies
In their own words.[8]

सोफ़िया

दारअस्सलाम
को ख़ुदा हाफ़िज़ कहने के
चन्द महीनों बाद
ख़त मिला
परीन का
आख़िरी लाइन थी –
"सोफ़िया को सलाम
न दे सकी तुम्हारा––
सोफ़िया तो तुम्हारे जाने के
बाद ही
गुज़र गई थी
एड्स का केस था"

space to act on my sense of accountability to the people and issues I had studied in Dar. Any efforts to make my work "travel" beyond the Anglophone academy in ways that could become meaningful to people that mattered in Dar or Delhi were deemed extracurricular—in the same way that politics surrounding Roop Kanwar and Rushdie were declared extracurricular at Poona.

My work in Tanzania also made me aware of other difficulties pertaining to the question of relevance in scholarly knowledge production. In challenging the dominant image of all Tanzanian Asians as exploitative male traders, I highlighted the narratives of people from varied caste, class, religious, sectarian, and linguistic locations. In highlighting the relationality of identity, space, and power, I focused as much on the lives of cabdrivers, sex workers, and "racially mixed" people (who were both accepted and shunned by the "pure" Asians) as on the prosperous merchants, professionals, and community leaders. However, the sociopolitical power wielded by affluent Asians in Tanzania—combined with my position as a non-Tanzanian—meant that I could not share the critiques of communal organizations and leaders articulated by Asians who lived on the margins, without risking the latter's social lives or livelihoods. While my research could have proved helpful for those interested in fostering progressive interracial alliances in Tanzania, this fear of backlash by community leaders prevented me from publishing a book on my research. A critical ethnographic focus on the practices of the elite, however exciting theoretically or empirically, seriously limited the spaces available to me for producing knowledges that could contribute to advancing progressive politics in Tanzania "on the ground."

कैसे
मर गई सोफ़िया?
वो तो अभी
सत्रह की भी नहीं थी
वो तो रोज़ाना
पेट के भीतर
बच्चा लादे
पैदल आती–जाती थी
मागोमेनी से किसूटू तक––
शहर के काले हिस्से से
शहर के भूरे हिस्से तक

वो सोफ़िया
जिसे बात बात में
ख़ुराफ़ात सूझती थी....
जो किस्वाहिली में
मेरी ग़लतियां सुनकर
ज़ोर–ज़ोर से
हँसती थी.
जो मुझे काली–भूरी
चमड़ियों के रिश्तों के
अनेकों भेद बताती थी
और मेरा अपने शोध को
"काम" कहना
जिसे दुनिया का सबसे
बेहतरीन
मज़ाक़ लगता था

वो ही सोफ़िया
जो कहती थी
कि उसे
अपने बच्चे की
परवरिश के लिये
एक भी बाप की
ज़रूरत नहीं––
(न अपने बाप की
न बच्चे के)

कैसे मर गई
सोफ़िया
उन बेधड़क ख़्वाबों
गूंजते ठहाकों
और धमकते हुए क़दमों
के बावजूद?
वो तो अभी
सत्रह की भी
नहीं थी.

Struggling with these questions made it necessary for me to ask why I wanted to be in the U.S. academy, and what kind of academic work I wanted to do. Conversations with colleagues at Jawaharlal Nehru University, as well as a project with David Faust that focused on discursive and material divides produced by English-medium education in postcolonial India added new layers of complexity to this struggle. As I tried to work through these layers, I became frustrated with limitations posed by narrow conceptualizations of reflexivity in critical scholarship that rarely addressed how to generate conversations (and produce knowledges) that could move across the borders of the academy, classes, and continents. Incidentally, Susan Geiger, who was finishing her book *TANU Women* was also becoming disillusioned with popular approaches to reflexivity. Together, our mounting dissatisfaction created fertile ground to sow the seeds of a collaborative project, titled "Reflexivity, Positionality and Identity in Feminist Fieldwork: Beyond the Impasse."

And somewhere in the middle of all these searches, I decided to shift my institutional home to women's studies—a field where I felt I could blend commitments, genres, and theories in a more undisciplined way. Through a mix of exciting developments, I found myself returning to Minnesota in the fall of 1997 to make a new beginning in Women's Studies.

From *Mujhe Jawab Do* to *Playing with Fire*

Susan Geiger's tragic death in 2001 brought our collaboration to an untimely end. But the leukemia that destroyed Susan's body could not kill the quest that our conversations had inspired: a quest to cre-

SOFIA

A few months after saying good-bye to
    Dar es Salaam
Parin's letter came
Her last line was—"I could not give your
    salaam to Sofia; Sofia passed away
    soon after you left
It was a case of AIDS."

How could Sofia die?
when she was not even seventeen yet?
    when she trekked everyday
baby in her belly
from Magomeni to Kisutu
from the black part of the city
to the brown part of the city.
The mischievous Sofia
who laughed loudly when I made mistakes
    in Kiswahili
who told me of the secret bonds between
    brown and black skins which no one
    else could
who thought it was the world's most
    sophisticated joke
that I called my research, "work"
the same Sofia who said
that she did not need any father to raise
    her child (not her own, not her
    child's).
How could Sofia die?
despite those fearless dreams, those
    ringing laughs, those continuously
    vibrating feet
she was not even seventeen yet.

. . .

*Kailasha of Khanpur village does not know her
age. But many saathis respectfully call her
Kailasha Amma, in the same way that they
call Bitoli, Bitoli Amma. Like Bitoli, Kailasha
also has encountered life in such a way that
the distance between childhood and old age
seems to have shrunk into a few moments. No
matter which meeting, rally, or dharna, Kailasha Amma is always there. But she is often*

ate new forms of accountability in feminist
knowledge production not only through a
self-reflexivity about how researchers are
always inserted in politics of identities
and categories, but also through a serious
interrogation of how our institutional and
geopolitical positions contribute to rendering our work relevant—or irrelevant—across
the boundaries of the northern academy,
wherever that north might be geographically
located. For me, this quest—combined with
long-term prior associations with feminist
activists in India—translated into a process
of imagining new collaborations with nongovernmental organization (NGO) workers
and activists in Uttar Pradesh.

The process began with *Mujhe Jawab
Do*, a study of a rural women's street theater
campaign against domestic violence in Chitrakoot District. This work shared the ongoing commitment of postcolonial feminists
to destabilize ethnographic practices that
perpetuate the idea that it is only "women"
who live in the third world—not the institutions or subjects of feminism. But as I
faced the reality of how NGOs and donor-
driven visions of empowerment were deradi-
calizing grassroots feminisms, it became
clear to me that any effective intervention
in transnational politics of knowledge production would have to be accompanied
by a reshaping of dominant intellectual
practices. It would require—among other
things—collaborative agendas created with
grassroots activists, to concretely grapple
with the forms and languages in which new
knowledges ought to be produced, and the
ways in which those knowledges can be
shared, critiqued, used, and revised across
multiple sociopolitical, institutional, and
geographical borders. These concerns found
expression in a journey with eight NGO

quiet. Even when she is asked a question, she remains quiet.

When the saathis first won the battle of bringing irrigation water in the Sharada Nahar in 2007, the Sangathan organized a movement-wide conference in Khanpur for two days. The preparations for this conference were proceeding in earnest. Donations were coming in from village after village. A few volunteers had just sat down to calculate how much cash and grain had been contributed when Kailasha Amma came up and, undoing a knot at the end of her sari's pallu, she pulled out a fifty-rupee note and extended it—"Here is my contribution!" Upon delivering the note, Kailasha returned quietly to the spot where she had been sitting.

Everyone was stunned. Kailasha, who has no flesh on her bones, has to struggle hard to manage even two rotis for herself at the end of the day. Sometimes the saathis hesitate to include her in the movement's work because her body tires easily. The conference became so important for that same Kailasha Amma that she gave away her whole day's earnings to this Sangathan. Kailasha's silent support spoke louder than the support of the most vocal saathis. Her refusal to name or to draw attention to her act translated her gesture into a sacrifice that inspired the saathis. It produced an affect through which the political meanings of a hungry body became inseparable from the relationships that were emerging in and through the movement. This affect had the power to convert the rage generated by hunger into a profound hope of possibilities.

I have worked on various versions of the above text in Hindi and English for three years now, but it was only in October 2009 that I first met Kailasha Amma at a meeting attended by forty or so saathis. The story

activists in Sitapur District, which resulted first in the creation of *Sangtin Yatra*, and then its English version, *Playing with Fire.*

Both *Sangtin Yatra* and *Playing with Fire* advanced a collective struggle against depoliticization propagated by donor-driven programs that seek to "empower" rural women in the global south. These collective struggles gave birth to SKMS, a movement of peasants and laborers, which quickly spread across Mishrikh and Pisawan blocks of Sitapur District. As my companions in SKMS and I continue to travel together, we remain convinced that despite the risks that accompany alliance work, it is only by embracing more collaborative journeys across borders that we can create new intellectual and political possibilities to grow and flourish on our own terms, in our own spaces, and in our own languages.

. . .

Theater of Hopes

Richa Nagar and Tarun Kumar

Sunshine spread like warm gold into our laps on that cold January morning in the Kunwarapur village. About twenty members of SKMS had gathered outside the Sangathan's dairy to explore their interest in using *rangmanch* as a way to advance the movement's struggle. There was an excitement and sense of anticipation in the air as the faces of the more vocal members of the Sangathan such as Pita and Shammu mingled with the less-known faces of Sunita, Tama, and Saraswati Amma. The movement's fight against the corruption and everyday humiliations associated with the government of India's recently launched National Rural Employment Guarantee Act about Kailasha's role in the Sangathan is based on an episode that Richa Singh narrated to me in 2007, which I subsequently wrote up in my capacity as the Sangathan's "scribe." Kailasha's story—along with many others about the making of the Sangathan—has gone through continuous revision as it has been reread by, shared with, and translated for multiple meetings and audiences. Today, Kailasha and her two motherless granddaughters had also joined the other saathis so that they could listen to and give feedback on three draft chapters of what is now called *Ek Aur Neemsar*, a chronicle of SKMS's evolution since 2004 that I have been writing in Hindi with Richa Singh, with occasional participation from Surbala, Reena, and those who have been contributing to SKMS's newspaper, *Hamara Safar*.

Kailasha Amma silently nodded her approval when I paused after reading the Hindi version of the above passage. Other saathis clapped for Kailasha and said they wanted the second chapter of *Ek Aur Neemsaar* to open with her story. There was a brief discussion of how sacrifices such as hers constitute important stories because they allow for collective reflection, while giving courage and direction to the Sangathan's struggles.

However, I felt a restlessness that I had not encountered until that moment. I felt challenged by Kailasha's bodily presence in a way that I could not define. I wondered whether Richa Singh and I had violated Kailasha by deploying her hunger for the purposes of the Sangathan. Why was it that, even with all of our sensitivity and self-reflexivity, I had been unable to recognize the possibility of this coauthored text to commit violence until I read it before Kailasha and her granddaughters?

(NREGA) had turned a collective of a handful of people into a member-driven movement of more than three thousand people in just a matter of a few months. However, this "spectacular success" had also created serious challenges for the Sangathan: How could the depth and nuances of the political analysis that was emerging in and giving momentum to the movement be shaped by the struggles and circumstances of the membership in ways that the Sangathan's aims and agendas were not imagined and led primarily by just twenty or thirty people? Could theater become a vehicle for helping bodies and minds to remember, author, and own a collective struggle in ways that an ever-widening movement could also become an ever-deepening movement in terms of its political methodology, praxis, and poetics of engagement?

It was this search, perhaps, that made today's coming together so different from the ways in which the members had explored issues in the past. Instead of speaking through arguments, stories, and debate, people spoke in languages they had not shared before. Tama may not have been able to see the *dholak* he was playing, but his fingers danced crazily on it as the notes of Pita's voice rose higher and higher to match Tama's beats. Sunita left her feverish daughter with a neighbor so she could take the *dholak* from Tama to announce a collective rebellion against the block development officer (BDO). Reena let go of the worry that her husband would throw a tantrum if she did not behave like a proper *bahu* in her village; the papier-mâché glove puppet in the bright red sari became, with Reena's skillful maneuvers, a wild woman who laughed, jumped, and pulled the mustache of the Pradhan to protest his corrupt ways. And

But there is no easy escape from this thorny discomfort. Kailasha expects this story in the book just as she heard it. Is it because she does not know where, how, and among whom her story will travel? Is it because she doesn't really connect with the language and form in which her story is narrated? Is it because she thinks it will give her recognition in the Sangathan?

I am afraid that trying to pin down the answers to these questions may enact a greater violence than the possibility of violence that these questions seek to struggle with.

. . .

Dear Piya,

It's early morning of March 11th. I am sitting in a corner in Schiphol airport in Amsterdam. I have a couple of hours in hand before boarding my flight for Mumbai (a two-week-long trip to India to say hello to Babuji and Maa and to work on a film that Tarun and I have started to make with the saathis of SKMS). I feel a need to speak with you, even if it's in quickly snatched fragments here and there.

Your ways of telling and listening, absorbing and forgiving, are deepening our connection in ways that I find transformative for my soul. . . . For the last month and a half, even in the middle of my schizophrenic lives, I have been enveloped by the fierce power, beauty, and generosity of your letter. Perhaps the most compelling challenge you have articulated for us relates to the sparks of connection, magic, and possibility that cannot always be found through the written word, at least not in our immediate institutional contexts where "creative" gets morphed into the

Saraswati Amma, who had no patience with singing and dancing, designated Shammu as the BDO so she could grab his collar and give him a piece of her mind for all his lies and evildoings against the saathis of the Sangathan.

Eighteen months later, on a sweltering July afternoon in Minneapolis, ten Hindi- and Urdu-speaking people gathered in Divya's living room to read stories by Ismat Chughtai and Saadat Hasan Manto. Except for Tarun, our director from Mumbai, everyone else was a resident of Minnesota and earned a living as an engineer, professor, banker, scientist, or librarian. This was a group of confident people who believed that they had well-articulated perspectives on social problems affecting the subcontinent. We comfortably discussed the stories, stating what we found impressive or unimpressive about them, and tried to imagine what it would be like to dramatize one of them through our community theater workshop.

When it came to talking with our bodies, however, most of us turned into wood. Yasmin couldn't bring herself to swear nor scratch her calves like the sweeper in Chughtai's story, *Do Haath*, was supposed to. Richa became self-conscious when Tarun asked her to enact the labor pains of one of the daughters-in-law in the story. And as the authoritarian mother-in-law trying to uphold the dominant values of sexual morality, Meera struggled to enunciate things in a language she had spoken all her life. Yet, these challenges generated an excitement in everyone, from the newly married Subha and Navneet, who loved to play the romantic couple on the stage, to the ten-year-old Medha, whose crisp and confident delivery always got a reaction from the audience. And, from the soft-spoken Divya, whose "productive," even when that creativity seeks to resist the idea of productivity as it has come to be celebrated by our institutions.

At the same time, the promise of this continued dialogue, this patching and quilting between us—and between fragments of our multiple worlds that haunt us *and* make us—is precisely what makes me hopeful about narration through words—written, imagined, and *felt*; about sharing pieces in which chaos and dissonance, silence and mourning do not have to be analytically separated, translated, or made visible; about the process of finding faith, meaning, *and* languages together so that we can make ourselves radically vulnerable as we create an honest dialectic between our "internal" struggles—of making sense of our souls, our intimate silences, betrayals, nightmares (the uttering of which has been permanently postponed at times)—and our "external" struggles that involve our associations with other souls, their silences, hopes, fears, and sufferings. In linking the *khichdi* in Sitapur with the *mar-bhat* and *lal cha* and *biskit* in the *cha bagan*, you open up such a promising space of entanglements where our own bodies/spirits become inseparable from the bodies we want to commune with in our writing, organizing, healing, being. But how do we come to those entanglements if the spaces and languages available to us are acutely suspicious, even resentful, of that possibility?

Your discussion about the excesses we carry in our bodies reminded me of that seemingly endless moment when I stood at a bus stop in Nayi Tehri and watched a woman trying to nurse her inconsolable, hungry infant. I could

sarcastic and mischievous commentary as the narrator stunned her friends, to Brendan and David, who had lived in South Asia but who never had a similar opportunity to immerse themselves in the intricacies of a place-based context and characters. The two months of developing a staged reading of Chughtai's story became all-consuming as each of us struggled with not only what our bodies could be un/trained to un/do, but also as every meeting of the collective was followed by emotionally charged reflections: What did it mean to learn about the politics of untouchability, sexual morality, and economics through our bodies? What did it mean to claim to know, understand, or stand with struggles in the subcontinent from our locations? What light did this process shed on our own stances and rigidities and on how we had chosen to expose our children to, or shield them from, these issues? It became clear that enacting the story meant learning and unlearning how privilege and pride, humor and hopes, insults and humiliations are internalized and resisted through our bodies.

As organizers of this work in Kunwarapur and Minneapolis, we found it instructive to reflect on the commonalities and disjunctures in the passions, processes, and products that have emerged in and through theater in these two very different contexts. Among the most generative for us is the question of when theater becomes *community theater* and what makes community theater successful? Does success reside in the creative and affective processes that lead to the creation and enactment of an aesthetically powerful product? Or, does the real test of success lie in that which comes after the enactment through a coming-together of people who become a collectivity?

not know how hungry the woman was, but I could see that she did not even try to offer her dry breast to the child in her arms. She continued to thrust a nippled water bottle into the screaming baby's mouth. I stood there with my friend, Khajan, streams of milk flowing under my own shirt, for I had an eighteen-month-old on another continent waiting for me, and my body was responding to this child's call to quench her hunger. However, as a complete stranger accompanied by a man from the area, I couldn't even communicate to the woman the solidarity that I felt in my body. If the people on the *cha bagan* can offer their only protein to you, what stopped me from offering to that baby the protein that I had in excess?

That moment from Nayi Tehri has never left me. My need to process it once led to a fragmented poem in Hindi, interspersed with its translation into English, as I struggled to write a (non)conclusion to an academic conference paper that I was asked to present in Singapore; but a couple of harsh responses I received from two self-described "feminists" at that conference made me think that I should not try to communicate with academics through poems again. The memories of that child's screams, of the eyes of her mother, of my drenched shirt and a subsequent conversation with Khajan, and of the "feminists" who told me how my poem was emotionally manipulative, still howl in my face and make me ask again and again whether "we" will ever be able to confront the ways in which our bodies enable, complicate, and foreclose our political and theoretical commitments; and the manner in which this confrontation

If success implies advancing critical creativity, analysis, and vision through theater, then it is the emergence of the collective that makes such theater possible. This is a theater that is enabled and nourished by collective labor—the labor of grappling with and recognizing one another's journeys, silences, passions, and aspirations. The labor of working through the ups and downs of the creative process as well as the knots of our hearts, minds, and bodies. The labor of learning to dream together and to celebrate what emerges from laboring together so that those who draw inspiration and challenge from that theater can return to weave the next dream.

. . .

A long conversation with Özlem Aslan, Nadia Hasan, Omme-Salma Rahemtullah, Nishant Upadhyay, and Begüm Uzun in Toronto inspired me to think again about my role in SKMS.[12] Can the term *scribe* capture the work that I often do with SKMS? As someone who does not inhabit the immediate space of the movement all the time, perhaps *scribe* is exactly what I have been at many occasions. But that is not all that I am, since I am also given—and claim—the space in the movement to raise the toughest questions I can think of. This responsibility has come with obvious risks. Yet, I take it seriously because, when a movement is being celebrated as being unique and successful, it is easy to slip into the same problems that we have been critical of. As somebody who is outside the immediate space of Sitapur, then, I try to ask questions that remind the SKMS about these risks and slippages. Why do I think I have this space? Because I have the trust that allows me to can never yield answers, only questions and hauntings.

Saathis in Sitapur often remark on the well-intentioned members of the middle classes who visit their villages to support them and who condemn caste untouchability but who cannot operate without their own segregated bottles of purified water. Why is this practice not deemed untouchability, they ask. I feel that sangtins have a sophisticated gauge by which they determine whether or not someone can stand with them, to what extent, and in what ways; and the ability to eat and drink the same food and water that they are eating and drinking is a very important component of this gauge. I try to do well on the test but almost always lose my voice due to the air and water pollution, and sometimes get violently ill with gastroenteritis, at which point I am generously excused by my comrades for my body's refusal to comply with their standards. All of this keeps me perpetually journeying through the question of what it means to enact solidarity when, like a virus, the germs of my physical, material, and socioeconomic location have made a *pukka* house inside my body and made it unable to accept the same conditions of living embraced by those I want to stand, dream, and learn with? Is the body betraying the mind, or is it telling a harsh truth that the mind is refusing to accept? Maybe some of each? But how do we theorize this contradiction, and work with it in our beings and in the spaces available to us in, despite, and beyond our institutions?

■ ■ ■

carry out this responsibility. For, the saathis can also question my practices, and I am also available to do what the Sangathan needs me to do. For instance, I can write in Hindi and English for the movement, mobilize resources to advance SKMS's work, help build connections, and mobilize support of various kinds. So in some ways my role is carved out.

At other times, however, I have asked myself and have been asked by academics in the United States if my relevance for the movement is over. There was a time when this anxiety led me to repeatedly pose a question before the saathis: "There is all of this terrific stuff happening in SKMS, so do you think that it is time for me, 'the academic,' to leave?" Saathis tolerated my question patiently for a couple of years, and then threw a question back at me: "How important do you think you are that you keep talking about withdrawing from SKMS? Why don't you stand in the next rally before everyone and say that, oh you know, me Richa Nagar, I am so important that I have just decided to leave, sorry I can't think of anything I can do anymore."

To receive this response to my anxieties was extremely helpful for me. What the saathis were teaching me through this question is that anyone who is committed to a struggle will need to find something to do that they know how to do best; that an alliance means that everyone must figure out ways in which they can creatively contribute to the struggle as a whole.

Surbala sometimes comes after weeks of organizing meetings and rallies and laboring in the heat for hours, and then sits down to embroider as a way to relax. It is a creative skill through which she expresses herself,

Trust and Translation

In a coffee shop in Taksim, Ayşe Gül
Altınay was holding the Turkish script of
The Triggerman, written by Ebru Nihan
Celkan, and we had fifteen minutes in hand
before we had to enter the auditorium. In
those fifteen minutes, Ayşe tried to explain
to me in English the key pieces of the play
as well as the nuances of each scene. After
the play was over, Ebru asked me if I could
see India and Indians in this play, which
was about the making and nourishing of
terrorism by the Turkish state.

Ayşe's trust reminded me of that bus
ride from Aurangabad in 1989 when Shruti
Tambe read to me Gauri Deshpande's
Chandrike Ga Sarike Ga. Shruti knew that
I was only a beginner in Marathi, but every
time she lifted her eyes from the book to
meet mine, I saw a trust that moved and
overwhelmed. "Watch me speak," she said,
"listen to me, and you will understand.
You can feel the language." I remember us
discussing the book for days afterward. If I
close my eyes, I can still relive the curiosi-
ties and yearnings that Gauri Deshpande's
words brought to life—even though I
felt them only through Shruti's voice and
through Shruti's trust.

After an energizing morning with
twenty-two feminist activists who gathered in the office of Insan Hakları Ortak
Platformu (Human Rights Joint Platform)
in Ankara, Aksu Bora, Tennur Baş, and I
catch a cab to Ankara University. Aksu asks
when *Ek Aur Neemsaar* is coming out in
English. I tell Aksu what I feel confident
about after months of agonizing over—and
supposedly resolving—for myself: "I do
not want to translate *Ek Aur Neemsaar*

and the embroidered material is sometimes
sold by SKMS to help with the organizational work. Surbala once said, "Writing
to you is what embroidering is to me. My
embroidery supports the movement in the
same way as your writing does. If my embroidery does not cause a crisis for me, why
does your writing cause a crisis for you?"
Surbala's question pushed me to reflect on
the ways in which saathis process the same
dilemmas that academics struggle with. It
helped me locate my own labor as writer in
relation to other forms of labor that enable
the movement.

• • •

In November 2010, Dorothy Hoffman,
the principal of Laura Jeffrey Academy, a
girl-focused middle school in Saint Paul,
Minnesota, invited me to talk to her class
about the making of *Playing with Fire*, and
the subsequent journey of the sangtins. A
few weeks later, I received a letter from her,
where she said

> Sorry [for taking] so long in getting
> back to you after your visit with the 8th
> grade girls. Your time with them, and
> the manner in which you presented the
> experience of the Sangtin group, was
> exactly what they needed to take a gi-
> ant step into what the class (year-long)
> was/is all about. It brought them from
> the highly self-conscious state of ado-
> lescence into the greater world and the
> world of women in the world. Your ques-
> tion about "pity"—bringing them away
> from it into admiration—helped them
> begin to differentiate between sympathy
> and empathy. The power they heard of
> and saw in the slides gave them an im-
> age of what a collective can accomplish

into English, at least not in the form that *Playing with Fire* took. There are all these unintended and unforeseen consequences of circulating stories in a language such as English, which may not work for the alliance and the Sangathan at this time."

Aksu listens respectfully but disagrees that not translating is the way out. Translation into English, she says, is the only way readers in Turkey will be able to enter into critical dialogues about it. In the absence of *Sangtin Yatra*'s translation as *Playing with Fire*, the kind of conversation we had this morning would never happen. "I appreciate your argument," says Aksu, "but I think you cannot *not* translate." Tennur, who is intently listening to this conversation, agrees.

Less than a week later, I am in Diyarbakir. After an intense discussion session with more than sixty women of KAMER who read *Ateşle Oynamak*, the Turkish translation of *Playing with Fire*, Ayşe Gül and Nebahat Akkoç are excited about the possibility of having the conversation between KAMER and SKMS in person. Can one or two dalit women from the Sangtin Writers collective come to Turkey for a dialogue with Kurdish women in KAMER? I hesitate, having a sense of the kind of concerns I might hear at this proposal from members of SKMS. I also recall those tough moments in Minneapolis, Richmond, and New Delhi when well-intentioned desires of forging dialogues and exploring resonances between sangtins and other collectives working in very different worlds, but grappling with similar questions of marginality and justice, only led to pain and disappointments. Heart-wrenching events that taught me why and how the idea of bring-

in terms of support and change. . . . Jan Mandell, from Central High School Theatre, came in the afternoon and did some community building theatre activities with them—and it was evident that the morning with you had given them motivation to want to be together—to want/and dare to want to know one another better. They knew/know we have our own castes to wrestle with and that we avoid doing so every day in our classrooms and lives. The girls are hungry for guidance in how to go further—together—and I'm afraid they'll not get all they need right now. Sometimes, our accountability can only be for planting the seeds.

The responsibility to translate and represent implies continuously grappling with the question of whether we can represent ethically in ways that mitigate epistemic violence. But no matter how carefully one carries out that task, it is risky business to translate struggles in a manner that their complexities and insights can be recognized in locations far removed from where they are unfolding. While Dorothy Hoffman was able to do justice to my labor of representing sangtins' struggle, there are multiple examples of times when *Playing with Fire* has traveled with consequences that were in opposition to the spirit of the book.[13] Yet, the conversations with Dorothy generated hope precisely because, as a teacher and poet, she was already immersed in the labor of unlearning and relearning in ways that resist resolutions and closures; that seriously question dominant assumptions about, and desires for, expertise; that recognize the necessity of becoming radically vulnerable in order to build trust and to undertake the ing together struggles in the same room in order to learn from them is far easier than the imaginative, analytical, political, and creative labors of figuring out what it might take to make those struggles speak with one another. Not to mention the emotional labor of how to work through difficult moments in which there might be neither speech nor translation. Only the possibility of coming to terms with impossibilities.

But how can I communicate those concerns without oversimplifying them, or without violating my responsibility as a coauthor, as a member of an alliance, as a translator, and as a critic? How do I enact accountability without ignoring the truth that trust and faith in translation are the chief, perhaps the only, modes of communication available to me as I interact with members of SKMS and with those friends in Turkey and elsewhere who have chosen to listen to the sangtins' journey with open minds and generous hearts?

. . .

Every act of sharing is an act of translation, an act that contains the possibility of becoming radically vulnerable. It is impossible to "know" where the sharing might lead us without having taken the risk of exposing that intimate fragment that can only be translated inadequately. The journeys of embracing these risks are journeys of faith. Sometimes they give us courage to tell more. Sometimes, they teach us to withdraw. And at yet others, there is only the inevitability of sleeplessness, hauntings, tears.

In Cape Town, Elaine Salo, Sophie Oldfield, Koni Benson, and I spend three days

very hard work of *trying* to get to a place from where one can simply hope to kindle a faith in dialogues.

. . .

No Accelerated Passport for Rambeti

In 2012–13, members of the Climate Change, Agriculture, and Food Security (CCAFS) Program of the Consultative Group for International Agricultural Research (CGIAR) and the international network Promoting Local Innovation (Prolinnova) expressed an interest in learning how the methodology of the Sangtin Writers could help them develop more sustainable partnerships with grassroots communities. This encouraged me to organize a series of email, phone, and Skype conversations between members of SKMS and CCAFS. The conversations focused on two points: whether and how CGIAR and Prolinnova could learn from SKMS in addressing the politics of social inequity and difference while addressing issues of access to livelihoods; and whether it was worthwhile for SKMS to devote its energies to building a dialogue with CCAFS and Prolinnova despite the violent histories and geographies against rural peoples that institutions such as CGIAR have enabled. The conversations led David Edmunds and Lini Wollenburg from CCAFS and Chesha Wettasinha from Prolinnova to extend an invitation to Rambeti, Richa Singh, and me to attend a workshop titled "Climate Change, Innovation and Gender" in Phnom Penh. Hosted by Prolinnova's Cambodia country team, the workshop together, sharing pieces of stories that make us, and haunt us. Stories of those we have chosen to walk with. Of journeys that are necessarily interrupted and fragmented. Our conversations push me to search for some of those bits that remain unwritten in the pages of these translated fragments. They inspire me to bring a tentative closure to this chapter by making the fragments, and the translations, messier and by becoming more radically vulnerable.

Ek Aur Neemsaar (Another Neemsaar) is the title of the book, published in 2012, that documents Sangtin's journey from the writing of *Sangtin Yatra* to the making of SKMS. Namisharanya, the holy town that attracts many Hindu pilgrims to Sitapur District, has a nickname—Neemsaar, which literally means the essence of the Neem leaf—an essence that is bitter but cures illnesses. *Ek Aur Neemsaar* also carries bitter truths that lie at the heart of sangtins' struggles.

Muddying the Waters emerged from a decision to not translate *Ek Aur Neemsaar* into English. *Ek Aur Neemsaar* taught me how telling stories across borders can trigger desires and dreams that might betray the "original" dream and commitment of *Sangtin Yatra*. I sensed how translated and published words can turn into both wounds and weapons. I felt paralyzed by the mobility of my own body and by my own ability to play with words. I could "know" and "feel" the drama of the political theater that I participated in with members of SKMS, but I could no longer claim to responsibly represent the everyday drama that was unfolding in the ever-expanding movement in the villages of Sitapur.

organizers stated their aims, and their vision of SKMS's role in the workshop thus:

> The purpose . . . is to stimulate research, development projects and information exchange networks that strengthen the ability of rural women and men to test and implement their ideas for improving agriculture in ways that simultaneously reduce poverty, food insecurity and greenhouse gas emissions. Addressing climate change in a way that is fair to rural women and men in the global south, who have contributed relatively little to the problem, will require two important social reforms. First, rural women and men must take on active leadership in designing projects and programs. SKMS has been remarkably successful in mobilizing rural women and men to change their lives, often in remote areas and with little or no support from outside organizations. Second, large research and development organizations must not undermine local initiatives once they are underway. SKMS has a unique, critical perspective on the work of international NGOs, research institutions, and development agencies and how they interact with grassroots movements. SKMS thus can help our grassroots partners in improving their mobilization efforts, and help large research and development organizations make reforms necessary so that they can enhance rather than weaken local innovation.[14]

I had no difficulty convincing the hosts at CGIAR of the importance of Rambeti's involvement in the workshop, and in helping them craft an invitation that underlined the critical insights that only she could offer

The journeys that unfold on the pages of this book, then, are as much about what can be said or known in love as they are about the uncertainties that burden love, and that make solidarity perpetually fragile and uneven. They are as much about the political economy of truth making as they are about impure truths and polluted genres. They are as much about contaminated knowledges as they are about ruptured intimacies that enable and stifle us.

• • •

My first sleepless night in Cape Town. In the magnificent house where I am residing as a visiting professor from the United States. A stack of newspapers by the kitchen fireplace brings forth a long erased memory. Of burning hot summer afternoons in Lucknow when I put *leyi* to seal three sides of the envelopes that my mother made out of beautiful glossy pages of *Soviet Land*, the complimentary magazine that came freely to us as a perk associated with Dadaji's membership in the Indo-Soviet Cultural Society. I can almost feel each fresh stream of sweat that trickled down my legs even as the green Usha table fan sat on the floor blowing hot air at Maa and me. Was I five then?

Maa tied a string around each stack of fifty envelopes and then walked to Ban Wali Gali to sell them secretly to a shop owned by Guptaji. Guptaji liked the envelopes because of the special "imported" paper and their impressive size. He did not disclose to anyone that Nagarji's *chhoti bahu* sold those envelopes to him because his son's activism as a student had rendered him jobless with three children, a foreign

as a dalit agricultural laborer who plays a leadership role in SKMS. However, getting a passport for Rambeti in time for the workshop was a different story. Rambeti required special permission from her district authorities in order to get a passport in hand within three months of her application. The district magistrate and the sub-district magistrate of Sitapur refused to sign a letter supporting SKMS's request for an accelerated passport for Rambeti on the grounds that they did not know rural laborers well enough to support such a request. Ironically, neither Richa Singh nor I as "representatives" of SKMS would have had any difficulty receiving such permission. While we were optimistic that Rambeti's passport would come through, we were tormented by the same old question: even after all the victories of SKMS's rank-and-file members, how is it that those in power can dismiss a dalit member as a representative of her own struggle but have no qualms about accepting a sawarn as the narrator of the same struggle?

The journey continues, as does the commitment to wrestle with this violence.

• • •

My nineteenth sleepless night in Cape Town. I am thinking of death. How it comes easily and is accepted easily by saathis in Sitapur. When we met in July, Roshan could not join us for the rehearsals, and saathis said he might not live long. Two weeks later, Kusuma's husband died of an unknown disease before he turned fifty. And I received news a few days ago that Radhpyari's son died of a snake bite in his village because he could not be taken to a hospital in time.

language certificate in Russian, and an in-progress doctorate in organic chemistry.

How much money did those envelopes fetch? How did I manage to not remember those afternoons for almost four decades?

Does my forgetting of this truth betray my lack of intimacy with my own mother? Can I adequately mourn the loss that comes from the knowledge that my mother may not share my pain for what we could not be together?

Deaths that dramatically end life—and hopes. Yet, saathis often swallow the sorrow of deepest loss by death. There is no desire on the part of saathis to translate or communicate these sorrows in the scripts that we create together. There is no assumption or expectation that the intimacy or intensity of these sorrows can be apprehended, even partially, by the currently available registers.

What does that say about the discourse of hope that we—the saathis and their supporters—have collectively refined and mastered in our rallies, meetings, speeches, and writing?

Or maybe a praxis of love and radical vulnerability is contingent on learning to accept that which cannot enter the realm of translation?

2. Dar es Salaam

*Making Peace with
an Abandoned "Field"*

It all began in Dar es Salaam. The place I learned to love through stories of countless journeys. The place that entangled me forever with questions of expertise and knowledge making; of positionality and responsibility; of memories that haunt; and of promises that remained unfulfilled. Dar is the place where I first set foot in 1991 and to which I could not physically return after the completion of my dissertation fieldwork in 1993.

The reasons behind my initial immersion in Dar es Salaam had as much to do with the excitement generated by debates in postcolonial theory, African studies, and women's and oral history in the early 1990s as they had to do with my desire to resist a racialized system of creating "experts" where, as an immigrant from India, I was often expected to become a "South Asianist" in the U.S. academy. Little did I know that despite all the exciting rhetoric about the need to promote south–south research and postcolonial scholarship in postcolonial sites, the same academy would try to label me as an "Africanist" a few years later, while also frequently assuming that I studied Tanzanian Asians because I must be "one of them." At the same time, academics who were authorized as "one of them" in the United States, United Kingdom, and Canada repeatedly asked: "How did you as an 'outsider' get people in Dar to talk about all those things they would never tell us?"

Yet, these were not the assumptions or questions that deterred me from continuing my relationship with Dar es Salaam. My decision to not continue research in Dar emerged more from a combination of warnings and suggestions, ranging from "this research will land you in serious trouble with the rich East African Asians" to "why don't you develop this study as a comparative analysis of South Asians in Hong Kong and Tanzania so that you can diffuse the race and class politics while gaining access to an international market for your book?"

Despite the distance and agony that resulted, it is the relationships and promises that I made in Dar es Salaam that set everything in motion. Dar is where I began to understand scholarship as an intense creative and political journey that comes with certain responsibilities. I grappled, for the first time, with what it might mean to carry out those responsibilities when intellectual work hinges on getting entangled with people who share with the researcher their everyday lives and spaces, their festivities and mourning, their disappointments and longings. My "abandonment" of Dar as a research site resulted from the harsh truth that I did not have the tools at the time to adequately wrestle with the commitments that could do justice to such entanglements. And the inevitable and lingering restlessness that came from this abandonment put me on the path of searching for languages, translations, and representations that can be more ethical; that can try to better internalize the poetry of coauthored dreams and fires; and the critical analyses and visions that this ever-evolving search can make possible.

The following discussion of the research methodology that I adopted in Dar is derived from a longer essay that aimed to inject into the feminist geography of the early 1990s the vibrancy of the debates on positionality and location that were happening in African Studies, women's history, and critical ethnography (Nagar 1997). As such, this chapter is inserted in the terminologies and discussions of the 1990s. While much of my research in Dar came out in the form of academic articles in journals that the majority of my subjects or "life historians" were never likely to read, one research topic that was close to my heart—but that remained confined to the dissertation pages—concerned the everyday politics of language in the Asian communities. The sidebar accompanying this chapter is excerpted from a more detailed chapter of my dissertation on this topic (Nagar 1995).

Exploring Methodological Borderlands through Oral Narratives

What does it mean to situate fieldwork in the multiple contexts in which we, as politically engaged beings, operate? How are research and researcher both constituted in and through the "spaces of betweenness" that unfold in the process of making knowledge in the field? Can fieldwork be a form of resistance to dominant ways of acquiring and codifying knowledge? Feminist geographers have become increasingly immersed in these difficult conversations about the politics of fieldwork and representation (see Katz 1994, Nast 1994). Here, I contribute to this discussion on the basis of my own fieldwork experience in Dar es Salaam. Specifically, I explore how critical feminist ethnography has enabled me to explore issues of multiply juxtaposed social identities and their connectedness with social places.[1] I also emphasize the importance of relationality and reflexivity in my work by illuminating how my social and spatial situatedness with respect to different communities and individuals defined my relationships with them, and thereby, the knowledge that we produced. Finally, I show how my own attempts to expose power relations through my research, and to overcome them in my personal life, affected what I saw, heard, probed, and wrote.

Identities and Narratives: The Focus of My Research

The fragmented nature of subjectivity and the contingency of social experience is captured well by Stuart Hall when he compares identity to a bus ticket: "You just have to get from here to there, the whole of you can never be represented in the ticket you carry but you have to buy a ticket in order to get from here to there" (quoted in Watts 1992, 124). Racial, ethnic, gender, class, or sexual identities do not define a fixed profile of traits, but a fluctuating composition of differences, multiple intersections, and incommensurabilities that are historically, politically, culturally, and contextually constructed, and constantly transformed in continuous plays of history, culture, and power (Lowe 1991).

It is through an engagement with these complex and often contradictory constructions, expressions, and transformations of multiple and intersecting identities in people's everyday lives that I dismantle the homogenous category of "Asian" in postcolonial Dar es Salaam. This racial category—originally constructed in a colonial context to refer to people who immigrated from what are now India and Pakistan and to position "Asians" between the "native African" and the ruling British in East Africa—has continued to define Tanzania's social and political landscape. I explore how Tanzanian Asian men and women experienced, created, and modified their complex social identities and boundaries in the context of a rapidly changing political-economic environment and continuously shifting numbers and configurations of their communities between 1961 and 1993. In the course of this exploration, I examine essentializing descriptions based on race, gender, class, religion, sect, and language. I also highlight two other processes—namely, how individuals and organizations combined gendered discourses with discourses of race, caste, class, and religion to maintain or alter both social boundaries and gender relations; and the manner in which social places, such as community halls, clubs, beaches, mosques, and religious schools, reinforced existing identities and structures of power on the one hand, and became sites to challenge dominance on the other. Social places, communal organizations, languages, and various kinds of interracial, interreligious, and interclass relationships serve as multiple windows to reveal different facets of complexity and diversity associated with the lives of Asian women and men. Throughout my work, I intersperse my own narrative with the narratives of men and women from different classes and religious, caste, sectarian, and linguistic backgrounds, some labeled as "pure" and others as "half-castes," some respected and others shunned by their communities. This narrative challenges the dominant image of all Tanzanian Asians as exploitative male traders, and emphasizes how those in power (whether in state, communities, or organizations) tried to shape racial and communal rhetoric, and how the less powerful internalized or troubled their ideas.

A key question that arises here is whether a focus on identity is the best way to examine the diverse experiences and the hierarchies of power among people. Margaret Somers points out why an "identity approach" is necessary to understand social action. An individual or a collectivity, Somers maintains, cannot be assumed to have any particular set of interests simply because one aspect of their identity fits into one social category such as class or race or gender. Rather than imputing interests to people on the basis of a social category, an identity approach to action focuses on how people characterize themselves. It recognizes that people are guided to act by the multiple relationships in which they are embedded, and that the patterns of their relationships continually shift over time and space (Somers 1992).

Identities are formed and challenged within numerous and multilayered narratives and social networks. As Somers writes, "narrative identities are constituted by a person's temporally and spatially specific 'place' in culturally constructed stories that comprise (breakable) rules, (variable) practices, binding (and unbinding) institutions, and the multiple stories of family, nation, or economic life" (Somers 1992, 607). My research places the public and cultural narratives that inform people's lives in relation to spatial structures, institutional practices, organizational constraints, politics, and demography, all of which combine to shape the history and geography of social action. In this manner, Asians from different backgrounds can be located as characters in their social narratives within a temporally and place-specific configuration of relationships and practices.

A great deal of emphasis has been placed on race, class, and gender in recent feminist and identity-related literature emerging in the Anglophone academy. Although this emphasis may be pertinent in some contexts, race, class, and gender can, by themselves, be inadequate to understand experiences of peoples whose identities and social experience are defined just as saliently (if not more so) by religious, caste, sectarian, and linguistic affiliations. In the following discussion of the methodology of my research on identity politics among Asians in Dar es Salaam, I show that identity theory needs to be geographically and historically contextualized, allowing the range of social multiplicities we consider as researchers to expand and alter according to the places and time periods we study.

Problematizing Categories

Identities are often defined in terms of normative categories which typically take the form of fixed binary oppositions, categorically asserting the meaning of masculine and feminine, white and black, homosexual and heterosexual, etc. (Scott 1986). My study deals with normative categories based on race (African, Asian, Arab, half-caste), religion (Hindu, Muslim, Sikh), caste/sect (Ismaili, Ithna Asheri, Brahmin, Baniya), region of origin (Goan, Gujarati, Kutchi, Punjabi), class, gender, and language. I focus on four Asian communities in Dar es Salaam—"the Hindus," "the Ithna Asheris," "the Sikhs," and "the Goans." Although these communities distinguished themselves primarily along religious lines, their labels subsumed other identities as well. The word Sikh, for example, was invoked as a simultaneously religious, linguistic, and regional category referring to followers of the Sikh faith from Punjab who spoke Punjabi. The term Goan was generally used by Tanzanians to refer to Roman Catholics from Goa, which was a Portuguese colony until 1961 and is now part of India. The label Ithna Asheri referred to Khoja Shia Muslims who traced their origins to the Kutch and Kathiawar regions of India. Tanzanian Asians used the term Hindu to refer mainly to people from Gujarat, Kathiawar, and Kutch who were born in any Hindu caste. References to Hindus from other parts of India were generally qualified by terms such as Hindu Punjabi or UP Hindu.

Thus, the labels Sikh and Hindu gave primacy to religion, although regional and linguistic affiliations were also implied. The term Ithna Asheri gave primacy to a specific Muslim sect, but its regional origins were clear. The label Goan gave primacy to a region, but it had strong religious and sectarian connotations. There was no consistency, therefore, in the way names were applied to different groups. It is to highlight the inconsistent and unproblematized nature of these frequently used designations that I use the phrase *normative categories* in describing these communities. I chose these four communities to complicate the too-often-made distinctions among Hindu, Muslim, Sikh, and Christian as if they are internally homogeneous, self-contained, and disharmonious categories. I challenge this simple classification of communities on the basis of religious affiliation by highlighting the manner in which social experience shapes and is shaped by various layers of social identities in different geographical and historical contexts. At the same time, I explore how organizational, institutional, and societal processes as well as ontological, public, and cultural narratives operate in people's lives over time and in different places to strengthen and reinforce their identities as members of specific categories (see Nagar 1995).

Creating a "Feminist Ethno-geography" to Explore Social Boundaries

Dominant paradigms in the social sciences have largely treated subalterns as a residual category since they are not immediately visible participants in politics, trade, and matters of state (Ngaiza and Koda 1991). Through personal narratives, oral and life historical researchers have grappled with the experiences of those who do not have access to means of publicity and whose feelings, thoughts, and actions get hidden behind the experience of dominant male middle class, which incorrectly acquires universal significance. Behar (1993), Mbilinyi (1989), and Ngaiza and Koda (1991) point out how oral narratives can make "private" oppressions more public and more shared, challenging dominant patriarchal definitions and the silencing of subalterns. Furthermore, a critical awareness of relationality is central to any study of community and identity. Personal narratives, strengthened by participant observation, provide insights into the complexities of intersecting social relationships and the manner in which these construct communities and identities in different contexts.

My research deploys feminist ethnography, with sensitivity to the role of place and space in constituting identities and communities as well as in the production of knowledge itself. Between 1991 and 1993, I spent twelve months in Dar es Salaam, collected fifty-eight life stories, and conducted 150 shorter interviews/conversations with Goan, Sikh, Ithna Asheri, and Hindu men and women from different backgrounds.[2] Shorter interviews centered on people's family and occupational histories, experiences of and opinions about various political events since 1960, participation in community activities, daily schedules, and mental maps, as well as histories of communal institutions and organizations as narrated by both leaders and common people. Most life stories emerged from several long conversations with each informant over a period of time and involved (in addition to the topics mentioned above) discussions on family, marriage, and relationships; personal, familial, and economic issues; race and gender relations; community politics; attitudes toward individuals and groups; and reflections on informants' multiple and contextual identities. Additionally, I collected information from historical and contemporary newspapers, community records, and family archives.

Participant observation formed the core of my research and the heart of my experience in Dar es Salaam. There was no clear line of separation between my personal life and my research. I spent most of my time in the Asian-dominated city center with friends and acquaintances from different communities in temples, mosques, clubs, halls, playgrounds, beaches, religion classes, and community houses; in weekly community gatherings; at celebrations of secular/religious festivals and weddings; and in people's homes, where I frequently spent

Photo 3. Beaches became sites of lively debate about multiparty politics in Tanzania. Dar es Salaam, 1993. (Photo: Richa Nagar)

time or lived as a guest, friend, researcher, or "adopted" family member. There was hardly a street in the city center that I did not know intimately. Many Asian families welcomed me as one of their own and gently insisted that if they ever found me paying for a meal, they would be offended. The deeply segregated nature of the city along racial and class lines meant that I was totally cut off from Asians when I lived away from the city center on the university campus. However, once I entered the Asian area, I ate my meals in people's homes, participated in family and neighborhood gossip, and caught up with everyday events in the communities. Being in Asian residential and social places allowed me to experience and identify the rifts and alliances along the lines of religion, class, caste, race, and gender that defined these places.

Dar es Salaam became a kaleidoscope of social sites for me, as I traversed its segregated gendered, classed, raced, and communalized spaces in the course of my daily life. With every turn of the kaleidoscope, I was conscious of my changed position, both geographically and socially. Not only did I behave differently in each situation, but people in each place textualized me differently, and dialogical processes between me and my informants in different places continuously shaped the structure and the interpretations of the narratives that were produced in the course of my work.

My methodology attempted to infuse feminist ethnography with a geographical understanding. A combination of oral narratives, observations, shorter interviews, mental maps of informants, and newspaper and archival sources helped me construct "life-historical geographies" that combined a geographical approach with a historical sensibility, explored complexities of lived culture and subjectivity, and examined how individuals were positioned within complex social relations in time, place, and space.

Reflexivity and Intersubjectivity in a Geography of Positionality

My research topic and methodology made reflexivity and intersubjectivity central to my work.[3] At the heart of both reflexivity and intersubjectivity lie issues of positionality. Understanding positionality entails an analysis of the locations of the researcher and the "researched," and of their relationship with each other. As Visweswaran notes, "the relationship of the knower to known is constituted by the process of knowing. Conversely, the process of knowing is itself determined by the relationship of knower to known" (Visweswaran 1994, 48).

My exploration of the politics of communities and social identities is intertwined with the complex ways in which my own identities and background situated me in relation to my informants. An examination of these intricate positionings in the following pages reveals how my aim to analyze normative categories through my research did not preclude people from labeling me and putting me into categories to which they directly or indirectly related. The ways I was perceived by individuals or by a whole community, for example, shaped the degree to which they accepted me and what they shared with me. These positionings were profoundly affected by place- and space-specific phenomena and processes, an aspect often overlooked by ethnographers.

Reflexivity also necessitates that I analyze my own personal and political commitments with respect to my informants and my research project. Such an investigation on my part can be defined as "an effort at 'accountable positioning' . . ., an endeavor to be answerable for what I have learned to see, and for what I have learned to do" (Visweswaran 1994, 48).

How "Communities" Perceived Me

Some things about me were quite apparent to almost every Asian with whom I interacted—I was a single woman, in her early twenties, from a lower-middle-class Hindu family in India, doing doctoral research in Dar es Salaam. Other aspects of my background I revealed in diverse ways, depending on the context, and different things were perceived as important by different communities. Despite these divergences, however, I never felt that the desire to build relationships with the communities was one-sided. From the beginning, all the communities sought common ground with me on which to build a foundation for our relationship. People's imagined and symbolic connections with geographical regions—whether it be the United States, the Indian states of Gujarat or Uttar Pradesh, or the city of Lucknow—and the manner in which they placed me with reference to those places, played an important role in defining their attitudes towards me.

Gujarati speakers, who formed an overwhelming majority of the Asian population of Dar es Salaam, easily guessed my Gujarati ethnic origins by my last name and my knowledge of the Gujarati language. My Hindi accent, however, often required me to clarify that although my family has retained a "Gujarati" identity in the state of Uttar Pradesh (where my ancestors migrated from Gujarat several centuries ago), my first language is Hindi/Urdu, and I was born and raised in the old part of the city of Lucknow, which has been deeply influenced by a significant presence of Shia Muslims.[4] My "Gujaratiness" as well as my "Hinduness" and "Brahmanness" (which the Gujarati Hindus and Muslims were able to guess by my name) were always questionable, however, and possibly considered fake when I was interacting with people in Dar es Salaam who considered themselves more Gujarati or more Hindu than myself. At the same time, the doubtful state of my Hinduness allowed me to come closer to Muslims.

Among the Hindus, I was recognized as a "Gujarati" even though my family has had no contact with Gujarat for more than a century. Although I consider Hindi/Urdu as my mother tongue, my ability to speak and read Gujarati was appreciated as "respect toward my own mother tongue." No one ever openly questioned my beliefs or habits—often it was assumed that I was a believer, a vegetarian, and that I felt uncomfortable eating or living with Muslims, or with lower-caste Hindus who ate meat. The upper-caste Hindus who discovered that I was not religious, ate meat, and had close relationships not only with lower-caste Hindus and Asian Muslims, but also with Africans, often called me "a young, overenthusiastic radical," but even this assessment never seemed to have any outward effect on my personal relationships with these people. In lower-caste homes, my willingness to eat nonvegetarian food with them often evoked expressions of pleasant surprise and contributed to making me more welcome in their homes by weakening the caste barriers.

Members of the Ithna Asheri community were often impressed that my hometown was Lucknow. Although my knowledge of Gujarati made communication with informants easy, they were fascinated by the fact that I could speak Urdu, since Urdu is the language in which religious gatherings are held. Many times I was complimented for my familiarity with the Shia culture by statements like: "When I saw you in the mosque, I thought you were an Ithna Asheri," or "I was surprised to know that you were not an Ithna Asheri—you look like one." My Hinduness was also questioned by many Ithna Asheris on the grounds that I ate meat with them, lived with Ithna Asheri friends, and visited the mosque. I was often told that I did not "act like a Hindu" or that I would "make a good Ithna Asheri." Thrice I was also asked whether my interest in their community meant that I intended to convert to the Ithna Asheri faith. At such points, I explained that I was similarly trying to understand the Hindu, Sikh, and Goan communities, too.

Despite my warm acceptance by both Hindu and Ithna Asheri communities, however, I was often aware of being looked upon as an oddity. In an environment where people's religious identities mattered greatly, my informants often assumed that I was a practicing Hindu and seemed perplexed by my participation in the religious ceremonies of non-Hindus, especially of Ithna Asheris and Goans.

In the Sikh community, my being perceived as a Hindu did not raise doubts, as it is quite common for Hindus in Dar es Salaam to attend Sikh religious events, and vice versa. Most Sikh men and women I met in Dar es Salaam were fluent in Hindi/Urdu and our conversations were, therefore, in my first language, not theirs. A large proportion of Sikhs in Dar es Salaam, especially women in their thirties and forties, had immigrated to Tanzania within the last twenty years. These women developed an affinity with me the moment they discovered that I was from North India. I was seen by the Sikh men and women as a sister or daughter "from our region" due to the physical proximity of the states of Punjab and Uttar Pradesh. I was often invited to weekly gatherings and to people's homes: "This is your home. Come over whenever you miss your own food or people." I was also pampered by older Sikh women who fed me, gave me advice about looking after myself in Dar es Salaam, and urged me to get married before I got too old.

My connection with the "prestigious" United States seemed to matter more in the Goan community than anywhere else. I was often introduced by Goans to other Goans as "a scholar from the United States who is studying our community." There was also an expectation that I would dress in a trendy western style and would know all about western dancing, and some people seemed disappointed when I seemed to fail on both counts. Quite a few Goans had relatives in Canada and said that they could relate to my life and environment in the United States based on what they had seen or heard about Canada. Some others were interested in migrating to the United States or Canada and were therefore eager to know about my life in the West. My familiarity with Bombay and Poona, where quite a few Goans received their education or had relatives or friends, also brought me close to them in some ways.

Except in the Goan community, I introduced myself as a scholar from a U.S. university only when I interacted with businessmen, professionals, and house-

Photo 4. The weekly *langar* preparations in the Gurdwara allowed Sikh women from all classes to combine collective labor with gossip and political analysis. Dar es Salaam, 1993. (Photo: Richa Nagar)

wives from the upper classes, and with university students and faculty. To most others, my affiliation with the United States did not matter in the first instance and only became clear when we talked about ourselves in greater detail. Some of my working-class informants who had assumed that I was a student from India seemed to me to become more distant once I disclosed my U.S. affiliation. This made me cautious about when and how I revealed to them my connection with the United States.

My living situation significantly influenced my relationship with the various communities. My attempts to build connections within each community frequently took me to those who were prominent in their communities. These included the families of a Hindu lawyer, an Ithna Asheri journalist, a Sikh dentist, a Goan businesswoman, and a Hindu architect. We quickly built good personal relationships, I often shared meals or spent my weekends with them, and in one case I lived with the family for more than a month. During this close interaction, I visited community centers, temples, and mosques with my hosts, and they introduced me to their friends, acquaintances, and leaders of community organizations as someone who was "like a family member." Making my first entry into community spaces from the homes of well-known members of those communities proved invaluable for me, and the respective communities invited me in with their doors wide open. I often felt overwhelmed by the trust and confidence that many people placed in me unquestioningly. It was as if my trustworthiness had already been tested and they did not have to worry about me anymore. Yet, I was always aware of being looked upon as a Hindu. While this made me feel completely free to argue, disagree, or agree with Hindus in discussions around communal issues, it also made me feel burdened with being looked upon as a Hindu "other" in non-Hindu communities. No matter how close I felt to people in the Goan, Ithna Asheri, and Sikh communities, I was careful not to do or say anything that could be construed by them as overstepping my limits as someone who did not follow the same faith.

Ethnographic Research and Betrayal

For me, fieldwork in Dar es Salaam was, in many ways, like knitting a large familial net. Differences, whether religious, political, or ideological, were part of the same multi-textured, multicolored net where threads did not match perfectly. Amid my many friends, "mothers," "aunts," "uncles," "sisters," "brothers," and "grandparents," I never felt that Dar es Salaam was not my home. At the same time, however, some of these very individuals who trusted me with their personal stories, fed me regularly, showered affection on me, and received my affection in return, might disapprove of the manner in which I have used their words in my academic work. The dilemma this situation posed for me has been well-articulated by Lila Abu-Lughod:

> Does using my knowledge of individuals for purposes beyond friendship and shared memories by fixing their words and lives for disclosure to a world beyond the one they live in constitute some sort of betrayal? As someone who moves between worlds, I feel that confronting the negative images I know to exist in the United States toward Arabs is one way to honor the kindness they have shown me. So is challenging stereotypical generalizations that ultimately make them seem more "other." Yet how will my critical ethnography be received? This is the dilemma all those of us who move back and forth between worlds must face as we juggle speaking for, speaking to, and . . . speaking from. (Abu-Lughod 1993, 41)

The task I undertook in my research involved challenging the negative imaging and stereotyping of Asians not only in the West and among Africans, Arabs, and Europeans inside Tanzania, but also *within* the Asian "community" among people of differing religions, languages, classes, castes, and sects. This second challenge created a major ethical quandary. The communities that I studied were heterogeneous not only in terms of "race" and class, religious, sectarian, regional, and linguistic affiliations, but also in terms of their access to power. An understanding of power hierarchies and the struggles around them in these communities necessitated that I engage with the privileged and the deprived, the dominant and the dominated. For example, wealthy businessmen, traders, professionals, and their spouses had as much to do with my study as did taxi drivers, shoemakers, street vendors, school teachers, seamstresses, and middle-class housewives. On several occasions, I felt a real tension between my ties of affection with particular people and my commitment to certain political beliefs, and was forced to reconcile two kinds of ethical commitments—the ethics associated with my political beliefs and the ethics of respecting the trust that each life historian or informant had placed in me. I tried to maintain my commitment to people who shared their stories and thoughts with me by accurately representing their words and opinions, and by respecting the need of many of them to remain anonymous. At the same time, my political commitment to examine relations of power in communities and homes required me to use the words of several community leaders, husbands, and wealthy women and men in contexts where they might not have liked them to be used.

Reconciling Political Ethics with Cultural Ethics?

The dilemmas I confronted were not confined to the issue of betrayal, however. My biggest difficulty in the field was reconciling my antiracist commitment and my ideas about sexual intimacies with the need to accept and respect my informants' opinions on these issues, particularly when I spent time in their homes like a family member. Having lived most of my life in a lower-middle-class joint family in a religiously mixed, old neighborhood of Lucknow, I felt perfectly at home in middle-class homes of Hindus, Muslims, Sikhs, and Christians. I had a good sense of what was proper or improper to talk about before elders, men, or women, when to avoid wearing jeans or tight clothes, when to cover my head, take off my shoes, sit on the floor, or help in the kitchen. But my ability to adapt myself to the homes and environment of my informants also led them to think that I fitted their definition of a "good girl," that being unmarried I had no sexual experience, and that I "kept away from homosexuals." In a way, this situation was no different from situations that I had often faced growing up in old Lucknow—where the need to show respect to elders superseded the need to shock them. In Dar es Salaam, therefore, I resorted to the same option that I did in Lucknow—I stayed silent except before those who I knew would understand or engage with me. With the exception of three women friends and their families, no one knew about my involvement with a white man with whom I had been living for some time in the United States.

My position as a young woman also sometimes caused me agony. There were times, especially in families that I was close to, when I was seen as too young to take care of myself in a "harsh place like Dar es Salaam." For example, I often got advice about what I was supposed to do or not do, how it was important for me not to venture alone into "African" areas, whom I should be interviewing, and whom I should not be wasting my time with. I frequently had to address such situations by direct confrontation, or by ignoring what I was being ordered to do.

The racist attitudes of many "Asians" toward "Africans" caused me to make a bigger adjustment, however. When I first started my fieldwork, I spent almost all my time living, working, and socializing in the Asian-dominated city center, which was segregated from African residential areas. With the exception of African domestic workers in Asian homes, shops, and offices, I had no chance to interact with Africans. Although living in the Asian area allowed me to collect a wealth of information, its social environment stifled and angered me. As a result, two months after I started my fieldwork, I moved to the university campus, which was located far from the city center. Many Asians in the city center expressed fear of going to the university alone because it was "a totally African area." I commuted back and forth between the university and town, mostly by dala-dalas. Asians, whether rich or poor, rarely used dala-dalas and perceived them as dangerous because they were "full of lower-class Africans." Asian girls and women, supposedly because of their relative inexperience and vulnerability as compared to Asian men, were especially warned off from venturing into African areas on dala-dalas. When I did what other Asian women were not supposed to do, however, it was attributed to my being westernized, as people from the West were thought to "like to mix with the locals and do 'exotic' things like climbing on dala-dalas, which they can't do in their own countries."[5]

But choosing to commute to the Asian communities instead of living with them did not really take me away from racism. It showed me, sometimes through personal pain, the other side of the same coin. I tried to express my anguish in a letter to a close friend back in the United States:

> At times it pains me . . . to have brown skin here. I take the bus every day to town and most of the times I am the only Asian riding in the bus. Sometimes I am greeted sarcastically, "Kem chho?" I feel angry . . . because I can hear and feel the resentment against the brown skin in the voice that is greeting me. And I feel like screaming: "I am not . . . [a] *Muhindi* from here. Don't look at me like that . . ."
> . . . But then my position here as an Indian student from India is not quite the same as a [politicized] *Muhindi* from Tanzania either. My problem is that I am a foreigner here, and at times I want to be recognized as such. But anyone who does not know me thinks that I am just an arrogant . . . *Muhindi* who does not

know enough Kiswahili in spite of having lived in Tanzania all her life. It hurts me so much to be resented here. . . . And what really frustrates me is that the nature of my research keeps me away from the *Waswahili* . . . because I am too busy [immersing myself in] the Asian communities.[6]

In Dar es Salaam, where the divide between African and Asian residential areas was sharp, the shift in my spatial location from the Asian-dominated city center to the African-dominated university significantly changed my lifestyle and the politics of fieldwork. It affected what I saw, what I considered important, and the manner in which I perceived things. The politics around multiparty elections had made the situation between Africans and Asians exceptionally tense around the time when I started living on campus. Living with African students and commuting for several hours on buses as a sole Asian made me acutely aware of the fury that many ordinary Africans felt against Asians. It also provided me opportunities to explore with several faculty members contemporary racial politics and their relationship with political and economic changes in the country.[7] These discussions enabled me to grapple with how raced, classed, and gendered discourses developed in Tanzania in different political and economic contexts since independence. Members of the Women's Research and Documentation Project at the University of Dar es Salaam gave valuable feedback on my research ideas through both group and individual discussions, and emphasized the importance of situating my study in the context of Asian African "realities," as well. My previous research focus around Asian community politics shifted as a result of these interactions to encompass issues related to race and how they affected political discourse and social attitudes of those living in Dar es Salaam. While so far I had seen Asians simplistically lumping all Africans together, I could now understand how it was also difficult for many Africans to recognize or acknowledge the complexities of the Asian communities.

Dressing for Ethnography?

One issue that consistently posed problems for me throughout my stay in Dar es Salaam was the question of appropriate dress. In her "Sari Stories," Kamala Visweswaran describes how a gendered body is "(ad)dressed" intimately by history, place, culture, age, and class. She observes that "nothing could be more 'ordinary' for many South Indian women than wearing a sari, yet the stories underscore my own confrontations with this most unremarked activity: getting dressed. Of course, the idea of 'dressing up' has a history in feminist ethnography, for what we female (as opposed to male) ethnographers wear has some bearing on how we are received as social actors and as anthropologists" (Visweswaran 1994, 14).

Feminists from Beauvoir to Butler have drawn attention to the body as a locus of cultural inscription (Beauvoir 1973; Butler 1987, 1990). The body is a material reality that has already been culturally located and defined within a social context, and it is also the site that receives cultural interpretations (Butler 1987, 133). Through the act of dressing, the gendered body becomes a textualized site for the construction, imposition, and reception of preexisting identities and cultural meanings on the one hand, and for challenging the dominant categories and meanings on the other.

My confrontations with dressing were continuous. Public dress codes and gendered communal identities were intimately related among Asians in Dar es Salaam. Although *salwaar qameez* and western-style dress were popular among the Hindu women in their young and middle ages, it was only a sari or a bindi on the forehead that automatically branded a woman as a Hindu. Most Goans saw both sari and *salwaar qameez* as "old fashioned" or "too Indian," and the majority of Goan women wore western-style dress. Among Sikhs and Ithna Asheris, *salwaar qameez* with a *dupatta* was the most popular dress, although *hijaab* was practiced in public places by most Ithna Asheri women.

On a day-to-day basis, *salwaar qameez* was the most practical dress for me in the Asian neighborhoods even though it made many Goans and most Hindus of my age group think that I was "too old-fashioned." It was a dress I had worn all my life, it was considered respectable in all the communities without making me an "insider" to a particular one, and it allowed me to interact spontaneously with Muslims, Hindus, and Sikhs of all ages without fearing that my clothes would offend anyone's sentiments. I was always aware of how easily many Ithna Asheris, Sikhs, and elderly Hindus granted me trust and respect on the basis on my being dressed "properly" in *salwaar qameez*. I did not want the same people to feel cheated by me if they spotted me in the streets in anything that "inappropriately" revealed my arms or legs. Thus I had to bear the distaste of being looked upon as "old-fashioned" by some in order to avoid being seen as disrespectful or phony by others. But even this balancing act did not work entirely because *salwaar qameez* always made me the odd one in the homes and community places of the Goans.

Wearing a *salwaar qameez* also made me acutely aware of my Asianness when I commuted across the racially marked social spaces between the university and town. I tried to resist everything that would encourage an African to categorize me as an Asian from Dar es Salaam. As part of my struggle to challenge assumptions, I often tried to disrupt dress codes by wearing western-style shirts with my *salwaar* or long skirts with loose, long-sleeved tops. This was easier for me to do when I spent most of my day in the newspaper archives rather than talking to people and walking from street to street. While this way of dressing discouraged Africans from looking at me as a "regular *Muhindi*," it also made me too strange an Asian to be able to move freely in the streets of the downtown area among Asian acquaintances.

Sometimes, negotiating between these conflicting expectations and needs made things quite complicated. For example, when I initially met a Goan school teacher, he commented on my *salwaar qameez*, saying, "We Goans are far more westernized and progressive than most Indians. You will find no Goan woman in Dar wearing a dress like yours." His judgmental tone troubled me so much that I wore my U.S.-bought pants, T-shirt, and tennis shoes when I visited him for our second interview. But dressing according to the codes of one community left me inappropriately attired for a gathering I was to attend in a different community and classed space. That same evening, I wanted to attend a big Hindu celebration and my upper-class hosts had told me that none of my cotton *salwaar qameezes* would do because it was going to be a "nice gathering." So, I had to walk all day on the streets with a heavy bag that carried not only my tape-recording equipment and papers but also a silk sari, a matching blouse and petticoat, a bindi, and another set of footwear. Before entering the wedding hall, I had to go to the house of a Hindu woman and undergo the necessary transformation of appearance in order to become a part of the gathering.

The question of dress, therefore, intimately linked the gendered body with the everyday politics of communal, class, and race identities in social spaces. My need as a researcher to associate simultaneously with different communities, without being seen as solely identifying with only one of them, compelled me to negotiate the gendered dress codes without showing disrespect toward people and without making undesirable compromises. Such a negotiation, however, was not easy. It required me to deal with contradictions associated with my social and geographical position throughout my stay in Dar es Salaam.

Situatedness and Social Relationships in the Making of Life Stories

Far from being the creation of a single individual, a life story results from a collaboration between two individuals. From the start, a life story embodies the agendas, purposes, and interests of the narrator and the interpreter, both of whom are socially and spatially positioned subjects whose positions influence not only their perspectives but also their relationship with each other. The mutual situatedness of these positioned subjects has a profound influence on the shape of a narrative (Rosaldo 1989, Mirza and Strobel 1989, Geiger 1986 and 1990, Popular Memory Group 1982, Personal Narratives Group 1989). For instance, my study of multifaceted, contextually constructed identities is itself shaped by the complex identities of those who participated in the production of life histories. Every brief or long-term relationship that was established with each informant was characterized by the complex intersections of our personal histories and geographies, which in turn influenced whom or what we talked about and how. To explore this point further, let me discuss the process by which life stories of two individuals, Francis and Nargis (both aliases), were produced.

In terms of the normative categories described initially, Francis was a married Goan man in his forties, Tanzanian by nationality, a motor mechanic and school-bus driver by vocation, and a resident of Dar es Salaam since birth. I can describe Nargis as a divorced Ithna Asheri woman, also in her forties, who was born in Dar es Salaam into a wealthy business family but spent more than a decade in Britain, where she acquired U.K. citizenship. In the late 1980s, she returned to Dar es Salaam with her father to fight a case against the illegal acquisition of his property by his relatives. But these sketchy descriptions by themselves reveal very little about why the stories of Francis and Nargis took the particular forms they did. In order to understand that, one has to consider how I, as a positioned subject, shaped their narratives.

Although Francis and Nargis did not know each other, they were introduced to me by a friend who thought they would each be a good informant for my research.

Nargis and I had some long conversations. We often disagreed on issues pertaining to race and racism but agreed on matters related to gendered religious communalism. We soon developed affection for each other and became good friends. A few months after we were introduced, Nargis was shattered by the death of her father, who lived with her, and she invited me to stay with her. I lived with Nargis for more than two months, and her life story was the end product of many conversations that we had in a variety of social and personal contexts.

The life story of Francis, in contrast, was obtained in a single, half-hour meeting followed by a five-hour meeting the next day. For the first interview, I met Francis in the lounge of the YWCA, which I found to be a safe public space to talk with men I did not know well. The second conversation took place in Francis's home and was more casual, although my presence as a visitor with a tape recorder and a notebook clearly established the terms of our relationship: Francis was the narrator, I was the researcher, and each of us was an "outsider" to the other person's life.

Despite his racist and sexist ideas, I was impressed by Francis's openness and his well-formulated perspective on many social issues that I was interested in. I was aware that his ideas and experiences would greatly enrich my study of social identities. The Goans I had interviewed prior to Francis were considered important in the community and supposedly "knew all there was to know about Goans." Francis was different. No Goan was ever likely to send me to him, and no Goan did. In fact, when a Goan community leader found out that I had spoken to Francis, he chided me for wasting my time on a taxi driver who knew nothing. I felt that I had a lot to learn from Francis, but unfortunately, our relationship could not develop much. At the end of our long conversation, Francis directed at me what I considered to be improper sexual remarks, and we did not speak again.

Until that moment, I felt safe with Francis. His position as a married man in his mid-forties, who saw himself as a working-class person and who was introduced to me by a close friend, encouraged me to ask him sensitive questions about his family life and about issues such as sex work, interracial relations, and Asians' involvement in underground economic activities, such as smuggling. Francis's response to my questions was significantly influenced by my position as a twenty-three-year-old single woman who was seen as an "Asian" but who was simultaneously perceived as westernized because of her connection with the United States. The assumption that I was westernized led several men, including Francis, to think that they could openly discuss their personal, intercommunal, and interracial sexual relationships with me, a topic they would have felt uncomfortable to discuss if I had arrived directly from India to do the same research. For example, when Francis shared that he and his wife were planning to have more children, he also told me about his extramarital relationships with three women, two of whom had abortions as a result. My status as an "outsider" encouraged Francis to discuss people openly. For instance, he expressed his dislike for his neighbor, Linda (alias), because he considered her a bad influence on his wife. He mentioned Asian sex workers and their clients by name, and told me about his ex-boss, who was once engaged in smuggling. He freely discussed his love affairs and his differences with his wife because I was unlikely to meet his wife if he did not want that to happen.

In Nargis's case, the distinctions between my status as an "insider" and "outsider" became increasingly blurred with time. In the beginning, we were outsiders to each other. While Nargis freely talked about her community and her life to me and I shared many things with her, our relationship remained formal, and both of us were aware of my position as a researcher who did not belong to Nargis's home or community spaces. While discussing events and issues, we both avoided mentioning people by name, and I was careful to not disclose to her anything about my other interviews. When I started living with Nargis, however, the barriers of public and private and home and community that previously existed between us collapsed. As the sites of our interactions shifted from formal spaces of the living room and dinner table to informal spaces of Nargis's kitchen, bedroom, and neighborhood streets, our conversations became too personal and sensitive to be tape recorded or jotted down verbatim. Although I continued to be a social outsider for Nargis at times when she observed religious fasts or participated in *maatam*, in most other spheres we became insiders to each other's lives. We regularly discussed everything that happened in our lives.

She talked about the developments of her court case, as well as her relationships with her relatives, community leaders, lawyers, and friends. I told her about the people I met and interviewed, and we spent a considerable amount of time discussing Asian-African relations in the context of multiparty politics and the social and political issues specific to the Ithna Asheri community.

As was often the case with my interviewees, my "Asianness" frequently led Francis and Nargis to consider me an insider in the context of discussions around race. Both felt free to voice their prejudices and racist sentiments against Africans in front of me because they assumed that I shared their opinions. Although such views made me angry, I reacted quite differently in each case. Beyond posing some questions to challenge Francis's position, I did little to voice my disapproval. First, the nature of my brief relationship with him did not allow me to risk offending him. Moreover, being unfamiliar with Francis's social milieu, I wanted to know as much as possible about his background, his work, his social relationships with Asians and Africans, his perspectives on gender, race, and class relations among Goans and non-Goans, his attitude and stereotypes about people of different communities and regions, and his perceptions of "Goanness," "Indianness," and "Africanness."

With Nargis, things developed quite differently. In the initial interviews, she shared with me many personal stories that she had not previously told anyone outside her immediate family. I valued the trust she had placed in me as a researcher, and even when I disagreed with her sometimes racist and homophobic ideas, I was careful not to say anything that might make her feel uncomfortable. Later, however, my close relationship with her, particularly at the time when I was living with her, allowed me to disagree and argue openly with her. Nargis's position as a "subject" or "informant" for my research took a back seat then. She was first and foremost a good friend, like an older sister, with whom I felt a need to communicate honestly and to make her understand my position on issues as I tried to understand hers. Once the barrier of formality between Nargis and me was broken and we became a part of each other's daily lives, I also felt responsible to decide in each instance whether a particular piece of information about her life was shared with me as a researcher, friend, or housemate.

Earlier in this chapter, I argued that in order to understand adequately the complexities of identity politics, we must be sensitive to the diverse and multiple social and geographical contexts in which those identities are constructed. The analysis of my relationship with Francis and Nargis goes a step further. It demonstrates that not only is a contextualization of identity theory crucial to our understanding of identities, but that the narratives that researchers produce are themselves shaped by our own social and geographical positions with respect to the subjects or "informants" whose identities we study. As Prell notes, "In the life history, two stories together produce one. A hearer and a listener ask, respond, present, and edit a life . . . One must know oneself through and in light of the other. The subject-subject relationship is itself a reflexive event in which a self is presented with a full knowledge of reporting, or constructing itself" (Prell 1989, 254).

Naming and Claiming Languages: Mother Tongues, Homelands, and Community Politics in Dar es Salaam

> We need in particular to pay attention to those conditions of dia-
> logue in which the different powers, histories, limits and languages
> that permit the process of "othering" to occur are inscribed. This
> draws us into an endless journey between cultures, languages, and
> complex configurations of meaning and power.
> —Iain Chambers, *Migrancy, Culture, and Identity*

Fragments of Nuzhat Abbas's sentences written in English, Kiswahili, Guja-rati, and Urdu echo in my head as I grope to find a suitable beginning for the stories and arguments I want to share. Born in Zanzibar during the revolution, she was raised in Karachi and Toronto, and then moved to Madison, Wisconsin, to pursue a doctorate in comparative literature. Disrupting and complicating myths of origin and exile, she writes:

> There are multiple stories here. Multiple languages. And silences. Some
> that I can decipher, some that I can't. . . . I write my words in the Colo-
> nizer's language that I love and long to claim. The other languages drift
> in my mind and interrupt me as I read, as I write. Snatches of music, my
> mother speaking, sermons at the mosque, Swahili, Gujerati, Urdu, and
> differently accented Englishes crowd my mind. My own voice with its pe-
> culiar accent, intimate to my ears, speaks carefully, anxious not to drown
> out what I may hear from other voices. My tongue aches with the effort.
> Grows heavy, falters. . . . She imagines for herself a language that could
> mirror her constantly dividing selves, her multiplicity of national and cul-
> tural identities, without recuperating her for the needs of the centre. She
> longs for a language that would not automatically erase the dreadful pain
> of these splittings, a language that would not just celebrate hybridity as
> choice but would show the cultural struggle of which it is, itself, an after
> effect.[8] (Abbas 1993)

This cultural struggle that Nuzhat mentions is also a social, political, and economic struggle. Like social places and ideologies that define the "pures" and "impures" in different communities, languages are also key sites where power is exercised and contested, and where identities are defined and challenged. As situated encounters between subjects endowed with socially structured resources and competencies, linguistic interactions—however personal or insignificant they may seem—bear the traces of the social structures that they both express and help to reproduce (Thompson 1991).

Race, Power, and Language

The class-based conflict between Asians and Africans in Dar es Salaam was compounded by the Asians' segregated social lives. The failure of most Asians to adopt Kiswahili as their own language often added fuel to the fire, especially in times of political crisis. Just as Asian communal places became targets of African criticism during the 1960s, so also the linguistic isolation of Asians came under heavy fire during the indigenization debate of 1992–93. One newspaper article voiced a common "African" complaint against "Asians": "One does not need to go very far to identify the difficulties proven by the Asian community['s] attitudes, based on their extreme cultural isolation. They have completely failed to integrate . . . with the indigenous [peoples]. . . . If you enter into their business places . . . they will communicate among themselves through their Indian language knowing very well that you cannot understand their conversation, which is not the case with Europeans etc." (Mwakitwange 1993). The criticisms spread to other spheres, too. The Dar es Salaam Merchants Chamber was blamed for excluding its non-Asian members from its proceedings through excessive use of Gujarati (*Business Times*, 22 January 1993). Two months later, an African reader appealed to a leading English daily to stop publishing Gujarati advertisements (*Daily News*, 22 and 23 March 1993). Several Asians considered these criticisms as "blind attacks" (*Daily News*, 22 March 1993; also, *Business Times*, 22 January 1993), or as evidence of closed-mindedness and arrogance on the part of Africans (*Daily News*, 23 March 1993).

Many Asians I interviewed in Dar es Salaam, irrespective of class, gender, or community, shared prejudices against Africans when it came to marriage, religion, and food.[9] However, the issue of linguistic divides was complicated by the diverse immigration histories and social positions of Asians, which were generally not visible to "outsiders." For example, on the streets of Dar es Salaam, African youngsters often called out at Asian passers-by in Gujarati ("Kem Chho?") while thinking they were speaking Kihindi. Thus, Gujarati was often assumed to be Hindi, the language of Wahindi or Indians, and all Wahindi were taken to be Gujarati speakers, even though several Asian communities, for example, Sikhs, Goans, and Konkanis, did not identify with either Gujarati or Hindi. And for Asians like Farida, who felt close to Zanzibar and Kiswahili, such assumptions became painful:

> Since my childhood there was no language I knew more intimately than
> Kiswahili. Coming to Dar es Salaam was painful . . . I remember going
> to the market [once and] . . . telling the seller that I wanted potatoes
> and onions. And he just listened to me without giving me anything. . . .
> Then he said, "Mama, you are speaking excellent Kiswahili, you must be
> from Zanzibar." The seller was surprised that an Indian-looking woman
> was speaking fluent Kiswahili and I was surprised that this man was sur-
> prised! . . . You would never see this scene in Zanzibar. Whether you are
> Indian looking, or Chinese looking, or Arab looking, . . . everybody spoke
> Kiswahili. . . . Encounters like this made me feel uncomfortable in Dar es
> Salaam. Sometimes someone would say, "Wewe Muhindi, nenda kufa In-
> dia!" [You Muhindi, go die in India!] Initially, I used to remain quiet, but
> then I started returning such remarks by swearing in a very Swahili way.
> And I say, "Whether you like it or not, I will die here and you will come to
> my funeral." And they get very shocked. . . . They can't comprehend how
> these words are coming out of the mouth of an Asian-looking woman.[10]

Within Asian communities, racialized discourses marked attitudes toward
people who spoke Kiswahili. This issue acquired special relevance among
the Ithna Asheris, where a significant proportion of the community identified
strongly with Zanzibar and spoke Kiswahili at home. Nargis, who grew up in Dar
es Salaam, recalled the linguistic tensions in her community when Zanzibari
Ithna Asheris arrived:

> In 1965, something like two and a half thousand [Ithna Asheris] came
> from Zanzibar to Dar and we would say, "Look at them, they are talking
> Swahili." And we would call them "Golas" [derogatory label for Africans]
> . . . because they . . . never spoke in their mother tongue—Kutchi or Gu-
> jarati, and I really hated them because they used to talk in Swahili all the
> time. . . . I used to tell them, " . . . you come from India and you must
> know your mother tongue. I don't expect you to know French or English,
> but at least you must know Gujarati . . . I know, you are proud of your
> Swahili—it is a sweet language . . ., but at least when you are inside your
> home . . . you should preserve your culture. . . . [If you migrate to London,
> are you going to say,] 'Oh, I am in London now, so I should start speaking
> English and forget Gujarati and Kutchi?'"[11]

This tension between Kiswahili-speaking Ithna Asheris on the one hand and
Gujarati- and Kutchi-speaking Ithna Asheris on the other persisted across
class and gender lines. Farida (quoted earlier) remarked: "When we came to
the mainland, one of the first things we faced was that . . . if you come from
Zanzibar you are a Gola, an African, because you speak Kiswahili. The Zan-

zibaris were treated very badly by the Dar es Salaam Ithna Asheris. We were 'uncultured' because. . . . when we [Zanzibari Ithna Asheris] met each other, we spoke in Kiswahili. We still do that today, and they [mainland Ithna Asheris] still look down upon us."[12] However, these tensions between the Zanzibari and mainland Ithna Asheris were largely contained within the community. For many, Ithna Asheris exemplified "the highest degree of integration with Africans," in sharp contrast to the Hindus who were seen as the "least integrated" of all Asians. Maria, a middle-class Goan woman, remarked:

> About the Ithna Asheris, I would say that only their skins and hair are different but [from inside,] they are very African. . . . Most of them talk in Kiswahili at home, and even when they talk in Gujarati or English they use a few Kiswahili words in each sentence. I think that's because of the Zanzibar influence. . . . I think [Hindus] are very aloof people, especially when it comes to Africans. Maybe it is racism—because you hardly see a Hindu lady even talking to an African lady. And if I am talking to an African lady, or [worse still,] an African man, they look at me so [suspiciously].[13]

The aloofness of Hindus from Africans described by Maria was especially noticeable among the upper- and upper-middle classes. A Mnyakusa friend who had worked for Asian businessmen from different communities remarked: "Of all Wahindi, Ithna Asheris speak the best Kiswahili, and Banyanis [Hindus] undoubtedly speak the worst Kiswahili. They say 'Bana' instead of 'Bwana.' They say 'Kuja Hapa' for 'Njoo Hapa.' They insert a lot of Kihindi [Gujarati] words in their Kiswahili. . . . Banyani women are worse off than Banyani men."[14] Sujata, an upper-class Hindu woman, reaffirmed the popular notion that Ithna Asheris are closer than Hindus to Africans, while rationalizing the distanced behavior of Hindus in cultural terms: "Africans call us Banyanis, and non-Hindu Asians call us Gujarati, . . . because they know us from our attire, our *chandlo*, and our language. So, we have a more distinct culture. We speak very clear Gujarati, but Ithna Asheris mainly speak Swahili, and they mix Swahili in with their Gujarati. Among Ismailis those who come from Kathiawar speak very good Gujarati, but most of them either speak Kutchi, or broken Gujarati."[15] Several Hindu leaders accepted the charge of aloofness while defending themselves on the grounds that their distance from Africans was based less on racism and more on religious and cultural difference. Damji Rathod, the former general secretary of the Hindu Mandal, remarked: "Being Muslims, Ithna Asheris are not as different from Africans as Hindus are. [In our case,] the most distinct difference is the religion because mostly Africans are either Muslims or Christians. Then, there is also food. We are very strict vegetarians and Africans are meat eaters. That does not allow us to mingle with them as freely as Ithna Asheris can. That's why Ithna Asheris are linguistically and socially more integrated with Africans than we Gujaratis are."[16]

While constructing a singular Hindu and Gujarati identity and explaining Hindus' distanced relationship with Africans on the basis of cultural difference, both Sujata and Damji Bhai failed to consider how linguistic affinities are complicated simultaneously by class, caste, region, and gender. Jasu, a poor vendor from Rana caste, came to Dar es Salaam from Zanzibar in 1965 at the age of twelve. She noted linguistic differences not only between Hindus and Ithna Asheris, but also between upper-caste Hindus from Dar es Salaam and lower-caste Hindus from Zanzibar, and between women and men of her own caste:

> I can immediately tell a Zanzibari Asian by their language. . . . The Gujarati of Zanzibari laboring castes is quite different from the Gujarati of Dar es Salaam Hindus. We use many Swahili words, but they [Hindus from Dar] don't. . . . Also, most Zanzibari Asians speak perfect Swahili. But if you have remained inside the homes in Zanzibar, then you wouldn't know good Swahili. We Zanzibari Ranas do not know as much Swahili as Zanzibari Ithna Asheris or Sunnis do. People say, "You are from Zanzibar, then how come you don't speak good Swahili?" How could we know good Swahili? We [women] mostly worked in Hindu homes, and our men went to the *soko* [market] and did the outside work. All the people around us were Indians—who could I speak Swahili with? My children know everything in Swahili because they have grown up with Africans and Arabs here in Kariakoo [mixed lower-class neighborhood]. But . . . when I speak Swahili with the Golas [Africans], they laugh at me. But Zanzibari Ithna Asheris speak a lot of Swahili because they [spend a great deal] of time with Golas.[17]

Upper-caste Hindus often equated the lifestyles of lower-caste Hindus with that of Africans. Although I did not meet any Hindus who spoke Kiswahili as their first language, poor Zanzibari Hindus from Rana, Bhoi, and Divecha communities were frequently referred to as Golas. A wealthy, upper-caste Hindu woman echoed the sentiments of many upper-caste Hindus when she opined: "Koris [Divechas], Bhois, and Ranas are like Golas. Their Gujarati is very impure, and sometimes it is difficult for us to understand them. . . . You see, they have lived with Africans for a long time and so their talking, eating, drinking, and spending habits are similar to Africans. They eat meat, fish, all kinds of nonvegetarian food . . . they spend their money on chicken and liquor rather than on their children's education, or on improving their standard of living."[18] A similar process of othering also operated among Goans where

Photo 5. A barbershop in Jasu's working-class neighborhood of Kariakoo. Dar es Salaam, 1993. (Photo: Richa Nagar)

"Goans with Seychelloise blood" as well as working-class Goans who have moved from upcountry were frequently looked down upon as more Swahili than Goan. For example, Julie grew up in Tabora, where there were few Goans. Her friends were Hindus, Ismailis, Africans, and Arabs. Julie's mother ran a canteen to supplement her father's meager income, and this further exposed Julie to people of all backgrounds. She grew up speaking English at home, and Kiswahili, Gujarati, and Kutchi with her friends. After coming to Dar es Salaam, Julie married an Arab man from Pemba, converted to Islam, and had three children. She worked as a secretary in a computer firm and lived away from the Asian area in Ilala in an extended family that included her husband's parents and siblings. Julie felt too "odd" to be called a Goan.[19]

> I guess I am a lot more Swahili than most Goans. Since childhood, I haven't had much to do with either Goa or Konkani. But my Kiswahili was always excellent—that's why I had no problems adjusting with my parents-in-law. In the office, I talk on the phone in Kiswahili and people assume that I am African. . . . They don't believe that an Asian can speak that kind of Kiswahili. Before I joined my office as a secretary, none of the Asians got along with the African workers. When I came, I instantly won their love and respect. Asians asked me teasingly, "Do you bribe them to

do your work?" I said, "No, I *talk* to them." . . . Then an African worker said, "She knows how to speak respectfully, while you all just give commands even if you don't mean to. That makes all the difference."[20]

Zanzibari Asians such as Farida may have been considered "impure" and "inferior" by upper-class Ithna Asheris or by the elite Hindus of Dar es Salaam, and Goans such as Julie may have been seen as more "Swahili" than "Goan," but it was precisely such othering that allowed the Faridas and Julies to dislodge dominant assumptions about who and what a Gujarati, Swahili, Ithna Asheri, or Goan was supposed to be. Gujarati, the language of the rich and upper castes, was spoken by the Zanzibari Hindus such as Jasu, but with a difference—it was taken apart, and then put back together with a new inflection, accent, and a new Swahilized vocabulary. And the Julies and Faridas transcended the imposed languages and identities altogether—by reinventing mother tongues, by creating new communities, and by unsettling the very premises that were necessary to box them as Asian or African.

The Desire for Unified Identities: The Case of Ithna Asheris

The politics of community and identity among Asians in Dar es Salaam was entangled with the ways that community organizations affected people's access to particular languages, and placed those languages within specific religious and social discursive practices. The religious institutions of the Ithna Asheri community, for example, were essential in promoting the use of Urdu and Arabic. Arabic was taught with Gujarati in the madrassas, while most of the *majilises* in Dar es Salaam were held in Urdu even though the majority of people, including local preachers, were able to speak only a little Urdu and could read Urdu only in the Gujarati or Roman script. The introduction of Urdu as one of the main religious languages in the Gujarati- and Kutchi-speaking Ithna Asheri community dated back to the late nineteenth century, when the Ithna Asheris broke away from the Ismaili community. After the split, the new Ithna Asheris in East Africa invited Urdu-speaking Shia scholars from India to teach them the basics of Shia Ithna Asherism, and the Ithna Asheris in Zanzibar and Tanganyika were initiated into the faith through the Urdu language.[21] In the early 1990s, however, many young Ithna Asheris in Dar es Salaam found it hard to follow Urdu *majilises*, and the rate of attendance in the religious gatherings was dropping. Muhsin Alidina expressed the shared agony of the community leaders:[22] "If you send an Urdu preacher to Zanzibar, people don't come—they just can't understand Urdu. If you send a Swahili preacher, they come. Here [in Dar es Salaam], English is favored [over Urdu] in the *majlises* by the youngsters . . . if you have a *majlis* in English, the older people get upset . . . [but to the youngsters], Urdu is as foreign as Chinese."[23]

However, the relationship of the youngsters with Urdu was not so easy to summarize. While many Goans seemed to prefer western movies and music, other Asian communities in Dar es Salaam were hooked on Indian and Pakistani cinema, television serials, and music. Musicians and film stars were invited by wealthy Asian organizations, and their performances were attended by large Asian audiences.[24] No wonder, then, that when a preacher talked like a Pakistani actor, the Ithna Asheri youngsters came happily to the *majlis*. Mulla Asher, the only Urdu preacher who was reputed to draw youngsters in large numbers to his *majlises*, told Alidina: "One day I asked a boy, ' . . . whenever I preach, I see you inside the mosque. But why [don't I see you there] when someone else preaches?' He said, ' . . . You speak like those Pakistani actors. [That's why]."[25] The generational politics of linguistic affiliations threw the Ithna Asheri community leaders into a serious dilemma. As Alidina pointed out,

> You see, a young Ithna Asheri boy probably speaks Gujarati at home. But the moment he leaves home [for] school, . . . he speaks Swahili. . . . Then he comes to the mosque and it's Urdu. Now, all these languages . . . he has picked up from his environment. They are not taught Gujarati . . . [as] we were. . . . [If] you speak to him in Gujarati, he will reply to you but if you ask him to write or read a letter, he can't. . . . The same is true of his Swahili. It's like this lady [preacher] you heard in the Mehfil—she can [only recite memorized sermons in Urdu]. So naturally, when you try to speak to her in Urdu, she can't. This is the dilemma of the community—our children are exposed to various languages, but they are not perfect in any of them [except English]. . . . But you also have the older generation who must be catered for. . . . So, what [should] the community do? [Should] it have a bilingual policy? [Should] we . . . have what they have in London—[where] . . . during Moharram there [is] half an hour of preaching in English and then one hour of Urdu?[26]

The leaders of the Ithna Asheri Jamaats had constantly to deal with this dilemma of language in their effort to provide "appropriate" religious instruction and socialization to its younger members. In 1968, the first edition of *Elements of Islamic Studies* was published by the Bilal Muslim Mission of Tanzania in English for the Ithna Asheri community in Africa because it was felt that, with the radical changes in the East African educational system, the East African Ithna Asheri community was steadily losing contact with the Gujarati language and the new generation was unable to benefit from the religious literature written in Gujarati (Meghji 1968).[27] Soon, however, it was felt that the Ithna

Asheri children in Dar es Salaam required additional religious textbooks in Gujarati that were written in Roman script. Razia Tejani explained, "Most children speak Gujarati at home, and so they automatically pick up religious instruction in Gujarati, but they do not know the Gujarati script. So, if Gujarati language is written in Roman script, there is no problem because all of them know the Roman alphabet."[28]

But writing Gujarati in Roman script could not solve the more serious problem that Ithna Asheri leaders faced: The continuing emigration of Ithna Asheris from East Africa and their ever-expanding numbers in the United Kingdom, Canada, and the United States. While this trend necessitated increasing adoption of English, it also raised fears about the uncontrolled Anglicization of the community. In 1988, the international organizations of the Ithna Asheris introduced a common syllabus for religious instruction in English in the Khoja Shia Ithna Asheri madrassas all over the world so that their youngsters would not have to face language barriers in religious education.[29] Preachers from Tanzania, who had never delivered sermons in English, were also encouraged to travel to several U.K. and North American cities in order to preach to Ithna Asheris in English (Sheriff 1991). At the same time, the Ithna Asheri Supreme Council attempted to guard against over-Anglicization and westernization of the community by adopting a Common Language Preservation Programme and by resolving to make Gujarati a compulsory subject in all madrassas. Ithna Asheri leaders felt that the religious and cultural identity of the community could only be sustained through a common language, spoken and understood by all.[30] As Mohamed Khalfan, a sixty-two-year-old Zanzibari Ithna Asheri man who led the movement for the revival of Gujarati in the community, expressed, "the community . . . continues to grow still further in size [with] each succeeding generation while the memory of the origin, struggle and vicissitudes of the predecessors get fainter and fainter as it continues to spread and settle in other parts of the world under the stress and strain of alien influences and unfamiliar and frustrating environments" (Khalfan 1989). Westward emigration was a real fear, and even the most "ordinary" people in the Ithna Asheri community were acutely aware of the anti-Islamic sentiment in the West. The thought of "Anglo-Khojas," "Canadian-Khojas," and "American-Khojas" had alarmed the community leaders.[31] Khalfan warned the Ithna Asheris,

> There is a gradual increase . . . in the numbers of [Ithna Asheri] families
> . . . in some parts of the world including Africa, where the children are
> made to lose their mother tongue. . . . The close common identity will
> be eroded, communication will be hampered, the fraternity will weaken,
> the concern for each other at the global level will diminish and the com-
> munity and its Federations will become vulnerable to divisive forces and

pressures if this trend, innocent as it may seem, is allowed to catch up or continue to the danger point of no-return. (Khalfan 1989)

The same warning was repeated several times by the Ithna Asheri Jamaat in its effort to maintain Gujarati as the "carrier of culture and tradition" (Khoja Shia Ithna Asheri Jamaat 1989, 2). Nevertheless, this push from above to promote Gujarati as the "mother tongue" and "common language" was not supported by all segments of the Ithna Asheri leadership. Muhsin Alidina, who was on the opposite side of those who were promoting Gujarati, commented,

> If we need a common language . . . we must not be insular. We must look
> for a language that [embraces] a wider section of the [Shia] community—
> not just the Khojas [but also] the Iranians, the Lebanese, or whatever it
> is. You see, the idea is to preserve not only your traditional ethnic identity,
> but . . . [also] your religious identity. So, . . . why don't we adopt Arabic
> as a means of communication, particularly when we have to use this lan-
> guage to teach religion. . . . [The other alternative is to] adopt English.
> It is a universal language. People, whether they like it or not, learn the
> language . . . But this [view] does not seem to cut much ice. They [other
> leaders] say, "No, we are from the Indian subcontinent . . . our whole his-
> tory [is rooted] in this particular language and region, so we must have
> a common language that also shows our common ethnic identity. This is
> why [we need] Gujarati." . . . But most of the youngsters don't even care
> about Gujarati.

The struggle over the use of Gujarati in the Ithna Asheri community was primarily an intergenerational struggle. The older generation agreed with the leaders of the Ithna Asheri Federation that a common language needed to be preserved, while the younger generation saw Gujarati as an artificially imposed common language. The leaders, through their powerful international organiza-tions, tried to fight their community's "fragmentation." However, the younger generation—raised with English, Gujarati, Kutchi, Kiswahili, and Urdu—found it difficult to show allegiance to any one language. Linguistic mingling was part of its existence, and no single or pure form of language could take care of its need to express itself in plural ways. As Faizal, a nineteen-year-old Ithna Asheri man, born in Dar es Salaam of Zanzibari parents, remarked, "I am a *chautara* when it comes to languages—can't do without Kiswahili, or English, or Gujarati, or Kutchi. I need all of them, all the time. I have grown up think-ing that all these languages are mine. So, now suddenly, it is hard to relate to the idea of mastering Gujarati—learning how to read and write it—because we are told that it is superior to the rest. My mother tongue is not Gujarati. My mother tongue is a mixture of many tongues, and I have already mastered it."[32]

The struggles over naming and claiming multiple mother tongues and home-lands in Dar es Salaam were inseparable from contested histories of those who constituted a "community," as well as the changing interpretations of those histories, as they were invoked and challenged in multiple contexts. As Chambers puts it, "History is harvested and collected, to be assembled, made to speak, re-membered, re-read and re-written, and language comes alive in transit, in interpretation" (Chambers 1994, 3).

Conclusion

Theoretical engagements with identity and positionality, with their overwhelm-ing focus on the politics of race, class, gender, and sexuality, prove inadequate when we look beyond U.S. and British contexts. My discussion here underscores the point that in order to be of greater social relevance, such engagements must be geographically and historically contextualized. This chapter also argues that a keen understanding of the geography of positionality is crucial to feminist ethnography. Reflexivity and relationality enable us to understand more fully the ways in which the politics of social identities play out in our everyday lives and spaces, and the manner in which they influence the knowledge we produce. The preceding analysis reveals me as positioned subject, situated in specific ways, with respect to the communities and people that I studied. Francis and Nargis, like all other members of Asian communities who participated in my research, were positioned subjects, and their positions must be analyzed with respect to my own in order to grasp how their life stories came into being and how I have created academic knowledge on the basis of their stories.

Finally, the sidebar here, "Naming and Claiming Languages: The Politics of Mother Tongues and Homelands in Dar es Salaam," further illustrates my point about the need to grapple with identity and difference through lenses that do not rigidly adhere to race, class, gender, and sexuality. It also suggests that it is only through a self-reflexive and critical feminist ethno-geographical engagement that we can produce a multilayered and nuanced analysis of social identities and struggles around meanings of community.

3. Reflexivity, Positionality, and Languages of Collaboration in Feminist Fieldwork

Part 1 of this chapter is an abridged and revised version of a longer piece originally written with Susan Geiger between 1997 and 2001. The original piece was circulated widely in a conference paper format. It was first published in revised and condensed form in 2007, six years after Susan's death.

When two major journals in feminist studies rejected the original piece authored with Geiger, I continued my attempts to share our argument in feminist and critical geography venues. Part 2 of this chapter is a revised version of an article that first emerged in 2001–2 from one such effort; I deployed the arguments made with Geiger to interpret the responses of three different feminist audiences to a manuscript that I submitted to the journal, *Gender, Place and Culture*.

Part 3 is a revised version of a chapter that was first written in 2005–6, around the same time part 1 was being revised for publication. It can be seen as a postscript to the discussion on reflexivity and positionality, with attention to language and translation, themes that have continued to acquire increasing prominence in my concerns since then.

Part 1. The Original Argument: Beyond the Impasse?

Richa Nagar and Susan Geiger

> Some sort of reflexive identification of the academic writer with the "Other" interpreted, analyzed or written about, is so important in reestablishing critical authority in the rubble of paradigms precisely because the most powerful and paralyzing aspect of the critique of representation has been its ethical implications for the very mode of communication—discursive, impersonal writing—so basic to academic work.
>
> —George Marcus, "Commentary"

Since the late 1980s, the practice of fieldwork has been under heavy scrutiny. Although issues of power, privilege, location, and authorship pervade all research practices, "the crisis of representation"—that is, doubts about the "possibility of truthful portrayals of others" and "the capacity of the subaltern to be heard"—has been particularly paralyzing for those engaged in fieldwork-based research (Ortner 1995, 190). Feminist social scientists in the *western* academy, especially those focusing on *third-world* subjects, have responded to this crisis either by abandoning fieldwork, or by engaging in what Marcus calls "a reflexive identification."[1] Here, we argue that neither approach can adequately respond to the challenges posed by the crisis of representation and that discussions about reflexivity, positionality, and identity—the central concepts in feminist interrogation of fieldwork—have reached an impasse. Simply stated, *reflexivity* involves a "radical consciousness of self in facing the political dimensions of fieldwork and construction of knowledge" (Helen Callaway 1992, quoted in Hertz 1997, viii). In feminist conversations about fieldwork, reflexivity has often implied analyses of ways that ethnographic knowledge is shaped by the shifting, contextual, and relational contours of the researcher's social *identity* and her social situatedness or *positionality* (in terms of gender, race, class, sexuality, and other axes of social difference) with respect to her subjects.

As a way to reframe the discussions on reflexivity, positionality, and identity, we pose two key questions that lie at the heart of feminist research in third-world contexts. First, how can feminists use fieldwork to produce knowledges across multiple divides (of power, geopolitical, and institutional locations, and axes of difference) without reinscribing the interests of the privileged? Second, how can the *production* of knowledges be tied explicitly to a politics of social change favoring less privileged communities and places?

A widespread engagement with reflexive practices by feminist ethnographers has generated rich dialogues about the methodological and epistemological dilemmas endemic to fieldwork, as well as the challenges associated with identity politics as they affect academic, interpersonal, institutional, and intellectual relationships. Such reflexivity, however, has mainly focused on examining the identities of individual researchers rather than on how such identities intersect with institutional, geopolitical, and material aspects of their positionality. This limited engagement has foreclosed opportunities for grappling with the two key questions posed above. A further problem with existing approaches to reflexivity arises from a failure to distinguish systematically among ethical, ontological, and epistemological aspects of fieldwork dilemmas. Consequently, the *epistemological* dilemma of whether and how it is possible to represent "accurately" often gets conflated with *ethical* relationships and choices, and with *ontological* questions of whether there is a predefined reality about researcher-subject relationship that can be known, represented, challenged, or altered through reflexivity.

Producing knowledge across social divides in ways that are explicitly committed to a transformative politics necessitates that researchers rethink reflexivity, identity, and positionality, as well as the ends toward which these notions are deployed. Below we describe how challenges we faced in our own work led us to reflect on and articulate the current impasse. We then elaborate two interrelated approaches to reflexivity, positionality, and identity—a *speaking-with* model of research, and crossing boundaries with situated solidarities—for consideration by scholars who, like us, think that there is much to be lost by abandoning this face-to-face and necessarily problematic interactive research practice called fieldwork.

Articulating the Impasse

This essay began in early 1997 as an email conversation in which each of us sought to articulate our struggles with the theoretical and methodological terrain of reflexivity, positionality, and identity in the context of field research for a dissertation (Nagar 1995) and a book (Geiger 1997b) in Tanzania. Our respective projects made us aware of contradictions inherent in a major recent trend in feminist social sciences. While feminists invoke a commitment to challenge pre-given social categories, an emphasis on "positionality" requires reference to those very categories they seek to question. This embodiment of categorical identities in an individual is problematic because the social forces that name and reproduce categorical identities are continually in conflict with the necessary inauthenticity of the experience of those identities (Kawash 1996). In our cases, dismantling the homogenous category *Asian*—as constructed in a colonial context between "native" African and ruling British in East Africa—was of particular concern for Richa, while the categories and genders of Tanganyikans, supposedly responsible for anticolonial nationalism in the 1950s, were of greatest interest for Susan. Ironically, validation of our work to western feminist academic audiences seemingly made it necessary to position ourselves using the very categories (middle class, upper caste, white, Indian, woman, etc.) that we sought to problematize and disrupt.

There is a difference between an intellectual project that seeks to uncover complexity and a situation where an author feels that her work would be discredited if she is unable to establish herself as a legitimate researcher in the eyes of the experts evaluating her work. This scenario is exemplified by the following comment that Richa received from an anonymous reviewer in 1996 on an essay about marriage, migration, and religious ideologies among Asians in Tanzania that she submitted to a feminist journal: "Without knowing anything about the author, it is difficult to evaluate his/her use of the term *Hinduness*—a term that is probably insulting to the Hindus. . . . Especially in the light of considerable work on interviewing, [the lack of a self-reflexive account] is simply not acceptable. . . . Is the author male or female? The same goes for religion, caste and interviewing Hindus, Muslims and so forth." If Richa had merely revealed herself as a "Hindu woman," the question of legitimacy probably would not have arisen. We want to challenge and resist this demand to uncover ourselves in specific ways for academic consumption, because uncovering ourselves in these terms contradicts the purpose of problematizing the essentialist nature of social categories, which are, in reality, created, enacted, and transformed.

Gillian Rose addresses this ontological problem when she argues that the search for positionality through transparent reflexivity is bound to fail because it assumes that the messiness of the research process can be fully understood. Such a search, argues Rose, "depends on certain notions of agency (as conscious) and power (as context), and assumes that both are knowable" (Rose 1997, 311). She sees an inherent contradiction when "a researcher situates both herself and her research subjects in the same landscape of power, which is the context of the research project in question" because "the identity to be situated does not exist in isolation but only through mutually constitutive social relations, and . . . the implications of this relational understanding of position . . . makes the vision of a transparently knowable self and world impossible" (Rose 1997, 312).

Apart from this contradiction, we want to note at least three other problems. First, while many scholars expect ethnographic and life-historical research to be accompanied by a discussion of the author's identity and positionality, no such expectation applies to scholars using other research methods (e.g., quantitative, archival, and textual analyses). This unevenness assumes that researchers who do not engage in ethnographic or life-historical research do not need to respond to critiques of representation and, at worst, results in further marginalization of personal narratives in producing knowledge. Second, to squeeze into a few paragraphs or pages multifaceted and changing relationships with our subjects in Tanzania or India entails a translation that necessarily does injustice to their complexity. Finally, discussions of reflexivity generate feelings of paralysis among feminist scholars because the politics of representation often results either in a "rather puritanical, competitive assessment among scholars" (Marcus 1992, 490) or in "tropes" that are sometimes seen as "apologies," and at others as "badges" (Patai 1991, 149). And even these tropes do not always work. For example, Daphne Patai argues that self-reflexivity "does not redistribute income, gain political rights for the powerless, create housing for the homeless, or improve wealth" (Patai 1994, quoted in Wolf 1997, 35). Terms like *appropriation*, *exploitation*, and even *surveillance* are often attached to the very concept of "western" research among "nonwestern" subjects, leading many western scholars, especially students, to conclude that they cannot step into "other" worlds and societies for research purposes, or that it should not be done because it is inherently unethical (Geiger 1997a).

How can we take positionality and reflexivity out of misplaced struggles over legitimacy and transparent reflexivity and turn them into more meaningful conceptual tools that can help us advance transformative politics of difference in relation to our own research agendas? In the next two sections, we elaborate upon two interrelated and complementary approaches to reflexivity: A "speaking-with" approach that treats both reflexivity and positionality as processes evolving over space and time; and crossing borders to build "situated solidarities" rooted in our specific (multiple) contexts and place-based locations.

Speaking with Research Subjects

If the workings of power in fieldwork relationships cannot be fully understood, and the researcher's complex and shifting identities cannot accurately be captured, revealed, simplified, translated, or transposed across contexts, how can we approach difficult questions of power, privilege, political engagement, and social change? Feminist social scientists have often sought a *speaking-with* model of engagement between researcher and researched—an approach that involves talking and listening carefully, and openness to influences of people from varied sociocultural locations (De Vault 1999). These insights often remain vague, however, requiring extension of reflexivity from an identity-based focus to a more material and institutional focus. Rather than privileging a reflexivity that emphasizes researcher's identity, we must discuss more explicitly the economic, political, and institutional processes and structures that provide the context for the fieldwork encounter and shape its effects—an aspect that has often taken a backseat in reflexive exercises. Exploring the overlaps and disjunctures between these two kinds of reflexivities is essential for grappling with the theory/praxis divide, engaging in feminist knowledge production across multiple borders, and moving beyond the impasse.

Feminist scholars engaged in fieldwork are acutely aware of the dilemmas they face (see Wolf, 1997), but the popular practice of writing about these challenges has largely been a post-fieldwork (even post-analysis) exercise—one in which the author critically reflects on the difficulties (including power differentials) pertaining to social relationships, reciprocity, and responsibility encountered in the "field" in an article or a section of a book or dissertation. While this allows researchers to problematize the notions of bias and objectivity, it does not necessarily create spaces for critical reflection on the factors influencing the research process, its relevance to those to whom we are politically committed, the mutual benefits and enrichment exchanged, the use value of the work, etc. In other words, there has been little discussion of how to operationalize a speaking-with approach to research that might help us work through negotiated and partial meanings in our intellectual and political productions. These questions must be addressed by thinking about reflexivity and positionality as processes.

Crossing Borders with Situated Solidarities

> The problem of voice (speaking for, to or with) intersects with
> the problem of place ("speaking from" and "speaking of").
> —Arjun Appadurai, "Introduction"

> The challenge [is to redefine and execute] research strategies
> that move towards a "collaborative knowledge" that is
> self-consciously representative of border-crossings—of the
> combined insights of different persons, places, and research
> contexts . . . which simultaneously embrace different
> perspectives, voices and places, and which deliberately cross
> and re-cross multiple spatial, social and economic borders.
> —H-NET List for African History.

Crossing borders is on the agenda.[2] Foundations wish to fund projects connecting the global with the local, academics with practitioners. Editors are excited by cutting-edge scholarship that blurs disciplinary boundaries, and emphasizes hybridity. This is energizing, but the popularity of these border crossings in the present political climate should give us pause. As Shohat cautions, "A celebration of syncretism and hybridity per se, if not articulated in conjunction with questions of hegemony and neo-colonial power relations, runs the risk of appearing to sanctify the fait accompli of colonial violence" (Shohat 1996, 330). For feminist scholars simultaneously located in institutions and communities of both north and south, it is critical to ask what borders we cross, in whose interests, and how our practices are interwoven with processes of imperialism and neocolonialism.

Feminist fieldworkers have variously grappled with traversing borders, especially those separating the first and third worlds. Ong finds it necessary to "describe a political decentering . . . in Western knowledge as it allows itself to be redefined by discourses from the geopolitical margins" (Ong 1995, 367). Such redefinition involves "a deliberate cultivation of a mobile consciousness," engaged in a dialectical process of "disowning places that come with overly determined claims and re-owning them according to different (radical democratic) interests" and of "critical agency shifting between transnational sites of power" (Ong 1995, 368; see also Pratt 2004).

Those of us who believe that the intellectual and political value of engaging in face-to-face learning across borders outweighs the problematic context (global capitalism, northern imperialism, structural inequalities) in which such work necessarily takes place are responsible for developing critical analyses of our multidimensional struggles with such crossings. Tamara Jacka (1994, 663), self-described as a "White, urban Australian woman," does this by describing the questions and criticisms received from Sinologists and Chinese men on one side, and feminists and postcolonial theorists on the other, as she carried out research on changing gender relations in rural China. Acknowledging that she has drawn on "western" theories as well as a decade of "studying Chinese and things Chinese," Jacka asserts: "my focus on work and work relations derives as much from my interactions with Chinese women and from the Chinese Marxist emphasis on these issues as from western feminism. . . . from a dialectical shifting between Chinese and western approaches and an attempt to synthesise the insights of each. This moving between cultures, gaining insights from both, is . . . one of the most valuable aspects of the kind of research I am engaged in" (Jacka 1994, 665). Jacka rejects the notion that there is an "insurmountable gap" between her research and "the concerns of rural Chinese women," not because she believes that all women share common oppression or a common set of needs and values, but because she recognizes "the danger of essentializing the differences between East and West" (Jacka 1994, 665). She insists that her research has been centrally shaped by the concerns and thinking of women with whom she has worked, and refuses to back away from her research findings:

> I *do* think that women in [rural] China are doubly exploited by the peasant family and by socialist patriarchy. . . . And . . ., while this, no doubt, does reflect my concerns as a westerner, I think it also reflects the concerns of Chinese women. In addition, I maintain that while my work may contribute to western discourses on the backwardness of the non-western, non-modern world, it also offers something more positive . . . I think western feminists have much to learn from the experiences of women in eastern societies, and, as Gayatri Spivak asserts, not only must White women do their "homework" and learn about other women's experiences, their responses to other women's experiences will also allow White feminists to interrogate their own speaking positions. . . . I recognize that, regardless of my individual motivations, in terms of world power relations, I work from within a dominating and colonising discourse which imposes western, first world values on others, not the least by defining them as "non-western" or "third world." I would hope, however, that we are not all completely trapped in the "first world" or the "third world"—that there is some possibility of developing counter discourses by sharing and working with others, by repositioning ourselves at least temporarily, both literally by doing fieldwork and metaphorically, and by "smuggling ideas across the lines." (Jacka 1994, 667)

This kind of effective participation in border crossings necessitates a processual approach to reflexivity and positionality, combined with an acute awareness of the place-based nature of our intellectual praxis. The goal must be to build *situated* solidarities, which seek to reconfigure our academic fields in relation to the "fields" that our "research subjects" inhabit. Similar to Jodi Dean's (1995, 69) "reflective solidarities," situated solidarities aim to understand the larger interconnections produced by globalization of economies and labor forces while challenging the colonialist prioritizing of the West. They are attentive to the ways in which our ability to evoke the global in relation to the intimate, to configure the specific nature of our alliances and commitments, and to participate in processes of social change are significantly shaped by our geographical and socio-institutional locations, and the particular combination of processes, events, and struggles underway in those locations. As Wendy Larner suggests, it is inadequate for us to position ourselves only in theoretical and ideological "place"; we must also recognize our "geographical location, and by implication, the politics of that place" (Larner 1995, 177). Through her involvement in feminist discourses of difference among Maori and Pakeha women in Aotearoa/New Zealand, Larner recognizes that there will probably be multiple situated knowledges rooted in different (and often mutually irreconcilable) epistemological positions in any particular context. Thus, for her, the measure of contemporary feminist theory can neither be "'Who is making this theory?' nor 'What is the epistemological basis for the theory?' but rather 'What kinds of struggle does it make possible?'" (Larner 1995, 187).

Importantly, Larner maintains that despite the inevitable disjunctures, working with an understanding of positionality involves developing theoretical and political frameworks that integrate conflicts and contradictions:

> The goal is not unity based on common experience, or even experiences, but rather some sort of a workable compromise that will enable us to coalesce around specific issues. . . . If positionality is to be more than a recitation of one's personal characteristics, or a textual strategy, [we must address the dilemmas that] arise out of . . . the politics of negotiating not just multiple, but discrepant audiences. Moreover, it may be that out of such engagements will come alternative theorisations, generated not out of abstract discussions about theoretical correctness, but rather out of the efforts of academics who are engaged with, and speak to, specific political struggles. (Larner 1995, 187–88)

Moving toward this goal, we would add, requires an ongoing and open dialogue across geographical and disciplinary borders on how alternative theorizations can emerge from speaking to specific political struggles, and how inevitable disjunctures can become necessary pieces of reconfiguring the modes, purposes, and meanings of knowledge production.

Beyond the Impasse?

Dominant definitions of academic research automatically label as "extracurricular" (e.g., service, outreach, or creative work) much intellectual production that falls beyond the sphere of certified university scholarship. In the absence of enduring connections with specific political struggles, and of spaces for critical dialogues with those whose interests progressive research seeks to serve, the sole-conceptualized and sole-authored model of research will have little value for those who live in the fields of academics and NGO workers. Challenging normative definitions of knowledge and knowledge producers inevitably entails the reflexive reshaping of meanings embedded in different sociopolitical contexts, languages, and institutional cultures, as well as meanings that emerge, are stifled, or realign themselves in the course of specific struggles.

The difficulties of speaking with collaborators across borders are rooted in the structural realities of fieldwork—a research practice that frequently entails disjunctures between the sites of face-to-face encounters with people whose stories we want to tell, and the institutional locations from which we produce knowledge about them. For feminist researchers who travel back and forth between structurally unequal worlds, this aspect of fieldwork has to be replaced by innovative and dynamic processes of collective knowledge production that are valued as sociopolitically pertinent by those in the field with whom we share political commitments. Indeed, in our view, the dangers of relinquishing responsibility for acquiring, producing, and disseminating knowledge about and by people inhabiting the rest of the world have never been greater. To leave total control of what is said, and therefore widely "understood" (whether about India, Tanzania, Iraq, or Palestine) to those whose interests lie within the spheres of global capital, an increasingly homogenized media, or the political status quo (as long as it serves U.S. purposes) is to facilitate those very interests. Nor is it enough to simply criticize these processes and interests, and discuss them among ourselves—favorite academic pastimes.

Processual reflexivity and crossing borders with situated solidarities require openness to rethinking dominant standards of academic productivity. Orchestrating such a shift entails challenging traditional academic norms that inhibit collective and collaborative research—except in the classroom; value national and/or western theorizing over the thinking of all but a handful of third-world theorists; and caution graduate students and early career academics against pursuing intellectual interests that coalesce around political concerns, issues, people, and modes of analysis that challenge institutionalized ways of knowing and thinking. Many feminist/women's studies departments and programs have already celebrated thirty-year anniversaries, signaling more than a generation of scholarship within the academy. Feminist scholars can become important change agents within academic institutions. Anti-disciplinary feminist scholarship can support and facilitate collective and collaborative research across difficult borders, and take the lead in redefining the relationship between scholarship and community-based engagement and how academic merit gets evaluated. It can be critical in moving us beyond the impasse by creating institutional spaces promoting a far broader view of what counts as significant scholarship, and by encouraging graduate students and faculty to take intellectual and political risks—including that highly charged and thoroughly scrutinized practice known as feminist fieldwork.

Part 2. The Reframed Argument: Footloose Researchers, Traveling Theories, and Transnational Feminist Praxis

> When feminist scholars from western countries come here
> to do their research, they often try hard to do everything in
> our local language and idiom. But why is it that when they
> return to their institutions, they frequently write in ways
> that are totally inaccessible and irrelevant to us? . . . The
> question of access is not just about writing in English. It
> is about how one chooses to frame things, how one tells a
> story . . . [Suppose] you tell my story in a way that makes
> no sense at the conceptual level to me or my community,
> why would we care what you have to say about my life?
> —Discussion with feminist scholar-activists in Pune,
>   27 July 2000

Reflexivity, positionality, and identity have become keywords in feminist field-work in much of Anglophone academia. Indeed, it is now rare to find fieldwork-based feminist research that does not engage to some degree with the "politics of fieldwork." Despite this proliferation of self-reflexivity, however, feminist social scientists have largely avoided the most vexing political questions that lie at the heart of our in/ability to talk across worlds. The above quotation suggests that at the most basic level these questions have to do with the theoretical frameworks and languages that we deploy in our work. But the concern about the utility of theory and theoretical languages in transnational feminist praxis is entangled with at least three other complex issues: First is the question of accountability and the specific nature of our political commitments: Who are we writing for, how, and why? Second, it involves a serious engagement with questions of collaboration: What does it mean to coproduce relevant knowledge across geographical, institutional, and/or cultural borders? Third, it entails an explicit interrogation of the structure of the academy and the constraints and values embedded therein, as well as our desire and ability to challenge and reshape those structures and values.

Existing models of "doing" positionality and reflexivity fail to engage adequately with the above issues. This inadequacy led Susan Geiger and me to argue that much important theoretical work on the concepts of reflexivity, positionality, and identity has led to an impasse with respect to feminist research. This impasse is reflected, among other things, in the abandonment of fieldwork by some researchers in favor of textual analyses, and in criticisms that self-reflexive exercises amount to mere "navel gazing" and serve to prove the researchers' legitimacy (Patai 1991; see also Wolf 1997). By identifying these problems, we do not dismiss the importance of understanding how our situatedness as researchers and our multiple and shifting contextual identities and agendas shape the knowledges we produce. Rather, we maintain that such reflexivity does not go far enough in terms of political engagement, especially when it comes to feminist fieldwork in third-world contexts.

Here, I return to some of the arguments that Geiger and I make about the nature of this impasse by analyzing varying responses that I received in 2000 to my manuscript "*Mujhe Jawab Do* (Answer Me!)" from three different feminist audiences. These audiences were located respectively in the U.S. academy and in two NGOs in India—one being a grassroots organization of women in rural Bundelkhand, and another a research and documentation center in Pune. When juxtaposed and compared with one another, the three responses are instructive in not only rethinking issues of reflexivity, positionality, and identity in feminist fieldwork, but also in concretely identifying and grappling with some of the key challenges associated with transnational feminist praxis. But before I discuss the responses, a few words about *Mujhe Jawab Do* are in order.

Mujhe Jawab Do: Juggling Multiple Feminist Agendas

After eight years of research and writing on the gendered community and racial politics among South Asians in Tanzania, I significantly shifted the course of my intellectual journey and embarked in 1998 on a new research project in Chitrakoot district of Bundelkhand region in Uttar Pradesh. The reasons for this shift were related to my own struggles with what constitutes politically relevant research. Despite the theoretically and empirically exciting nature of my work in Tanzania, the material, institutional, and ethical constraints associated with this research seriously limited the spaces available to me for radical collaborative efforts with socially marginalized Asian and Asian African communities in Tanzania. These factors led me to shift my focus to rural women's activism and social spaces in Uttar Pradesh.

One of my central goals was to examine the spatial tactics adopted by rural women in Bundelkhand, often described as one of the most impoverished and violence-ridden areas in the country. Bundeli women's activism over issues of water and literacy had made a big splash in Indian newspapers, and I was eager to learn about these struggles and about the ways in which women's activism on the ground was shaped by institutions such as the Dutch government, the World Bank, the government of India, and the state- and district-level governmental and nongovernmental organizations.

However, as I became immersed in the two grassroots organizations working in this area, activists from one of these organizations, Vanangana, expressed that they wanted their emerging street theater on domestic violence to be a major part of my research inquiry. Accordingly, the first publication to come out of this research focused on charting the discursive geographies of women's resistance through Vanangana's street theater (Nagar 2000).[3] I explored the manner in which activists used social spaces to analyze the interrelationships among intimacy, marriage, and violence and to develop political discourses for their own mobilization, and how they creatively used kinship and gendered materialities of women's natal and conjugal villages to trouble the masculinist spaces of their communities.

The original version of the paper hinged on two main issues. First, it high-lighted how rural women's activism on issues surrounding access to water and literacy led them to critique an instrumentalist vision of empowerment in de-velopment organizations and how they theorized and acted upon their under-standings of the interconnections between empowerment, violence, space, and politics. Second, it argued that feminist social scientists located in the northern academy cannot choose to remain silent on third-world women's struggles about sensitive issues such as domestic violence simply because there is a messy poli-tics of power and representation involved in the fieldwork encounter. Rather, they should accept the challenge of figuring out how to productively engage with and participate in mutually generative knowledge production about those struggles.

Responses to the Paper

On finishing the initial version of *Mujhe Jawab Do* in March 2000, I sent off one set of copies to *Gender, Place and Culture* (GPC) and another set to the two (and only) Vanangana members who were fluent in English. Later, when I visited India in July 2000, I presented the same paper—in a mixture of Hindi and English—to feminist scholar-activists at Aalochana, a women's research and documentation center in Pune. While the overall responses from all three audiences were enthusiastic, each group emphasized quite different things in relation to the politics of positionality, reflexivity, and identity.

Response from Gender, Place and Culture

Two out of the three reviewers of *GPC* were disturbed because they assumed that my argument about the need for U.S.-based feminist scholars to engage with sensitive topics such as violence in the homes of rural women in India was coming from a white researcher. They wanted to know why the author did not explain how s/he dealt with cultural and linguistic differences, and why s/he did not highlight the contributions of Indian feminist scholars who were trying to engage in similar research endeavors. Both reviewers suggested that I either say more about my personal background and positionality, or drop the argument about why U.S.-based feminist researchers should not turn away from a deep engagement with marginalized women's struggles in the global south.

Response from Vanangana, Chitrakoot

The two English-speaking organizers at Vanangana expressed excitement about my ethnographic analysis of their street theater campaign and said that it helped them think about their political and spatial methodologies in a different light. However, they had reservations about the theoretical section of the paper. While they understood how a discussion of power and representation and of relationships between U.S.-based feminist scholars and poor women's activism in the third world could be important to other academic feminists, this subject was not interesting to them for two reasons.

First, it was inaccessible for the members of their organization. The readers suggested that I eliminate the theoretical language and write a shorter version of the paper in Hindi so that women who were active in the street theater campaign could read, reflect, and respond to my analysis of their movement.

Second, they wished to share my paper in English with other women's organizations in the country and with prospective funding agencies because they themselves did not have the time or resources to produce such an analysis. They believed that the paper would serve this purpose better if I could substitute the section on representation with a more detailed discussion of the relationship between empowerment and violence in development thinking and in women's social movements in South Asia.

Response from Aalochana, Women's Research
and Documentation Centre, Pune

When I presented the paper at Aalochana, an organization comprising feminist thinkers who are active in women's development NGOs and social movements, its members responded with passion. Several of them expressed an interest in building bridges with Vanangana members, in exchanging ideas, and in discussing future collaborations or strategies with them. Most women saw me as being from North India, and did not raise any issues about whether I was an authentic enough researcher to undertake the project. One scholar activist from New Delhi, however, who was the only other North Indian in the room besides me, asked why "American" researchers like me did not leave such research projects to "Indian" feminists and choose to do research on Indian communities living in the United States instead.

Comparing the Responses: Implications
for Transnational Feminist Praxis

None of the above-mentioned groups questioned the relevance of the struggles that I narrated and analyzed in *Mujhe Jawab Do*. Yet, the divergent nature of their responses uncovered the messiness associated with attempts by feminists

located in the western academy to talk across worlds—worlds that are separated
not just socially, geopolitically, and materially, but also in their understandings
of what constitutes meaningful theory and politics. Working through this messiness necessarily implies making decisions regarding which—and whose—understandings about meaningful theory matter the most to "us" and why. These
divergences also open a space to grapple with what Geiger and I call *the impasse*.
For instance, the response from the two *GPC* reviewers exemplified the central
problems that we identify with existing models of doing reflexivity. Reflexivity
in U.S. academic writing has mainly focused on examining the identities of the
individual researcher rather than on the ways in which those identities intersect
with institutional, geopolitical, and material aspects of their positionality. In so
doing, such identity-based reflexivity fails to distinguish systematically among
the ethical, ontological, and epistemological aspects of fieldwork dilemmas. Far
from viewing social categories as created, enacted, transformed *in* and *through*
specific encounters, a simple identity-based reflexivity demands that we uncover
ourselves in terms of certain predefined and coherent social categories that
can exist prior to those interactions. The response from the scholar-activist at
Aalochana indicates that the tendency to reduce reflexivity to simply an identity-
based reflexivity is by no means confined to the western academic establishment.
In raising questions about who constituted an authentic feminist researcher, the
above-mentioned member of Aalochana was clearly reducing positionality to
the retrogressive kind of identity politics that allows only "Xes to speak to X
issues" (di Leonardo and Lancaster 1997, 5).

It was the constructive criticism from the two Vanangana readers that I found
to be the most generative for my project at hand, *and* for further grappling
with the two key questions that Geiger and I identified as lying at the heart of
feminist research in third-world contexts. First, how can feminists use fieldwork to produce knowledges across multiple divides of power, locations, and
axes of difference in ways that do not reflect or reinforce the interests, agendas,
and priorities of the more privileged groups and places? Second, how can the
production of those knowledges be tied explicitly to a politics of social change
in favor of the less privileged people and places?

Like Larner's work with Maori and Pakeha women in New Zealand, Vanangana's critique was based in an implicit recognition that in any given context
there are likely to be multiple situated knowledges rooted in different and often
mutually irreconcilable epistemological positions. The question that Vanangana
members posed, then, was neither "Who was making the theoretical claims
about power and representation?" nor "What was the epistemological basis for
those theoretical claims?," but rather "What kinds of struggles did my analysis
make possible for them?" (paraphrased from Larner 1995, 187). In so doing,

Vanangana members circumvented the problems of a simple identity-based reflexivity that characterized the responses by the *GPC* reviewers and the critic from Aalochana. Instead, they articulated a more complex critique—grounded in a deeper political reflexivity—that pushed me to rethink the sociopolitical implications of my theoretical framework, and how my choices regarding analytical languages were explicitly tied to questions of accountability and responsibility in transnational feminist praxis.

Let me give an example to highlight this key difference in the two kinds of critiques. One of the *GPC* reviewers (who had assumed that I was white) thought it was pretentious of me to claim that the problems surrounding representations of the subaltern should not deter feminist scholars from getting involved in messy issues such as violence in the intimate lives of poor women in the third world. The reviewer also expressed irritation that at one place I used the term "talking to" instead of "talking with" when elaborating on the need for feminist academics located in the global north to seriously engage with theorizations of grassroots activists working in the global south. In order to please this reviewer, then, all I would have had to do was to claim an authentic status as a "real native" from Uttar Pradesh, and use the correct lingo that replaced "talking to" with "talking with" without changing my argument. Ironically, however, these modifications would have made no difference to the usefulness of my analysis to Vanangana. In fact, it was precisely the abstract discussion of subalternity, representation, and talking with, talking for, and talking to which made it hard for my initial analysis to speak directly to Vanangana's concerns. The concrete *practice* of talking with the campaigners, however, led me to reorient my story away from what was fashionable in the academic realm, into the direction of the Bundeli activists' political and intellectual priorities. This entailed rethinking the ways in which the discussion about the politics of representation could be interwoven with an intersectional analysis of empowerment, violence, space, and gender in South Asian development politics.

Ultimately, however, our ability to talk across worlds—to align our theoretical priorities with the concerns of marginalized communities whose struggles we want to advance—is connected to the opportunities, constraints, and values embedded in our academic institutions. Next, I turn to this structural issue and identify some areas that must be addressed in order to create institutional spaces that can facilitate more productive dialogues among feminists located in materially, geographically, socially, and politically diverse worlds.

Academia, Theory, and Transnational Feminist Praxis

> If you ask me what is the object of my work, the object of the
> work is to always reproduce the concrete in thought—not to
> generate another good theory, but to give a better-theorized ac-
> count of concrete historical reality. This is not an anti-theoretical
> stance. I need theory in order to do this. But the goal is to un-
> derstand the situation you started out with better than before.
> —Stuart Hall, "The Toad in the Garden"

Transnational feminist conversations, especially between worlds as far removed from one another as the ones I have described above, cannot be productive unless feminist academics based in northern institutions produce research agendas and knowledges that do not merely address what is theoretically exciting or trendy in their institutional locations, but also what is considered politically imperative by the communities we work with or are committed to. By making this distinction between theory and politics I am not implying that people who "do" theory are not engaged in political work, or that political activists are not simultaneously engaged in important theory building. Rather, I am echoing the manner in which each group commonly states its priorities: for feminist academics in major research institutions in the United States, the primary concerns are often articulated in terms of theory, while NGOs such as Vanangana or Aalochana are mainly interested in the political and strategic ramifications of a given concept or analysis. In other words, widening the notion of what constitutes theory should form the core of transnational feminist praxis. At a time when our students and colleagues are increasingly drawn to the elegance of "high" theory and the headiness of the abstract, it might be helpful to go back to theorists, such as Stuart Hall, who remind us that concrete political engagement does not translate into an antitheoretical stance.

Equally, it is critical that such knowledge be produced and shared in theoretical languages that are simultaneously accessible to multiple audiences in locations that may seem distant from one another. While many academics accept the idea that working with NGOs or social movements requires producing written products other than scholarly books or articles—for example, workshops, organizational reports, and newspaper articles in local languages—I believe that it is increasingly important for us to also produce *scholarly analyses* that can be accessed, used, and critiqued by our audiences in multiple social and institutional locations. This kind of scholarship is necessary not only to trouble the existing hierarchies of knowledge but also because, as we know so well, scholars in U.S. research universities are often too overcommitted to devote much time to developing "nonacademic" products.

At the same time, however, we must continue the struggle to create new institutional spaces that favor, facilitate, and give due recognition to alternative research products and to new forms of collaboration. Workshops, organizational reports, newspaper articles, and creative work in local and regional languages that emerge from our work, for instance, must be institutionally recognized—not as extracurricular activities that we do on the side but as research products that require special skills and time and energy commitments, and that are central to scholarly knowledge production. Similarly, we must carry on fighting for institutional recognition that knowledge is never produced by a single individual. This involves troubling the notion of sole authorship with one that genuinely recognizes and encourages knowledge making with actors such as grassroots mobilizers, life historians, and research assistants—not only in shaping the outcome of research—but also in articulating and framing our research priorities and questions. In the context of research that focuses on feminist organizing at the grassroots level, it is also important to interrogate predominant assumptions about "women's groups" and examine how such groups not only build critical alliances with men, but also the ways in which men, as research assistants and coresearchers, can play a critical role in yielding insights about activism, gender, and space, particularly in gender-segregated contexts.

Finally, I would like to draw upon Cindi Katz's notion of translocal "counter-topographies that link different places analytically and thereby enhance struggles in the name of common interests" (Katz 2001, 1230). If particular sociopolitical processes can be imagined as contour lines of constant elevation, connecting places that are being shaped through those processes, then conceptualizing new solidarities requires us to trace counter-topographies. This task involves the simultaneous labor of following contour lines across places, while also grappling with the ways that global processes are embedded in particular places (Pratt and Rosner 2012, 18). For feminist research to produce such counter-topographies, researchers must seriously consider how they can serve as useful channels of communication between scholars and activists located in different places. For example, organizations working on environmental and economic policies in Uttar Pradesh may want to understand how local organizations coordinated and developed their strategies during the WTO (World Trade Organization) protests in Seattle, while women's organizations in Pune may want to examine gender and caste with women's organizations in Bundelkhand. Combining such concerns in our own reflexive process can be generative in building situated solidarities, while also opening up spaces to dialogically explore the meanings, possibilities, and limitations of our own locational, material, and institutional specificities vis-à-vis the specificities of those with whom we wish to stand and speak.

Part 3: Postscript: Reflexivity, Positionality, and Languages of Collaboration

> Berlin of 1884 was effected through the sword and the bullet. But the night of the sword and the bullet was followed by the morning of the chalk and the blackboard. . . . The bullet was the means of the physical subjugation. Language was the means of the spiritual subjugation.
>
> —Ngũgĩ wa Thiong'o, "The Language of African Literature"

> Is it the inevitable conclusion to the formation of an interpretive community that its constituency, its specialized language, and its concerns tend to get tighter, more self-enclosed as its own self-confirming authority acquires more power, the solid status of orthodoxy, and a stable constituency? What is the acceptable humanistic antidote to what one discovers, say, among sociologists, philosophers and so-called policy scientists who speak only to and for each other in a language oblivious to everything but a well-guarded, constantly shrinking fiefdom forbidden to the uninitiated?
>
> —Edward W. Said, "Opponents, Audiences, Constituencies and Communities"

Language resides at the core of any struggle that seeks to decolonize and re-configure the agendas, mechanics, and purposes of knowledge production. I juxtapose the above statements by Ngũgĩ wa Thiong'o and Edward Said to connect two forms of discussion around language that often remain isolated: those in the realm of cultural and identity politics and those about the inclusiveness or exclusiveness of sites from which knowledge and norms of expertise and professionalism are produced. Here, I reflect on how these two struggles around language inform my ongoing intellectual and political journeys as a feminist thinker and writer located in the northern academy who works with nonacademic actors in the global south. Specifically, I consider how transborder collaborations can create critical opportunities to seek liberation from the "spiritual subjugation" of dominating languages, and help to carve out alternative interpretive communities that challenge the "fiefdoms" generally forbidden to the uninitiated.

Two Fields, Two Worlds?

My intellectual commitment and attachment to the question of language are rooted in my own battles since childhood with disjunctures between the worlds of elite and vernacular languages. With the beginning of an academic career as a geographer in the United States, the landscape of the same struggle that

I associated with my lower-middle-class upbringing in old Lucknow became wider and more complex. In the context of my critical ethnographic research in Tanzania and India, the implications of this reality were sobering: On the one hand, academics in the north who read and critiqued my work were automatically deemed as intellectuals worthy of the right to use and evaluate the knowledge I produced. On the other hand, the life historians, interviewees, and public intellectuals in the fields (located in the south) who enabled me to produce "new" knowledges for northern academia were automatically classified at worst as sources and at best as research subjects without having much power to access, evaluate, or demand revision of my ideas or the knowledge that I produced about them.

This, in turn, created further splits between the field inhabited by the members of the discipline(s) and the field inhabited by the research subjects: if I cared to make the latter a salient part of my interpretive community to which I wanted to be accountable, I was free to record any such work in my faculty annual report as service, outreach, or creative work. But such efforts could not legitimately guide my research agenda in the eyes of the northern research university if I wanted to be seen as a respectable scholar. Conversely, from the perspective of those located in the global south, north-based researchers mostly used the south as a source of raw materials (data) to be processed, packaged, and marketed according to the demands of their professional fields, with little or no engagement with the sociopolitical and intellectual debates or struggles that are considered pertinent in the places that their research sources and subjects inhabit.

The overlapping dichotomies between the field versus academic discipline, and sources or subjects versus intellectuals, emanate from a categorical distinction between production and popularization of knowledge that serves to accelerate professionalization while disregarding how "the very process of making knowledge is coterminous with the diffusion of knowledge" (Bender 1998, 21). When the north/south divides get intertwined with this general phenomenon of estrangement between production and use of knowledge, the problem becomes even more serious. First, there is little opportunity to grapple with questions such as, Who controls the production and distribution of the knowledges produced? Who forms its intended and actual audiences? How do these productions intersect with the political economy of publishing, literacy, access to and distribution of literature, and implied and empirical audiences (Williams and Chrisman 1994, 373)? Second, it impairs our ability to confront the basic problem of the production of knowledge in and for the West where the very act of writing for the West about the Other implicates us in projects that establish western authority and cultural difference (Abu-Lughod 2001, 105).

Commu(nica)ting across "Fields"

My struggle with these interrelated issues of "real" and theoretical languages
in the production and dissemination of knowledge began in 1996–97 with two
quite different collaborative articles, neither of which got published until much
later due to the resistance they encountered from academic reviewers in development studies and feminist studies. One was a preliminary exploration
of how the politics of English-medium schooling was shaped by processes of
modernization and social fracturing in postcolonial India. It suggested that the
very existence and well-being of an English-speaking techno-managerial and
professional elite (considered as experts) hinged on the presence of sociopolitical and discursive divides between the worlds of English and the vernacular
(Faust and Nagar 2001). The other essay written with Geiger (which constitutes
the first part of this chapter) argued for a need to extend academic reflexivity
in feminist fieldwork beyond the realm of the individual researcher's personal
identities to the sociopolitical and institutional locations in which researchers
were operating. Such reflexivity, we argued, could become a basis for forming
situated solidarities with third-world subjects to produce potentially (more)
meaningful knowledges across geographical, institutional, and sociopolitical
borders. As my research on communal and racial politics among Asians in
Tanzania gained visibility and I received invitations to display my credentials
as a specialist on the South Asian diaspora in East Africa, my immersion in the
above-mentioned concerns translated into an active distancing from the label
of "expert" on that subject.

Thus began the search for long-term partnerships with grassroots activists
in India to push at the definitions of cutting-edge knowledge in U.S. feminist
studies, and to highlight a need to produce frameworks that can meaningfully
travel across the two fields identified above. This project of expanding the idea
of "the cutting edge" also required another type of transnational partnership:
that between academic feminists who collaborated with community members
in different parts of the global south to complicate dominant discourses about
key concepts such as intersectionality, empowerment, and sexual politics (Nagar
and Swarr 2004, Swarr and Nagar 2004).

While these projects gave me intellectual stimulus and sparked productive
conversations with academic colleagues and students, my increasing involvement in yet another field—the field of women's NGOs in North India—was
helping me unpack three additional layers in the global politics of knowledge
production. First, the race for professionalization and estrangement of "experts"
from ordinary people and their struggles is not confined to the northern academy; NGOs in the global south are in the grip of the same processes. What
Bender remarks in the context of academic disciplines in the nineteenth century,

then, can also be applied to the twenty-first-century NGOs: "Professionalized disciplines or the modern service professions that imitated them [did not become] socially irresponsible. But their contributions to society began to flow from their own self-definitions rather than from a reciprocal engagement with general public discourse" (Bender 1993, 10).

Second, as officials, consultants, trainers, and specialists (who conduct case studies, run workshops, write reports, formulate grant proposals, etc.) have come to occupy a center stage in the donor-driven NGO sector, northern academics are no longer the only experts who have the means to go into the southern fields with funding from international donors (Benson and Nagar, 2006). Knowledge production about the majority who inhabit the margins of the south has become part of a globalized network of institutions and actors who share ideas, collaborate, and make critical decisions in international conferences and planning meetings. This implies that practices of both academic institutions and NGOs need to be subjected to scrutiny and redefinition so that dominating knowledges that can travel globally do not end up stifling other frameworks and languages that interpret and explain social realities and struggles from more local or translocal perspectives. Collaboration across multiple institutional sites and socioeconomic locations and in multiple languages and genres can play a critical role in undoing and remaking various layers that constitute transnational politics of knowledge production, and in interrogating and expanding the notions of skills and expertise in intellectual productions.

Third, rather than seeing elite research institutions and foundations as powerhouses from where knowledge about the so-called underprivileged emanates and then trickles downwards, it is important to disrupt and complicate the routes of circulation by which knowledges are produced and disseminated: vernacular and/or nonelite languages that have been unevenly empowered or systematically impoverished through processes of globalization and professionalization in both the academy and NGOs have important roles to play in shaping the nature and outcomes of this disruption.

Critique, Coauthorship, and Translations in the Journey with Sangtins

Even as I began to write for academic venues on the class, caste, and gender politics of NGOization and knowledge production (Nagar and Raju 2003, Nagar and Swarr 2004), I realized that such critical analysis was more or less meaningless for the NGO workers in rural Uttar Pradesh with whom I had been having sustained conversations on these issues since 1996. If the goal of critique was to find resonance on the "other" side, it could not happen merely through the efforts of academic collaborators writing for academic outlets. It had to emerge from a collective process of reflection and analysis with those who were being inserted in processes of professionalization and NGOization at the lowest rungs of the NGO ladder, with an explicit aim of generating dialogues in sites where everyday struggles with those issues were being articulated and enacted.

These churnings sowed the seeds of collaboration with eight members of Sangtin, a small collective of women in the Sitapur district of Uttar Pradesh, which was trying to define its goals by critically reflecting on the NGO-driven field of women's empowerment. Seven of these collaborators—Anupamlata, Reshma Ansari, Vibha Bajpayee, Ramsheela, Shashibala, Shashi Vaishya, and Surbala—made a living as village-level NGO workers, and the eighth, Richa Singh, as a district-level NGO activist in Sitapur. We began in 2002 by focusing on internal processes and politics of NGO work and the labor of activism, social change, and knowledge production from the perspective of the village-level NGO workers who undertake the main labor of translating donor-funded projects of empowerment on the ground. This collective analysis resulted in writing and publishing *Sangtin Yatra*, which braids autobiographical narratives of the seven rural activists to highlight how caste, class, religion, and gender enmesh with the processes of rural development and underdevelopment, empowerment and disempowerment (Anupamlata et al. 2004).[4] *Sangtin Yatra* was warmly received by progressive intellectuals and activists, but the authors were also subjected to an angry backlash from the director of Mahila Samakhya, Uttar Pradesh (MSUP), the state headquarters of the organization where seven of the nine authors were employed. An analysis of these contrasting sets of responses to *Sangtin Yatra* and our struggle to fight the backlash offered us another critical opportunity—this time in English with a countrywide and international readership in mind—to explore the themes of NGOization and global feminisms, while also suggesting new possibilities for (re)imagining transnational feminist interventions and globalization from below (see chapter 5; also, Sangtin Writers 2006).

But the aftermath of critique revealed to us, in jarring ways, the differential price that must be paid by people located at different places in the global hierarchy of knowledge for claiming a space as valid knowledge producers. At the individual level, it pushed us to seek allies and linked us with supporters in multiple institutions whose sociopolitical concerns intersected with ours. At the institutional level, it marked the beginning of new relationships and exchanges with educational organizations, publishers, and aid workers in India and the United States. These new encounters made us recognize that the structures and processes of elitism, classism, and casteism that we highlighted in the context of donor-driven empowerment projects are present in varying configurations in all institutional spaces. Reimagining and reconfiguring them requires critical dialogues in all the sites—including our collective—where intellectual and political work is being carried out (see chapter 5).

Within Sangtin, there have been several dimensions of internal critical reflexivity: One concerns the varied roles, social locations, and privileges enjoyed by different members of the collective and how these shape the politics of skills and labor within the group. Another pertains to the personal struggles of each member with her own casteist, communalistic, and/or heterosexist values, and how these affect our collective work. Finally, our collective imagination tends to get constrained by the same frameworks of donor-sponsored empowerment projects that we identified in *Sangtin Yatra* as NGOization of grassroots politics.

As the nine authors scrutinized prevailing discourses about what and who constitutes so-called legitimate knowledges and knowledge producers, we saw tight connections with the same cult of professionalism and expertise whose exclusionary and paralyzing effects we had highlighted in *Sangtin Yatra*. We could only continue the collaboration by establishing our labor and enterprise as simultaneously activist *and* academic. The decision to write *Playing with Fire* and to publish it with Zubaan Press in New Delhi and University of Minnesota Press in Minneapolis emerged from these struggles.

The issue of coauthorship was peripheral and somewhat artificial for the collective in the early phase of our partnership. At this time, some members of the collective felt that the need for coauthorship was emerging from my disciplinary ethical and political anxieties, rather than from the goals of our collaboration. However, when we embarked on a journey that was invested in imagining Sangtin's future by reflecting on the activists' own lives, coauthorship was embraced and fought for by each member of the collective—sometimes in the face of grave social and economic risks, and sometimes as a way to resist assumptions (or market considerations) of publishers and scholars about who could appear as authors of expert knowledge.

However, our ongoing journey is also teaching us that what is coauthored as a result of an evolving struggle is never set in stone and is forever changing with political and social exigencies. Ideologies that seek to dismantle casteism, classism, heterosexism, or communalism cannot be forced on a dynamic collective just to pursue a desire for consensus. Like collaborative writing, formulation of political ideas and intellectual concepts in a collective with open membership is a constantly evolving process. It is only by making space and nurturing this dynamism (which includes the risk of moving backward at times) that we can appreciate knowledge as being produced in both place and time, drawing upon diverse sources of experience and expertise, in ways that the fields of the academy, NGOs, and social movements can become means, not ends. Such efforts might also give birth to new conceptual languages that are equipped to undertake what Abu-Lughod calls a fearless examination of "the processes of entanglement" (Abu-Lughod 1998, 16). Modernization projects that seek to emancipate and empower poor women can be creatively and collectively re-interpreted across multiple institutional sites through cultural and intellectual productions that resonate at the intertwined scales of the intimate, the local, the translocal, and the transnational. Such productions have a better chance of simultaneously challenging, in multiple fields, the binary constructions of modernity/tradition and East/West, while also uncovering how so-called liberation projects operate through an active politics of class under the label of feminist solidarity (Abu-Lughod 1998, Sangtin Writers 2006).

4. Representation, Accountability, and Collaborative Border Crossings

Moving Beyond Positionality

This chapter is a revised version of an article originally written in 2002–3 in consultation with Farah Ali and what we then called the Sangtin Samooh, or the Sangtin women's collective. The border crossings discussed here must be read in the context of the sociopolitical events unfolding in India and the United States between 2001 and 2003.

Interrogating "Relevance" with Border Crossings

In fall 2002, Ellen Messer-Davidow, professor of English and comparative studies in discourse and society at Minnesota, gave a talk in my department. She cited an incident where Donna Shalala, the former U.S. secretary of Health and Human Services, maintained that academic research was useless to the Clinton administration when it was reforming welfare policy because it was too slow in coming out, produced conflicting results, used impenetrable jargon, and failed to address questions that concerned policy makers. Shalala was not bad-mouthing welfare scholars, argued Messer-Davidow; she was simply calling attention to what the academy expects all scholars to do: "it expects us to complexify, theorize and debate problems that have been constituted by our disciplines . . . Such fields as feminist, cultural and GLBT studies use highly politicized rhetorics and espouse social-change objectives but produce knowledge that has little impact on real-world politics other than igniting backlashes" (Messer-Davidow 2002b, 17; also Messer-Davidow 2002a).

From another part of the world, Jean Dreze, a renowned development economist echoed similar sentiments after his sustained involvement with two people's movements in Rajasthan (Dreze 2002).[1] He noted that even after fifteen years of research on hunger and famines and feeling "perhaps entitled to feel like an 'expert' of sorts on these matters" (especially after collaborating with Amartya Sen, the Nobel Prize winner for economics), he did not always find himself better equipped than others to understand the practical issues that arose in these groups. In fact, he often felt "embarrassingly ignorant" compared with local people who had little formal education but a "sharp understanding of the real world" and for whom the main insights of his research delivered no more than a "fairly obvious" message. Underscoring an urgent need to produce more accessible and relevant social scientific knowledge, Dreze stated rather provocatively that

> social scientists are chiefly engaged in arguing with each other about issues and theories that often bear little relation to the real world. It is in this foggy environment, that common sense ideas have a cutting edge. Their power, such as it is, springs not so much from great originality or profundity as from their ability to bring some basic clarity to the confused world of academia. It is no wonder that these common sense ideas often fail to capture the imagination of people who are not exposed to that confusion in the first place. (Dreze 2002, 817)

Scholars who have undertaken or theorized border crossings have long struggled with such tensions and contradictions between the academic and nonacademic realms by highlighting the problems of voice, authority, and representation (Spivak 1988, Ortner 1995). At the same time, very few have grappled explicitly with what Visweswaran identifies as a main challenge for postcolonial feminist ethnography: "If we have learned anything about anthropology's encounter with colonialism, the question is not really whether anthropologists can represent people better, but whether we can be accountable to people's own struggles for representation and self-determination" (1994, 32). In this chapter, I engage with this issue by focusing on two heightened concerns: that the gulf between the theories produced in the northern academic institutions and the priorities of southern intellectuals, activists, and communities continues to widen; and that very few Anglophone feminist and/or postcolonial geographers are explicitly engaged with the challenge of producing knowledges that speak the theoretical and political languages of communities beyond the academy (Alatas 2001, Frisch 1990, Larner 1995, Peake and Trotz 2001, Raju 2002).

Of course, it is widely accepted that scholars must produce different kinds of products to reach different audiences in the multiple worlds they inhabit and research. There is also a partially shared understanding that we can guard against betraying people's sociopolitical interests by disseminating the views of the marginalized actors and by transferring skills and legitimacy from professional to community researchers (Abu-Lughod 1993, Ong 1995, Red Thread 2000). And there are also cautionary reminders that we must interrogate a rhetoric that valorizes these crossings too readily lest they mimic and supplement the language of the increasingly corporate university establishment (Pratt

2000). But when it comes to addressing the reasons behind our limited ability to excite the imagination of our "subjects"—subaltern or otherwise—located in those Other worlds, or to shift the forms and languages of what is regarded as meaningful academic discourse, there is very little out there to help chart new possibilities for postcolonial geographies and transnational feminisms.

Here, my goal is neither to rehash a critical analysis of previously attempted or problematized border crossings, nor to perpetuate a romancing of collaboration across borders. My aim is, rather simply, to share some evolving thoughts triggered in response to my repeated encounters similar to those described by Jean Dreze—encounters where individuals and groups I worked with simply failed to see academic insights on power, space, identity, or representation as anything more than what was fairly obvious to them, or as anything that could usefully contribute to their own struggles around these issues.[2] At the same time, rather than expressing disdain, mistrust, or indifference toward academic knowledge, I found these organizations and individuals to be quite sophisticated when it came to determining the parameters of their relationships with north-based researchers. Despite (or perhaps because of) being acutely aware of the turbulent politics of location and positionality that mold these relationships, these social actors often had a strong sense of the relative privileges (e.g., mobility and resources) that north-based academics had access to, and the role that successful dialogues and collaborative efforts could play in advancing the personal, organizational, political, and/or intellectual agendas of all involved parties.

Since 1996, then, I have actively identified specific groups and individuals who are interested in building collaborative relationships with me, and I have reflected with them on the conditions, goals, and processes that could give a concrete form and language to our evolving dialogues and collaborative agendas. My efforts have emanated from the belief that discussions surrounding the politics of representation—and of reflexivity, positionality, and identity as a way to address those politics—have reached an impasse (see chapter 3). It is only in and through such moments—successful and failed—of dialogue and representation, then, that we can hope to build situated solidarities and explore new possibilities for postcolonial *and* transnational feminist geographical knowledges that can be simultaneously theorized, accessed, used, critiqued, and revised across geographical, institutional, and socioeconomic borders.

In approaching this question of representation through collaborative border crossings, I am not concerned exclusively with the relevance or utility of research (done by north-based academics) in speaking to the agendas and priorities of activists (located in the south). Ethnographies, travelogues, media, and popular culture continuously produce and circulate a global south through their representations and, in so doing, act as discursive sutures for policies that have deep consequences for our everyday lives. This necessitates a perpetual insertion and immersion of the researcher in the politics of representation regardless of an explicit commitment to activism. One way to enable this insertion is to conceive transnational border crossings as dialogues where the researcher embraces the labor of translating her/his political investments, ethics, and representational strategies to his/her subjects and where the researcher and subject together wrestle with whether, how, and to what extent there is a possibility for the emergence of a shared agenda.

From Partial Knowledges to Collaborative Border Crossings

It is probably not an exaggeration to say that the idea of border crossings has now become a trendy prerequisite—at least in the U.S. academy—for any critical social scientific scholarship to be regarded as "cutting edge." The enthusiasm for such cutting-edge theories and accounts has undoubtedly encouraged an active and desperately needed interrogation of almost every conceivable border—borders of disciplines, methods, nations, and social categories. At the same time, however, relatively little concern has been expressed for the manner in which the products of such crossings can or should become socially or politically relevant—or the means and languages by which they are rendered irrelevant or exclusionary—across the boundaries of the northern academy.

In feminist geography, the discussion that has come closest to addressing this question of relevance across borders has focused on the politics of representation and reflexivity (Radcliffe 1994, Rose 1997, Pratt 2000, Nagar 2002). Sarah Radcliffe, for instance, discusses the connections between authorial representation and political representation and asks how can "Western First World geographers write about Third World women in their teaching/productions, without at the same time (perhaps by the same means) claiming to represent these women politically?" (Radcliffe 1994, 26). Gillian Rose suggests that this problematic of representation can only be addressed by moving away from the notion of a "transparent reflexivity" in which any attempt at self-positioning by the author only serves "the purpose of stabilizing interpretation and removing bias in order to uncover the truth" and thereby reproduces the idea of a detached, universalizing gaze (Rose, cited in Pratt 2000, 641; see also chapter 3). Geraldine Pratt responds to Rose's call to explore how the researcher herself is reconstituted through the research process within a fissured space of fragile and fluid networks of connections and gaps. Through an interrogation and problematization of her own "research performances" undertaken at and with the Philippine Women Centre in Vancouver, Pratt presents a reflexive account in which the researcher, instead of being firmly located, is marked by "absences, fallibilities, and moments that require translation" (Pratt 2000, 642).

These writings have contributed to a rich discussion of the concepts of reflexivity and positionality in geographical research, but their primary focus has remained on textual and representational strategies rather than on the theoretical, empirical, and political content of the stories that geographers seek to tell. This kind of focus on dismantling or interrogating power hierarchies through representational and textual strategies has often resulted in an unintended widening of the gulf between the theories produced by north-based academics and the priorities of their south-based subjects. In making this observation, I do not want to diminish the importance of acknowledging the partialities of the knowledges "we" produce and of the ways in which these are indeed ridden with gaps and fissures. Nor am I suggesting that the politics and strategies of representation should cease to be our concern, for, academic writing—especially when it crosses politicized borders of any kind—necessarily implies struggles as well as strategic choices around representation. However, I do believe that if academics' acknowledgment of partial and fissured landscape of knowledge production does not go beyond textual performances, it runs the danger of reproducing an unbridgeable gap created by our own practice, a gap not very different from the one that Messer-Davidow writes about:

> The problem was a gap I couldn't seem to bridge when I wrote about academic feminism as a change project. The change I had grasped from all those years of doing activism I couldn't reformulate in scholarly terms, and the change I knew from reading scholarship I couldn't deploy in activism. Eventually I realized that practice created the problem. The activist me had acquired know-how by planning, escalating and modifying direct action, and the academic me had acquired knowledge by analyzing, refuting, and reframing esoteric propositions. These very different sets of practice didn't provide two perspectives on the same thing; rather, they constituted change as two divergent things. Tactical practices engendered changes that were orchestrated, whereas intellectual practices generated schemas that were debated. . . . How could I bridge the divides between intellectual and tactical practices, academic and societal arenas, discourses and dollars? (Messer-Davidow 2002b, 2–3)

If our goal is to transform the power hierarchies embedded in knowledge production, it cannot happen merely through a discussion of how we represent others and ourselves. What we need is an opening up of the theoretical horizons so that the stories and struggles we write about do not always become completely inaccessible and/or meaningless in the contexts from where those knowledges emerge. This need to expand our theoretical frameworks is not embedded in a romantic or presumptuous idea that our work could always be relevant to the subjects of our research. Rather, I am suggesting that the analyses we produce remain theoretically and politically impoverished in the absence of close scrutinies and critiques by those postcolonial subjects whose interests we want to advance, or whose histories and geographies we want to (re)write. Such a reimagining of our theoretical and political frameworks is only possible in and through spaces of collaborative knowledge production—spaces in which academic agendas and frameworks can be interrogated and recast, and where we can generate new transformative possibilities in the fissures, gaps, absences, and fallibilities of our critical frameworks whose cutting-edge status we may have taken for granted.

This chapter, then, argues for a need to develop postcolonial and transnational feminist praxes that focus explicitly on conceptualizing and implementing collaborative efforts that insist on crossing multiple and difficult borders. It points to a need to reflect on the sites and strategies deployed to produce such efforts, and on the specific processes, ethics, and imagination through which such dialogues and collaborations can find their form, content, and meaning. To ground this discussion, I draw upon two recent dialogues that I began in Uttar Pradesh (UP). The first was with a woman who chose to be called "Farah Ali" and whose relationship with me was defined by her wish to be represented in and through my research in ways that I could serve as an advocate for her. Far from being dismissed as "instrumental," Farah's injunction to represent her—and my willingness to respond to that injunction to effect that representation—point to the dialogic formation of a text that cannot be understood through a simple definition of collaboration. Instead, this border crossing is better described as my attempt to carry out what I regarded as a responsibility arising in the context of an unplanned encounter, one that carried critical learning moments for me.

The second border crossing describes my initial meeting in 2002 with the Sangtin Collective, which gave birth to what became my long-term entanglement with SKMS described throughout the pages of this book. Painfully, the opening section of this border crossing also foretells, in the words of a woman called Maya, her own murder five years later. While the socio-spatial processes and interrelationships at work in each case are quite different, both dialogues deploy personal narratives revolving around multiple forms of violence in lives marked by gender, caste, class, and communal politics, and deeply intimate struggles around that violence. Instead of seeking to "uncover" the processes that constitute these experiences of violence and struggle, my aim is to highlight strategies that are available for producing new collaborative geographies; for exploring the ways in which these geographies are simultaneously embedded in and speak to multiple sites and landscapes of struggle and survival; and for imagining the processes by which we might begin to reevaluate and reclaim previously colonized and appropriated knowledges.

Border Crossings in Translation

First Border Crossing with Farah Ali

Speaking with Farah

> Do you know what my fight is about, Richa? I'm fighting to speak my way so that
> no family member, no community, no organization, no researcher, no media
> person gets to distort my story to sensationalize my life! . . . I am speaking to
> you, seeking you out, building a relationship with you so that I can help you by
> telling you what you want to know. But I do so with an understanding that you
> are committed to helping me out when I need you, whether you are here . . . or
> in America.[3]

In these four bold sentences, Farah Ali powerfully summarizes her own struggle
as well as the nature of my partnership with her. I met Farah in 2002 through
an NGO I will call Sahara, which serves as a legal counseling cell and support
center in Lucknow for women of all classes and religious groups on issues of
domestic and dowry-related violence and troubled marital relationships. As
such, Sahara works with not only women and their partners, but also with key
members of their families who often play an important role in the creation and
escalation of their "marital problems." Although I have known and sometimes
participated in Sahara's activities since my college days, it was only in 2001–2
that my focus on women's NGOs and their relationships with globalization and
communalism brought me to Sahara as a researcher interested in exploring the
possibility of a long-term collaboration with the organization.

Sahara officials wanted me to help them document, analyze, and collectively
reflect on their work, and initially I was excited about the potential embedded in
such a collaboration. After working with Sahara over a period of four months,
however, I recognized that there was little openness among the organization's
leaders to internal or external criticism, especially in relation to their strong
organizational hierarchy and a problematic underplaying (at times, negation)
of class- and religion-based differences. These factors affected not only the internal structure of Sahara but also the manner in which it reached out to and
intervened in the lives of the women who sought its help. The coordinator of
Sahara was aware of my reservations, and we often had long, sometimes uncomfortable, discussions on the subject. Although my relationship and limited
collaboration with Sahara is not a theme of focus here, this brief background
is necessary to contextualize the story of Farah.

One of the questions that interested me during my work with Sahara and
other similar organizations in India was the interrelationship between communal violence and domestic violence: for example, how were the rise of Hindu

nationalism and the state-sponsored instances of anti-Muslim violence shaping the manner in which questions surrounding domestic violence were being
addressed, recast, or stifled inside and across familial and communal borders?
Whenever this question came up in our discussions at Sahara, one name that
was repeatedly mentioned was Farah Ali, a thirty-seven-year-old woman who
had filed a case with Sahara but subsequently withdrew from the organization
because she refused to adopt any of the steps that Sahara counselors advised her
to take. One counselor described Farah as "a sophisticated, U.S.-returned Muslim woman" who was uncomfortable with the organization because she wanted
her matter to remain private, whereas Sahara believed in politicizing domestic
violence issues by making them public. The counselor gave me Farah's number
but also warned me that I should not expect a positive response from her.

As it turned out, however, Farah was living not too far from my parents'
house, with her own parents and brother's family, and was eager to talk to
me—not on the phone, but at a neighborhood restaurant. We each walked
a few blocks from our homes, met at a street corner, and rode together on a
loud *tempo* to the restaurant. As we began to sense and share fragments of our
histories and geographies, Farah and I recognized some striking similarities in
our social locations that neither of us had encountered before: our upbringing
in lower-middle-class families (hers Muslim, mine Hindu) in the same city;
our unexpected journeys to the United States; our shared status at the time as
mothers with very young daughters living with our parents, married brothers,
and their families—and the contradictions, joys, and pains associated with that
reality. There is much to be noted and analyzed along these lines about the
telling, recording, and retelling of Farah's story, but for the present purposes, I
summarize the complex strands of Farah's struggle and return to the question
of collaboration.

Why No One Can Give Farah a Voice

Let me summarize the pieces that contribute to making Farah's story sensational
and exotic in eyes of the "outsiders"—not just those outsiders who can gaze at
her from the West, but also the multiple gazes that stifled Farah's voice in her
own home, city, and country. Farah, a well-educated social worker from a liberal
middle-class Sunni family, married Aamir in 1994. The marriage was arranged
through their families, but Farah and Aamir spent ten months getting to know
each other during the period of engagement, and both consented happily to the
marriage. In 1995, Aamir had an opportunity to work as a scientist at a top U.S.
university, and Farah joined him after spending two months at his parents' home
in Meerut. Farah had serious reservations about how Aamir's family treated
her, but she chose to not discuss her feelings with Aamir, and instead focused
her energies on building a healthy partnership with him once she reached the

United States. Despite her suspicion and discomfort with Aamir's growing pull toward extremist interpretations of Islam, Farah mostly remembered herself as a happy, content wife and mother in New Jersey until December 1998, when everything turned upside down on a trip back to India.

By March 1999, Farah found herself abandoned with her five-month-old daughter, Juhie, in her in-laws' home in Meerut. Aamir took possession of her immigration documents and returned to New Jersey, which prevented Farah and Juhie from returning to the United States. He subsequently divorced Farah from the United States in April 2000 on the grounds that she had failed to fulfill her duties as a Muslim wife and woman. Farah and Juhie moved from Meerut to Farah's parents' and brother's home in Lucknow. Farah refused to accept the divorce, but the All India Muslim Personal Law Board declared it legal. She wanted to fight the board's decision, but then came 11 September 2001, followed by the reescalation of the Hindu fanaticism over building a Ram Temple in Ayodhya and the massacre of Muslims in the Indian state of Gujarat. Said Farah, "To tell you the truth, my voice has been snatched. From my brothers, their wives, and my parents to the rest of my community . . . and from the folks at Sahara and the Muslim Law Board to the white guys in the U.S. Embassy [in New Delhi] . . . I feel like everyone's hands are pressing against my mouth to silence me. . . . All I have to do is just let out one word, . . . and the media and the people will just find one more reason to dehumanize Muslims."[4] Farah was correct. She was suspicious of everyone who wanted to speak on her behalf. She was convinced that their speaking for her would only serve their sociopolitical or careerist agendas, while undermining her own objectives. In extremely delicate political times in North India, when the Muslim Personal Law Board and Farah's parents and brother were asking her to not talk about her issues in public, Sahara wanted Farah to challenge Aamir by shaming him and his family in the mainstream media. Embarrassing his family in public, according to Sahara, could have forced Aamir to reconsider—or perhaps, withdraw—the divorce statement. It should come as no surprise, then, that one well-intentioned Sahara worker proceeded to leak Farah's story to a producer at Z-TV, who approached Farah for an interview with a promise that he would give her tremendous publicity that would eventually help her win a parliamentary election!

Farah refused to believe that any of these people could give her voice. She considered Sahara's thinking to be too parochial to understand her case. She hated the guts of the Z-TV producer and saw him as no different from those who caricatured Khomeini in the 1980s and who demonized Osama bin Laden in the 2000s. Farah was incensed by the stance of the Muslim Personal Law Board but also appreciated why it was dangerous to publicly criticize the board. She also recognized how her parents' and brother's hands were tied; they had to ask her to be silent about Aamir in these times of state-sponsored repression of

Indian Muslims, but she also felt that she and her daughter were increasingly becoming unwanted burdens in her natal home.

In these circumstances, Farah believed that the only tool she had left to regain her voice and fight for justice was through an entry into the United States of America—where she could confront Aamir through U.S. law, not because that law was inherently more just or sensitive than the Indian law, but because U.S. courts would not recognize the *talaaq nama* and/or would require Aamir to provide adequate maintenance for Farah and Juhie. Farah, whose parents-in-law and sister-in-law effectively prevented her from having any direct communication with Aamir after March 2000, also wondered if meeting Aamir face-to-face would make him realize the implications of what (Farah thought) he did under his family's pressure. Her final reason for regarding the United States as her best option was familiarity; since Farah had lived and worked in the States before, it seemed to be the easiest place for her to start a new life as a single mother and to give Juhie the environment that she needed to blossom. But Farah also feared that 11 September and its aftermath had irrevocably injured her relationships with the U.S. Immigration and Naturalization Service (INS), with the U.S. embassy in New Delhi, and perhaps with the very place where she hoped to find hope.[5]

Reading/Retelling Farah's Story

Farah's story had several complicated strands. There were multiple actors embedded in multiple locations, though I name just three here. There was Farah, who angrily—and rather perceptively—stated that her fate was straddling between Lucknow and Meerut, between family and community, between the United States and India, and between the INS and the Muslim Personal Law Board. There was Sahara—an NGO committed to a particular strategy of politicizing violence against women at the local level—which failed to appreciate Farah as a transnational subject, while Farah dismissed Sahara as too localized and as lacking subtlety in its tactics. And there was me, a U.S.-based researcher working "back home," trying to build a complex alliance with Farah while also remaining committed to certain ethical and political stances.

In terms of the available academic frameworks that could be deployed to make a "cutting-edge" theoretical intervention on the basis of this story, the possibilities were tremendous. I could choose to enact a highly innovative textual performance; I could theorize the multiple border zones that were at work in this story; I could problematize existing theorizations of communalism, secularism, and the postcolonial state; and I could revisit the famous trope of colonial feminism about brown women being saved from brown men by white men. But I had to accept that none of these approaches had much worth for Farah, for women like her who battle with similar forms of violence in similar locations, or for organizations such as Sahara, which often struggle to find new conceptual frameworks that can enable them to better understand and address the kind of violence and silencing that Farah faced.

And here I return to the partnership that Farah described between her and me at the outset of this section. Farah wanted me to help her return to the United States by discussing her situation with individuals working with specific South Asian women's NGOs in New Jersey, New York, and San Francisco who could advise her about how to reclaim her green card, and how to sue Aamir through the Indian courts of justice. She needed my assistance in tracking down Aamir, and after placing her confidence and trust in me generously, Farah also expected me to be there for her as an ally and friend. To her, these were the most important parts of our collaboration.

For me—as for many other feminist scholars—the kinds of commitments and obligations described above come with any research that involves close relationships between a researcher and her subjects. Generally speaking, there is nothing wrong in believing or acting on this idea. However, we lose a critical opportunity to interrogate and extend our theoretical frameworks when we reduce such visions or expectations of partnership articulated by our research subjects to the status of commitments that are either post-fieldwork or independent of theory or academic production. What we need to do instead is engage in a serious examination of why the existing possibilities of framing and analyzing Farah's story contribute little or nothing toward advancing the struggles that concern Farah or Sahara. Why is it that the most sophisticated and complex theories—when translated into an accessible language—fail to deliver anything beyond a fairly obvious message to Farah, her family, and to Sahara? And what possibilities for expanding those theoretical frameworks emerge when creating relevant knowledge for actors such as Farah and Sahara becomes one of my main academic goals? The real test of the relevance of this analysis and the extent to which it can do justice to the enmeshing of local and transnational subjectivities, power relationships, and citizenships cannot be based merely on my ability to provide another twist to the existing academic debates on these themes. It hinges, instead, on my ability to responsibly represent Farah's story in ways that can allow her to draw some sustenance and hope, and that can enable new conversations on the possibilities and limitations of collaborative border crossings.

Second Border Crossing

Producing a Methodology to Speak with the Sangtin Collective

Maya: *The chamars and yadavs in my village are at each other's throats and everyone blames me*[6] *. . . It all started on March 13th when Hari and Kishan broke into my home and beat me mercilessly . . . I went to the police station and said, "I dare any man in this village to touch me or humiliate me again for the rest of my*

*life. . . ." Kishan screamed, "This woman is evil. She keeps three men." I said,
"Yes, I have three men. I will keep two more. Why are my men his responsibility?"
. . . But for some reason, Kishan got released and Hari was arrested under the
Harijan Act [for discriminating against a member of a scheduled caste]. Now it
has become a big caste war.*

Eighteen rural women workers of Mahila Samakhya-Sitapur discuss Maya's
intervention and the complicated political situation it has created in her village.
Reena and Anupamlata reflect on how caste and family politics enmesh to shape
Maya's current circumstances. Others draw connections among Maya's mis-
matched marriage arranged by her younger sister (who is more prosperous and,
therefore, more influential), the physical violence inflicted upon her by that sister
and the sister's husband, and Maya's intimacy with one of her husband's cousins.
Vibha argues that the humiliation Maya suffers is closely linked to the manner in
which agricultural land is divided between her husband and his brothers. Maya
agrees with some of these statements and modifies or responds to the others. She
fears that the caste politics in the village and accusations hurled against her will
result in her murder—in the same way as her friend Jinnati was killed last month.
There are tears. There is concern. The women sitting in the circle know that Maya's fear is grounded in something too real and familiar. The group decides to hold
a public meeting in Maya's village in a week.[7]

In June 1996, I had the opportunity to join Richa Singh, the coordinator of the
newly launched Mahila Samakhya program in Sitapur (MSS), where she and her
coworkers had begun training eight local women as Sahyoginis, or mobilizers.
Each Sahyogini was responsible for mobilizing women in ten villages, mostly
in the vicinity of her own natal and conjugal villages. The idea was to give birth
to a new model of education and literacy in these villages that allowed poor
women from the "scheduled castes" and "other backward classes" to collectively
understand, address, and change the processes and structures responsible for
their marginalization. Another goal was to enable the women to build their
own grassroots organization that would replace MSS at the end of the initial
period of activity funded by the government of India and the World Bank. In
1999, eight Sahyoginis, along with Richa Singh, registered as cofounders of a
new organization, called Sangtin, that would continue the work of MSS after
the latter stopped getting funds from the current donors.

By the time Maya and her friends came together to discuss the caste war in
Maya's village and the murder of her friend, Jinnati, MSS activists had become
well-known in Uttar Pradesh, especially for their sustained efforts to challenge
and modify specific festivals and rituals that sanction violence against girls and
women. On a somewhat smaller scale, these women also addressed the ways in
which violence inflicted on poor women's bodies is intricately connected with
their access to land and wages, and with local religious and caste-based politics. It

is not surprising, then, that Maya's narration of her conflict with Hari and Kishan developed into an insightful and multilayered discussion among MSS women, where they explored the connections among landlessness, untouchability, poverty, morality, and sexualized violence in Maya's life and in their own lives.

However, unlike the heavily researched work of some other similar women's organizations in India, most of the accomplishments of MSS and Sangtin remained undocumented partly because of the desire of the rural women to be centrally involved as researchers in any documentation and analysis of their work. This factor, combined with my previous work with MS programs in Uttar Pradesh, led Richa Singh to contact me in March 2002 with a request to visit Sitapur and explore with key MSS activists the possibility of planning and undertaking a collaborative project. Between March and December 2002, I interacted with approximately sixty MSS workers (face-to-face and through detailed letters) to collectively determine the goals and processes that would define such a collaboration. Three central decisions were made:

- First, since Sangtin was to continue the work of MSS, the collaboration must focus on giving a vision and direction to Sangtin for its future work in Sitapur.
- Second, to determine their future goals, strategies, and political stances as a collective, it was necessary for women to engage in an in-depth reflection and analysis of their past achievements and failures *through* the life stories of key grassroots activists in their own midst, whose work around gender and caste-based violence they found to be the most inspiring. At a time when rural activists were increasingly disillusioned with changing structures and agendas of government-funded NGOs, Sangtin resolved to reflect carefully on the organizational limitations that frustrated and paralyzed the NGO workers.
- Third, women whose life stories were to be collected and analyzed for this project were to simultaneously acquire training as community researchers so that they could continue to document, analyze, and reflect on their own work on an ongoing basis without relying on the expertise or agendas of outside researchers.

In December 2002, women who had worked with MSS in more than eighty villages of Sitapur collectively chose eight founding members of Sangtin as women whose life stories they considered most central for understanding and documenting their history of struggles and accomplishments as a collective.[8] These women invited me to work on this collective project as a part of their team. Together, we spent nine days and nights jointly laying out the methodology, process, rules, and budget for the production, sharing, and dissemination of the life stories and the analyses emerging from them. This process was marked by moments in which all of us wrote our autobiographical journals in the same space, laughed and cried together as we shared our accounts, confronted each other with difficult questions, and produced new dynamics where some people learned to listen more carefully while others found the voices and words whose presence they had never realized.[9]

This proposed border crossing with the Sangtin Collective sought to make an intervention in the theory and praxis of north-south collaborations in several ways: First, it chose to focus on how rural activists theorize, strategize, prioritize, and act on their own understandings of development, globalization, violence, and empowerment. Second, it allowed me to use my analytical and linguistic skills, mobility, and location to help meet the goals of the activists, while also gaining new insights into ways that collaborative theories and methodologies on questions of development and empowerment can be produced across borders. Third, it prioritized activists' own articulations of how they wanted their understandings to be recorded, written, disseminated, and deployed, and the kind of role they wanted the academic researcher to play in these processes. Finally, feminist social scientists and NGOs have come to regard life stories as a rich tool for understanding personal experiences, identities, and social relations, and how individual biographies intersect with social processes. Their efforts and agendas, however, have mostly remained separate. This second collaboration made a commitment to advancing methodological discussions in both NGOs and academia by interrogating the dualisms of theory and praxis; expert and nonexpert; and academic and community-based; and by confronting questions of voice, authority, and representation at each step of this project's conceptualization and implementation.

Imagining Collaborative Feminist Postcolonial Geographies

The idea that postcolonial researchers should produce diverse knowledges to reach different audiences in the multiple worlds they straddle has gained increased currency across disciplines. Important differences remain, however, among those who hold this position. While some argue that academics can protect people's interests by disseminating the views of the marginalized, others remain highly skeptical of the degree to which the agendas of academics and grassroots workers can be harmonized. These divergent positions emanate, in part, from a lack of intellectual and creative labor that is committed to exploring the reasons behind academic researchers' limited ability to excite the imagination of the people whose struggles we study in the south or to shift the forms and languages of what is regarded as meaningful academic discourse.

Peake, Trotz, and Kobayashi are among the few who have explicitly grappled with the question of how third-world and first-world women can work together "in ways that are authorized by dialogue with [Third World subjects] and not just First World audiences" (Peake and Trotz 1999, 28). Reflexive questioning of ourselves and of the techniques we use to develop multivocality, they remind us, must be accompanied by a continued interrogation of how our supposedly "improved" representational strategies might be constituting new silences (Peake and Trotz 1999, 35). Such an interrogation requires that we challenge the divide between politics "on the ground" and research as an academic practice *through* a geography of engagement that taps into the tremendous potential of activism, and produces critical analyses based on local feminist praxis, and the ways that these connect with broader relations of domination and subordination (Peake and Kobayashi 2002, Peake and Trotz 2001).

It is in the context of these broader struggles of domination and subordination under globalization that these feminist geographies of engagement become explicitly postcolonial, and of critical relevance to the theory and praxis of social sciences. As Spivak observes, the expansion since 1989 of a full-scale globalized capitalism regulated by the WTO, the World Bank, and the International Monetary Fund (IMF) has been accompanied by a complex politics of the state and the international civil society. International platforms such as the United Nations are dominated by a "global feminist" agenda rooted in problematic assumptions such as a sex-gender system, an unacknowledged biological determination of behavior, and an "object-choice scenario that defines female life" in terms of choosing between children or public life, population control or "development" (Spivak 2000a, 321; see also Sharpe and Spivak 2003). In this political scenario, the interventions made by powerful NGOs often end up serving the interests of global capital, despite being feminist in their professed interest in gender.

These processes, Spivak argues, demand both a revision of feminist theory and a rethinking of the "subaltern" within the feminist mode. The genetically reproductive body as a site of production questions feminist theories based only on the ownership of the phenomenal body as means of reproduction, and feminist psychological theories reactive to reproductive genital penetration as normality. Politically, this new understanding of subalternity leads to global social movements supported by a Marxist analysis of exploitation, calling for an undoing of the systemic-anti-systemic binary opposition, and requiring an engagement with global feminism (Spivak 2000a, 321). Thus, "If the dominant is represented by the centreless centre of electronic finance capital, the subaltern woman is the target of credit-baiting without infrastructural involvement, thus opening a huge untapped market to the international commercial sector. Here a genuinely feminist politics would be a monitoring one, that forbids the ideological appropriation of much older self-employed women's undertakings, and further, requires and implements infrastructural change rather than practices cultural coercion in the name of feminism" (Spivak 2000a, 322). Instead of invoking strategic use of essentialism, then, Spivak emphasizes a need to underscore how oppositions are being generated in dominant discursive formations of global feminisms, and a process of "learning to learn from below" (2000a, 327).

The border crossings that I initiated with the help of Farah, Sahara, and MSS/ Sangtin can be seen as efforts to further imagine and enact postcolonial and transnational geographies of engagement through collaboration. Such collaborative processes provide concrete spaces to envision ways in which feminist scholars working on questions of subalternity might conceptualize accountability to people's struggles for self-representation and self-determination. Thus, collaboration becomes a tool to understand how women themselves define and represent their "subalternity" in complex ways that challenge the problematic assumptions made by a UN-style "global feminist" agenda. It, furthermore, becomes a vehicle for the collaborators to conceive new ways in which they can resist processes that make the subaltern woman "the target of credit-baiting without infrastructural involvement" (Spivak 2000a, 322).

At the same time, the words, commitments, and obligations shared between these women, organizations, and me do not serve a predetermined agenda (theirs or mine). Rather, our exchanges continue to take place in the spirit of listening, sharing, and collaborative decision making about where these stories should speak, for whom, in what languages, and with what purpose. These collaborations have the potential to fruitfully extend existing academic conversations and to yield generative insights across national and institutional borders on how familial and caste structures, socioeconomic processes, spatial (im)mobility, and politicized religion intersect to shape the multiple forms of violence in the lives of North Indian women, the resources and strategies that women create to resist this violence, as well as the contradictions that remain buried in their efforts to overcome their silences. In so doing, these collaborations allow us to exploit the political possibilities created by discursive materialities of global capitalism and international civil society. They permit us to complicate assumptions of elite theory about modernity in postcolonial societies, and allow us to appreciate the dilemmas as well as the possibilities of dalit and women's struggles (John 1996).

But what about authorship? Why are Farah and members of Sangtin identified as "consultants" and not coauthors of this chapter? A simple answer is that none of them wanted to be a coauthor because the broader issue of what constitutes a postcolonial geographical methodology is not one they found particularly relevant to their concerns. While they were interested in the specific representation of their own struggles and of our collaborative process, (re) defining geography was not central to their struggles, nor were they interested in becoming token coauthors.

A more complex discussion of this subject, however, demands an in-depth interrogation of standard forms of collaboration where a research agenda—and its theoretical and methodological underpinnings—is either determined (fully or largely) by the northern academic researcher and her institutional context and the names of the nonacademic actors she worked with appear as a way to denote shared power and authority; or, where two or more academic researchers from different institutional and sociopolitical locations coproduce an academic text. In either case, the collaboration is represented narrowly in terms of formal coauthorship, with the names of the authors appearing below the title of the academic text. The practice of crediting only the formal authors of a text is itself a faulty one that gives undue credit to authorship of a *text*, downplaying issues of collaboration in the processes of defining and addressing the research questions themselves. The expectation that our collaborators would always want to be coauthors, furthermore, assumes that speaking to academic audiences is a priority for all involved and that, like northern academics, their nonacademic collaborators in the south are also invested in securing intellectual property rights and/or recognition by academic audiences.

A more radical and more complex idea of collaboration must problematize these assumptions. If the intellectual agenda, research questions, and approaches evolve as part of a collaboration between actors in different institutional, sociopolitical, and geographical locations, then the collaborators must also understand that as long as they maintain their commitment to a shared intellectual and political agenda, they might be required to produce knowledges and theories for different audiences, with different goals and strategies. This implies that the specific products emerging from collaboration will sometimes be written jointly, and sometimes by an individual or subgroup in consultation with others. Nonetheless, the knowledges produced, as well as the purposes for which they are deployed, remain inherently and deeply collaborative, irrespective of the formal coauthorship of the actual texts that are produced and circulated.

The challenge for postcolonial and feminist geographers, then, is to conceptualize border crossings that are committed to forming collaborative partnerships with academic and nonacademic actors in "other" worlds in every sense of the term—partnerships in which the questions around how power and authority would be shared cannot be answered beforehand, but are imagined, struggled over, and resolved through the collaborative process itself. Since the issues I raise here defy conclusion by their very nature, I offer as a *non-conclusion* to these thoughts-in-progress, another semi-translated border crossing, or the painful reality of a collaboration that could not happen.

चुप्पी

गढ़वाल के एक नुक्कड़ पर
हम दोनों इन्तज़ार कर रहे थे
एक ही बस का
और वो बैठी थी
दूकान की सीढ़ियों पर
अपनी आठ महीने की बिटिया को

छातियों से ज़बरन अलग किये
मानो कोशिश कर रही हो सारी भीड़ से
अपना सूखा जिस्म छिपाने की

बार बार बिटिया
उसके बदन से
अपना मुँह रगड़ती
और बार–बार वो ठेल देती उस
ज़िद्दी मुँह में
निपल लगी एक पानी की बोतल
लेकिन वो
नन्ही–दुबली ताकतवर ज़ान
बोतल हटा कर हर बार माँ की
छाती से चिपक जाती
उसका भूखा ज़िद्दी मुँह पहले उन्हें
चिचोड़ता, फिर भूख से बेकाबू होकर
बेतरह चीखकर रोता

दो ही क़दम दूर
मैं चुपचाप
सब खड़ी देखती रही
गुनाहगार बनकर
गुनाहगार
इस बात की नहीं कि
अपनी अट्ठारह महीनों की
औलाद को मैं "काम" की वजह से
अमरीका छोड़ आई थी
बल्कि गुनाहगार उस
कड़वी ग़ैर बराबरी की
जिसने उस औरत के बजाय
मेरी क़मीज़ दूध से भिगो डाली...
जिसने लाख चाहने पर भी
रोक लिया मुझे उस
बच्ची को अपने भीतर
समेट लेने से...
वो ही गैरबराबरी
जो ढीठ सी
चट्टान बनकर
खड़ी हो गई मेरे और उस औरत के दरमियान
और हमारे बीच गुज़रे इस अधूरे
कठिन संवाद को जिसने, एक लम्बी
बोझिल चुप्पी के आगे
बढ़ने ही नहीं दिया।

THE COLLABORATION THAT DID NOT HAPPEN[10]

On a street corner in Garhwal
There we stood, she and I
waiting for the same bus
And she sat
on the steps of a shop close by
holding her eight month old daughter
firmly away from her breasts
as if to hide from the eyes of the crowd
her drained, dried up body.

Over and over again, the baby rubbed her mouth against the woman's breast
and her mother stuffed the rubber nipple of a water bottle
into that stubborn mouth
And over and over again, the little baby girl
skinny and resolute
would push the bottle away, clinging only to her mother's breasts. Her thirsty,
    determined mouth first searched those breasts
and then cried out uncontrollably, screaming in desperate hunger.

And there I stood, just two steps away
quietly watching this like a sinner
a sinner, whose sin was not that I had had to leave my own eighteen month
    old daughter
in the US, to "research" women's struggles in India
but the sin of that cruel disparity
which, instead of wetting that woman
had drenched my shirt with milk
which, despite my intense pain
prevented me from holding that child against my own chest. That very same
    disparity that stood between me and that woman
like a rock, dead set on squashing out this difficult, partial dialogue between us
before it could become anything more than
a long, burdened muteness.

5. Traveling and Crossing, Dreaming and Becoming

Journeys after Sangtin Yatra

This chapter is based on writing undertaken with Richa Singh, Surbala, and other saathis of Sangtin Kisaan Mazdoor Sangathan in Hindi and English between 2004 and 2012.

> When a movement stops asking questions, of itself, of the world, it
> becomes orthodoxy—an idea that has run out of ideas. It becomes
> fixed, static, brittle, rather than fluid. Water can resist the most
> savage of blows, ice shatters. It is only armed with our questions,
> that we can change history.
> —Notes from Nowhere, *We Are Everywhere*

मन में सवाल उठता है कि कैसे हो सकती हैं सारी महिलाएं एक? हज़ारों किलोमीटर की दूरी चन्द घन्टों में पूरी करने वाली कुछ महिलाएं, और चन्द किलोमीटर की दूरी कई घन्टों में पूरी करने वाली महिलाएं, और वे जिन्हें कभी गाँवों में अपने घरों की दहलीज़ लाँघने का मौका नहीं मिलता, जिनका पूरा जीवन ससुराल और मायके के बीच के रास्ते में बीत जाता है – क्या यह सारी महिलाएं कभी एक हो सकती हैं? यह बहुत बड़ा भेद है और इस भेद के रहते इस भेद को बरक़रार रखने वाले लोगों को यह हक़ नहीं बनता कि वे सब महिलाओं के एक होने की बात कहें। इनके दर्द और अरमान कभी एक नहीं हो सकते। अक्सर उच्च– या मध्यम–वर्गीय महिलाएं यह कहती हैं कि हिंसा तो सभी महिलाओं के साथ है, हाँ, उसके प्रकार अलग–अलग हैं। बिल्कुल सही। लेकिन पेट की भूख, या बीमारी से टूटता शरीर, या कल कहाँ से खायेंगे की फ़िक्र, या भारी बारिश में अपने छप्पर को बचाती महिला के कष्ट क्या बिल्कुल अलग नहीं होंगे?

These thoughts, first written in Hindi by Richa Singh in April 2005, point to a personal and collective turmoil with questions of inequality and the im/possibility of women from unequal locations to speak in a unified voice.[1] Reflecting on her own recently completed (paid) air travel to a conference in Mumbai, and her return to a village in Sitapur on a *thelia*, Richa Singh wrestles with the question of how there can be "oneness" among those women who cover the distance of thousands of kilometers in a few hours, those who cover the distance of a few kilometers in several hours, and those who barely walk on any other paths except those that connect their *mayaka* to their *sasural*.[2] Her gut feeling tells her that people who participate in maintaining these gulfs have no right to claim that all women are one. No matter what the arguments about all women confronting similar forms of violence—the pains and concerns of a woman who has to think about the hunger of her belly, or a body-breaking illness, or how to feed her family the next day, or how to save her thatched roof from the heavy rains—can never be the same as those of upper- and middle-class women desirous of claiming commonality with her.

This turmoil with inequality and the impossibility of experiential commonality that we attempt to translate here emerges from an ongoing journey that began in March 2002 when nine women began a collective journey in Sitapur as activists, critics, writers, and close companions. Here we summarize some of the key segments of this journey, reflecting on the manner in which the collective's investment in the politics of women's development NGOs and the overwhelming response generated by our collaborative book, *Sangtin Yatra* (Anupamlata et al. 2004, Sangtin Lekhak Samooh 2012), opened spaces for the authors to participate in and critically interrogate the sites of formal knowledge production. Specifically, the collective's agenda in the aftermath of the reception of *Sangtin Yatra* has evolved through encounters and engagements with international solidarity networks, donor agencies, academic publishing, and national curriculum development initiatives.

We begin with a brief sketch of *Sangtin Yatra* and its meanings for our intellectual and political growth as an alliance across borders. The two subsequent sections consider the effects of *Sangtin Yatra*, and how these inserted the collective into struggles around the politics of knowledge production in institutional sites that the collective had not encountered before. Finally, we reflect on the manner in which the transnational nature of our alliance has enabled our critical engagements with structures and norms of professionalism and expertise locally, regionally, nationally, and transnationally, as well as the limitations and contradictions that remain buried in these engagements.

Can Analytical Frameworks Travel?
Border Crossings through and beyond *Sangtin Yatra*

संगतिन यात्रा क्या सिर्फ़ एक पुस्तक है? नहीं, यह तो हम संगतिनों का संविधान है। कुछ भी काम करते हुए—चाहे गाँवों में हों, चाहे किसी बड़े मंच पर—हम सबको यह बराबर याद रहता है कि हमने संगतिन यात्रा में क्या लिखा है। हमें यह अपनी बहुत बड़ी ज़िम्मेदारी लगती है कि हमने जो लिखा है उसी दिशा में आगे बढ़ना है।

Sangtin Yatra began as a journey of nine travelers. Five of them—Anupam-lata, Ramsheela, Shashi Vaishya, Shashibala, and Vibha Bajpayee—made a living as village-level mobilizers in MSS, a large and influential government-sponsored NGO, where they had worked together for six to eight years as close associates. A sixth member of the collective, Surbala, had quit her position with MSS in 2000 in order to focus her energies on building another organization that this group had registered under the name of Sangtin, so that the work of rural women's empowerment could continue after the guaranteed funding expired for the MS program in Sitapur. Reshma Ansari, the collective's seventh member, ran a literacy center in her village as an MSS worker. Of the remaining two members of the collective, Richa Singh, who had begun her activist career as an office staff in MS-Varanasi, was then serving as a district coordinator of MSS; finally, Richa Nagar, a tenured associate professor of women's studies at the University of Minnesota at the time, had worked with MS activists in different districts of Uttar Pradesh since 1996 and had also been active as a creative and journalistic writer in Hindi since 1983.

This group of nine women initially came together to critically reflect on internal processes and politics of NGO work and the labor of activism, social change, and knowledge production from the perspective and priorities of the village-level NGO workers who undertake the main labor of translating the projects of empowerment on the ground. Confrontations, dialogues, and ne-gotiations with multiple inequalities—of social hierarchies, status, education, resources, and language—within the collective and within the structures in which each member of the collective is embedded were the primary vehicles to advance this journey.[3]

The title *Sangtin Yatra* captures the essence of our collaboration while also highlighting the name of the organization, Sangtin, in whose name the collective wanted to continue activities that combined rigorous research, radical activism, and creative work in the villages of Sitapur. For the several thousand travelers who have become sangtins since this journey began, *Sangtin Yatra* is not simply a book; it is our constitution. No matter where the members of the collective are working or speaking as sangtins, we recognize that remaining faithful to the principles that we identified for ourselves in *Sangtin Yatra* is one of our key responsibilities.

The writing of *Sangtin Yatra* marked a significant moment of creation in the making of our collective. We learned to identify the classed, caste, communal, and gendered processes that had shaped our differentiated pasts and presents as well as our investments and embeddedness in structures of privilege and oppression. We recognized how these processes fractured both subjectivities and solidarities, and that the task of imagining transformative politics neces-

Photo 6. The nine authors of *Sangtin Yatra/Playing with Fire*. Mishrikh, 2004. (Photo: David Faust)

sarily implied engaging with and producing uncomfortable dialogues with and about difference within collectives and institutions. In part, these dialogues are targeted at troubling the discursive practices associated with projects of poor women's empowerment, and in part, they seek to imagine new ways of sharing authority, imagining reciprocity, and enacting accountability.

As a fissured and wounded "we," we braid and unbraid the lives and struggles of seven sangtins who work as village-level activists—their childhoods and coming-of-age, their marriages and encounters with motherhood, and their growth as NGO workers and feminists. We challenge the expressions and agendas of donor-sponsored global feminisms that equate impoverished or dalit rural women's oppression to "private" practices such as veiling and whose conceptualizations of "violence against women" refuse to recognize how the poor rural men themselves are excluded from the dominant order of development and patriarchy. We explore how the micropolitics of professionalism and expertise serve to reinforce and reconstitute elitism, casteism, and communalism in women's development organizations, albeit in the name of saving the monolithic "woman-as-victim"—the new globalized, subaltern "woman" who is the subject of justice (through "expert" intervention) under international capitalism. Through this process of interweaving words, silences, and critiques—spoken and unspoken, written and unwritten—we forge a collective identity as activists and thinkers who are committed to reclaiming the sites of "empowerment"—politically and intellectually.

The process that led to the writing of *Sangtin Yatra* was intoxicating and exhausting, inspiring and challenging, and it allowed us to dream and cry together. Little did we recognize before the launch of *Sangtin Yatra*, however, that the collective articulation of sangtins' stories and critiques was a relatively easy step in a tougher journey that was yet to unfold. The warm welcome received by the book in the Hindi media, in the homes and offices of NGO workers, and in the communities of progressive artists and intellectuals was overwhelming. But the wide media attention in these spaces generated an angry response from the director of Mahila Samakhya, Uttar Pradesh (MSUP), and her allies. These responses pushed the collective to invest itself in issues of knowledge production for multiple audiences in myriad and complex ways. Questions about power and privilege, mediation and translation, attention and representation have posed constructive challenges as well as political possibilities for sangtins to grow as an alliance of transnational actors—an alliance interested in understanding and transforming frameworks and institutional spaces and hierarchies in and through which knowledge about issues and processes such as difference and discrimination, oppression and resistance, justice and empowerment is produced, recognized, validated, questioned, or dismissed. While grappling with these more "abstract" concerns, the collective has also juggled more "concrete" priorities such as the relationship between intellectual critique, political journey, and livelihoods, and whether and how a multilocational and multi-institutional alliance can maintain a balance among these without centering the vantage points of more privileged members of the collective.

This chapter, enabled and energized at different junctures by the struggles and insights of hundreds of sangtins but penned by one or two members of the alliance, is itself a part of our ongoing battles and negotiations, not simply within the collective, but also with spaces of academia, NGOs, social movements, and think tanks. In merging our analysis from our specific institutional contexts and comforts and discomforts with respect to English, we are acutely aware of the limitations and contradictions of our locations.[4] We also recognize the responsibilities and possibilities that open up with the act of claiming this analytical space. Our coauthorship underscores Sangtin's collective position that in any long-term collaboration across unequal worlds, the accounting of the nature of benefits and losses cannot be undertaken from the perspective of a single institutional location or by a single member of the alliance. Rather, it is in and through the collaborative moments of reflection and writing that the alliance gains new energy and insights to advance the struggle, to reassess the meanings of what has been gained or lost, and to determine the directions in which new steps might be taken.

In linking various segments of our yatra in different institutional realms, then, we consciously blur the conventional definitions of academic, activist, and creative writing. To advance the collective's goal of widening the political and intellectual spaces for its struggles, we write with multiple audiences in mind, including those NGO workers, organizers, intellectuals, and readers who wish to know where and how our journey has advanced in the aftermath of the critique produced in *Sangtin Yatra* and those who want to assess the possibilities and limits of the kind of alliance work that we have undertaken. Many pieces of this analysis have found their way into our Hindi publications—Sangtin's newspaper, *Hamara Safar*, and its book on the making of the sangtin movement between 2004 and 2011, *Ek Aur Neemsaar* (Nagar and Singh et al. 2012). By crafting an analysis that attempts to advance dialogue with these audiences simultaneously, we hope to resist a common tendency to maintain a separation between the theoretical and political insights that are produced for national and international Anglophone academic audiences on the one hand, and for the activists, NGO workers, community members, and thinkers in the vernacular realms, on the other.

In order to achieve this simultaneous resonance and relevance across worlds, we continue to rework here the ways of knowing *and speaking*—that is, the forms and languages in which narratives and analyses are produced in conventional academic productions, NGO reports, and journalism. We share with you notes from a yatra that is continuously unfolding—notes that are interwoven with an evolving praxis in which travelers from diverse locations learn and grow together as we articulate our overlapping intellectual agendas, grapple with lessons learned, determine the trajectories of our political journeys as individuals and members of an alliance, and as we are inserted in new institutional spaces with familiar hierarchies and inequalities—of caste, religion, class, gender, and geographical location—and continue to evolve processes for understanding, challenging, and transforming them.

Journeys after *Sangtin Yatra*: Specifying and Translating the Politics of Knowledge Production

Within three weeks of its launch in Lucknow, *Sangtin Yatra* became a target of attack by the director of MSUP, where seven out of nine authors were employed: Ramsheela, Shashibala, Shashi Vaishya, and Vibha Bajpayee as mobilizers; Reshma as a teacher in a literacy center; Anupamlata as a junior resource person; and Richa Singh as the district coordinator. The backlash developed

into an intense controversy that focused on authorizing or discrediting the
"truths" of the sangtins as well as recognition or dismissal of the partnership
among the nine authors (see Sangtin Writers 2006). Here we briefly reflect on
MSUP's attack and how it led us to seek allies and supporters transnationally,
and subsequently to create *Playing with Fire*.

The following translated excerpts give a flavor of the critique that made
Sangtin Yatra controversial.

EXCERPT 1

Hasn't it been only six years since we first learned to ride our bikes and stormed
the neighborhoods, streets, and villages of Sitapur?[5] Who among us had imagined that we would so confidently rebel and march out of the same households
that caged us. . . . When we prepared to write this book, we again felt a sense of
adventure creeping into our bones. Would this world be able to see us formerly
uneducated women as writers? Would it give us the same respect and wisdom that
it accords to all its upper caste and elite scholars and thinkers? Would our readers
be able to value the courage and trust with which we have poured out our most
cherished and intimate moments, our deepest sorrows and wounds of humiliation,
and everything sweet and bitter that we have encountered in our lives? . . . We
knew all too well from working in a women's organization that it is much easier to
interrogate the definitions of honor, morality, and justice by giving instances from
the lives of others, rather than by applying those critiques to our own clans and
families. Even so, we unveiled details about our lives in our diaries and discussions because we believed that we would not be able to advance this struggle by
hiding things. We suspect that our readers will read with pleasure—and perhaps,
respect—the details we furnish here about our intimate lives and relationships,
our sexuality, our poverty, and the putrid swamps of casteism and communalism
that we live in. But we wonder whether they would be able to read with equal
pleasure or respect our analyses and critiques of women's and development NGOs.
But on this issue, too, we were inspired by the belief that if we couldn't muster
the courage to say everything even after arriving at this juncture in our journey,
then it would be difficult to fight the battles to come.

EXCERPT 2

The scope of work done by rural-level NGO workers is defined in a rather constrained way in every respect. We are not given many opportunities that would
allow us to link what is happening in our villages to the conditions and struggles
ongoing in other states and countries. Similarly, we are not able to fully connect
the violence against dalit women with other forms of violence. . . . Almost every

other day, new workshops are organized to ensure that our documentation is refined and polished in accordance with the wishes of our funders. But . . . we get
very few spaces or resources to grapple with a range of sociopolitical processes
that are discussed in academic seminars and make the national and international
headlines every day—e.g., globalization and the negotiations of the World Trade
Organization, the ever-increasing suicides of peasants in our country, or the priva-
tization of water. As a result, we face severe limits in our ability to relate these
processes to the kinds of violence that are wreaked regularly on the bodies and
minds of women in our villages. And it is precisely our inability to make these
connections that allows established experts and other researchers to carry out
study projects "on" us. . . . In Sangtin, we have decided to reflect in depth on
how violence that is targeted on women's bodies is interwoven with other forms
of violence, and to advance those reflections and understandings collectively with
members of our village communities.

The process of creating *Sangtin Yatra*, as well as its content, argue for empowerment through dialogue. The collaboration finds its shape, substance, and
meaning through an evolving process that challenges the framing rationales of
donor-driven NGOs. The idea that poor women must be empowered through
"feminism"—as defined and taught to them by the "experts"—is challenged by
a process in which everyone's needs and priorities are continuously interrogated
and negotiated with the goal of creating a level playing field, however impossible
it might be to create such a field. The collective grapples with how the lives and
struggles of seven women—conventionally lumped together as "rural NGO
workers"—are interwoven with local structures of caste, class, religion, and
gender, as well as with broader processes of development, NGOization, and
knowledge production. The autobiographers' varied encounters with poverty,
hunger, caste-based and communal untouchability, and their struggles to gain
access to education, place question marks on the idealized definitions of childhood and the "rural girl child" often assumed by policy makers. We note how
shifts in the caste, class, and communal configurations of each sangtin's natal and
conjugal villages shaped the ways in which different groups in her village were
centered or marginalized with respect to development resources. The collective
confronts the implications of the difficult negotiations over salaries in homes
where men do not have stable employment and where men's insecurities lead
to increased instances of gambling and violence, which are, again, infested by
caste and communal politics. At the same time, the collective recognizes that
connections among local patriarchies, caste-based structures of discrimination,
and broader political economic processes must be made in ways that address
dominant versions of feminism that often declare to the rural women that their
primary enemies are their fathers, uncles, brothers, and husbands.

The aforementioned dialogues produced a critique of NGO work that enabled the authors to understand the processes by which NGOs, despite their stated goal of empowering women on the margins, end up being dominated by Hindu upper-caste workers and how critiques of casteism, communalism, and untouchability remain confined to the official meetings. Consequently, elitism within NGOs reproduces the very hierarchies that the NGOs seek to dismantle and the village-based, less formally educated dalit workers consistently find themselves at the margins of institutional spaces. The dialogical journey of sangtins also enabled the collective to grapple with the manner in which professionalization of organizational processes makes NGOs accountable primarily to their funders who seek reports, statistics, and evidence of empowerment, where empowerment is visualized as a concrete thing that can be measured, replicated, and reduced to its component parts. Furthermore, the separation of gender-based violence from other forms of violence pigeonholes the activists into a narrow vision, foreclosing opportunities for them to engage with such issues as communalism, struggles over water and land, displacement, war, and imperialism. In this way, village-level NGO workers become "experts" of their local field sites only.

But *Sangtin Yatra* did not limit itself to a critique of development and NGO-driven empowerment. The dialogic processes opened spaces to accomplish two other forms of critical work: The first was the task of combining careful research, reflexive activism, and critical pedagogy, which allowed the authors to scrutinize our own practices and relationships (for example, the manner in which our caste and class locations shaped the relative meanings of hunger and untouchability and the intense—often violent—silencing around homosexuality and around extramarital and intercommunal intimacies, even in feminist circles), and at how hierarchies of caste, class, religion, and gender were replicated in our own collective, families, communities, and relationships. The second was the critical work of grappling with the question of how Sangtin should envision its work with local communities. The cycle of dialogue, writing, and reflection helped Sangtin to create a vision that emphasized the importance of enacting accountability and transparency to people; the need for projects to emerge from local priorities rather than the priorities of the donors or trainers; the necessity of understanding bodily violence as deeply intertwined with economic and sociopolitical violence, and of recognizing socioeconomic disempowerment as intricately interwoven with intellectual disempowerment. Together, these new understandings and critical energies translated into a deeply felt need and commitment to gain expertise beyond the local.

The insights coproduced in *Sangtin Yatra* parallel and complement critiques that have been reverberating for almost two decades on the changing configurations of NGOs under neoliberalism. NGOs' increasing dependence on foreign donors and government funding has gone hand in hand with their growth as an arm of the state; as a result, activism is increasingly privatized and resistance gets converted into jobs that fetch salaries (Armstrong 2004, Kamat 2002, Roy 2004). Furthermore, the structures and practices of information retrieval and knowledge production work in ways such that southern NGOs and their workers frequently become suppliers of intellectual raw materials for northern NGOs; the latter demand transparency and accountability from the former "while maintaining secrecy and no accountability in return" (Nnaemeka 2004, 367). Greater dependence and closeness to funders result in upward accountability and technocratic definitions of achievement in the NGOs, so that unit costs, quantifiable outputs, and detailed specifications of what partners are expected to do become organizational norms (Hulme and Edwards 1997, 8). This kind of instrumentalist approach where empowerment becomes a blueprint is inconsistent with claims to promote long-term qualitative change and forecloses possibilities of genuine partnerships. In the realm of women's movements, the professionalization of gender issues and a decline in feminist mobilization on the ground has often been accompanied by the NGOization of grassroots feminisms—a phenomenon marked by the rise of a class of "femocrats" that unilaterally tends to decide what is best for all women, at the same time when women's NGOs have been reduced to marginalized forces within corporatist civil society (Lang 2000, Spivak 2000a).

When nine sangtins decided to share their reflections on similar trends in lay language with local communities and NGO workers in *Sangtin Yatra*, it created a furor. On the one hand, readers and reviewers praised the book as an "extra-ordinary intervention in feminist thought" from the Awadh-region (Kushavarti 2004, 26; also Pushpa 2004, Srivastava 2004), and remarked on the "freshness of hypothesis and methodology" with which *Sangtin Yatra* fought against social orthodoxies, and offered a "natural invitation to . . . understand and do things in new ways that can enact . . . creative struggle" (Verma 2004, 26). On the other hand, such attention triggered the wrath of the director of MSUP, who questioned the truth of the sangtins' critiques; the credentials of rural NGO workers as legitimate intellectuals; the ownership of the collective's ideas and efforts; and the honesty of Richa Singh and Richa Nagar, who allegedly had—for selfish reasons—tricked the less privileged rural activists to "shamelessly" spill their personal stories and to bite the hand that fed them. Within a month of the book's launch, the director of MSUP began to verbally attack the authors based in Sitapur. This was followed by official notices that transferred Richa Singh out of Sitapur and threatened to fire Anupamlata, Ramsheela, Reshma Ansari, Richa Singh, Shashibala, Shashi Vaishya, and Vibha Bajpayee on the grounds that they had participated in a criminal act against MS by writing *Sangtin Yatra*.[6] As for Richa Nagar, the MS leadership concluded that her "research" was done, she had returned to her university, and the drama of collaboration was over. The director of MSUP sent a letter to the chair of women's studies at Minnesota accusing Richa Nagar of leading an unethical and exploitative research project and demanding disciplinary action against her. Specifically, the director of MSUP wrote to the autobiographers: "It is only because of your work in Mahila Samakhya that you were able to step out of the four walls of your home. Mahila Samakhya has tirelessly worked to build your skills . . . and . . . [enabled you] to reach a level where you can powerfully connect with village women and make your voice heard on all platforms. Thus your . . . behavior is an act of betrayal and a gruesome criminal act against the organization."[7]

This attack led to a strong response in support of *Sangtin Yatra*. For example, Krishna Kumar, professor of education at the University of Delhi and then the director of the National Council for Educational Research and Training (NCERT), stepped forward in support of the book in *Jan Satta*, a major Hindi daily published from New Delhi: "In essence, this book is an evidence of the success of MS program, but it also symbolizes a rebellion against the formalities of constituting evidence. This rebellion is performed by the words themselves. Accepting those words, deriving happiness from their sculpting requires a generosity which if present in a governmental program can make it revolutionary" (Kumar 2004a, 2). Why did *Sangtin Yatra* become a cheeky mistake for which the authors had to be punished, when similar arguments have been made by prominent critics writing for highly educated audiences? As Krishna Kumar aptly notes, *Sangtin Yatra* and its aftermath illuminated the ways in which "rural woman's voice becomes dependent on business people of international funding. It is heard only when translated by licensed middle people. When it rarely emerges on its own, it is declared unruly, and therefore, intolerable" (2004a, 2; also Kumar 2004b).

Sangtin Yatra explicitly contests representational practices where rural women are "solicited, cajoled, encouraged to speak" so that "developed" urban women "may speak to one another about 'them'" (Lazreg 2002, 127). The authors had formed alliance in 2002 to critically reflect and write about the lives and work of the seven village-level NGO activists—not to produce entertaining stories for consumption by the urban middle class—but to make our self-critiques the basis for envisioning new directions for the activists' future political work with the poor communities in rural Sitapur. After considerable reflection on the division and definitions of "skills" that went into the book's writing and production in 2002–3, each author believed that the work was written and owned by all sangtins and the book was self-published in 2004 in the name of Sangtin, the organization that the authors based in Sitapur had cofounded in 1999.

The sangtins articulated their strategies of representation as an intervention into the politics of knowledge production. However, it was not until the visibility of *Sangtin Yatra* made our collaboration suspect and a source of insult to the state-level leadership of MS that the collective began to grapple more deeply with the political meanings of knowledge, and the relations, conditions, tools, and languages through which its producers and content are legitimized or eliminated. The attacks in the aftermath of our initial critique revealed to us that the norms and culture of expertise that we had critiqued in *Sangtin Yatra* were a tiny piece of a much larger picture; continuing the yatra necessarily entailed a commitment to disrupt the order of dominating knowledges and of the hierarchies of status and authority from which expertise is produced.

Edward Said draws our attention to the ways in which the cult of professionalism and expertise has created a doctrine of noninterference among fields so that the most crucial policy questions affecting human existence are left to "experts" who speak a highly specialized language (Said 2002, 119). As professionals are bestowed special privileges of knowing how things really work and of being close to power, argues Said, what emerges is an interpretive community whose constituency, specialized language, and concerns "tend to get tighter, more airtight, more self-enclosed as its own self-conforming authority acquires more power, the solid status of orthodoxy and a stable constituency" (Said 2002, 127–28). To counter this cult of professionalism, Said calls for a "politics of interpretation" that demands a dialectical response. Noninterference and specialization must be replaced by *interference*, "a crossing of borders and obstacles, a determined attempt to generalize exactly at those points where generalizations seem impossible to make" (Said 2002, 145). According to Said, this exercise entails the recovery of a history hitherto either misrepresented or rendered invisible. The next phase requires "connecting these more politically vigilant forms of interpretation to an ongoing political and social praxis . . . For to move from interpretation to its politics is in large measure to go from undoing to doing, and this . . . is risking all the discomfort of a great unsettlement in ways of seeing and doing" (Said 2002, 147).

If *Sangtin Yatra* was an attempt to articulate and circulate a critique by those who are frequently misrepresented and rendered invisible by the development industry, the journey in the aftermath of *Sangtin Yatra* can be seen as a move from undoing to doing. This move brought a new set of challenges—that of recognizing and politicizing the locations and languages from which the undoing can be simultaneously translated into doing. MSUP's attack on the authors' livelihoods and freedom of expression was worsened by the reality of a collective scattered across two continents, two districts, and six villages. Meanwhile, the authors in Sitapur were incessantly maligned in their workplace and by some of their "gender trainers":[8] not only had they "stripped themselves naked," they had also overstepped their "auqat" by critiquing the very institutions that had taught them how to "speak" and to "step out" of their "cages." Moreover, MS's

tremendous influence at the state and national levels and its credentials as an
organization dedicated to the empowerment of "most marginalized" women
made it difficult for the collective to garner overt support of individuals or organizations who had codependencies with MS. The sangtins in Sitapur became
convinced that it was time to mobilize pressure from supporters in a way that
could bypass the politics of MS at the state and national levels, and yet make the
government feel responsible for the actions of MSUP. The result was an online
petition prepared with the help of supporters in Uttar Pradesh, Maharashtra,
Minnesota, Washington DC, and New York. Signed by Indian professors and
activists in India, Nepal, United States, and the United Kingdom, the petition
was dispatched to seven departments of the state and central governments in
India, where it also coincided with commentaries written by prominent educa-
tors and critics in national dailies and periodicals. MS's attacks on the village-
level NGO workers stopped within days of receipt of petition and publication
of commentaries, but Richa Singh's transfer was not withdrawn.

Arguably, both the backlash and the petition and commentaries supporting
Sangtin Yatra can be seen as paving the way for new solidarities on the politics
of NGOization and knowledge production. The issues of elitism, exploitation,
and accountability that we raised in the book now acquired more gravity and
visibility. As reviews and excerpts from the book kept appearing in the Hindi
press beyond the borders of Uttar Pradesh, we grew confident that our analysis
was converging with the struggles and concerns of many. Ultimately, it was the
courage derived from this kind of wide support that galvanized Richa Singh to
deliver her protest resignation to MS and return to Sitapur to continue the collective journey with sangtins. With this resignation also came critical support
from the Minnesota chapter of the Association for India's Development (AID-
MN). Members of AID-MN familiarized themselves with *Sangtin Yatra* and
associated politics, initiated conversations with members of the collective and
with AID chapters in other parts of the United States and India about Sangtin's
future directions in light of its changing relationship with MS, and decided to
provide a saathiship to Richa Singh so that she could focus her energies to work
toward the goals articulated in *Sangtin Yatra*. Closer to home, the struggle was
honored by the NCERT, which invited Richa Singh to participate in the review
of national curriculum framework as a member of the National Focus Group on
gender issues in education. Furthermore, NGOs and activist networks working
within India recognized Sangtin as an ally in struggles against communalism,
casteism, violence against women, economic globalization, and imperialism.
Alongside these developments, there also arose an interest in translations of
Sangtin Yatra—into Telugu, Marathi, Urdu, and English. With the onset of MS's
attack, the collective instinctively knew that an English translation would be
necessary as a shield in case of intensified hostility, and Richa Nagar began to

translate the text. The online petition yielded greater urgency to this task. For the petition to work across borders, we needed the English translation so that our potential allies could familiarize themselves with the book before signing the petition.

The politics of language and translation acquired new meanings in each advancing phase of Sangtin's yatra. The journey began by interrogating the meanings of development, violence, and literacy as the activists wrote their lives across the borders of their mother tongue, Awadhi (which is often regarded as spoken, rural, and "traditional"), and Hindi, the language in which most people of rural Sitapur become literate and "modernized." Later, at the time of creating *Sangtin Yatra*, we also felt it necessary to complicate the communalized compartmentalization between Hindi and Urdu by identifying the language of sangtins as Hindustani. After the publication of *Sangtin Yatra*, the backlash against the authors took us into another realm of translation: across the borders of Hindustani (commonly regarded as vernacular, ordinary, and regional) and English (often seen as elite, national, and transnational). Initially aimed at gaining support for our constitutional rights to claim a space as authors, intellectuals, and critics, this translation subsequently became invested in communicating the meanings of our labor across the borders of people's organizations and movements (often regarded as political and grounded) and academia (often considered intellectual and theoretical). On the one hand, the excitement of those who read the English translation convinced us that the process through which we had grappled with the politics of knowledge production and NGO work enabled *Sangtin Yatra* to speak across borders.

On the other hand, the collective recognized the inseparability of the intellectual and political, of theory and praxis, and the need to creatively politicize these interwoven strands for members of the NGO sector, educational institutions, and the communities where we live and work. The harassment targeted at the eight sangtins in Sitapur frequently took the form of accusations that the sharp analysis and language of *Sangtin Yatra* could not have been produced by them since they were not highly educated or qualified intellectuals. However, Richa Nagar's work with the collective—especially the work that did not acquire a familiar academic form (e.g., preparing petitions, networking with supporters, writing official responses to MS, facilitating conversations between AID-MN and Sangtin)—was deemed as belonging to the nonacademic realm (of activism). As the nine authors scrutinized these prevailing discourses about what and who constitute legitimate knowledges and knowledge producers within academia and activism, we saw tight connections with the same cult of professionalism and expertise whose exclusionary and paralyzing effects we had highlighted in *Sangtin Yatra*. We could only continue the yatra by establishing our labor and enterprise as simultaneously activist *and* academic. The decision to write *Playing with Fire* and to publish it with Zubaan Press in New Delhi and the University of Minnesota Press in Minneapolis emerged from these churnings.

New Institutions, Old Discomforts: Sangtin's Struggles for Survival

The journey after *Sangtin Yatra* taught us that it is not sufficient to tease apart multiple layers of politics that define every act of knowledge production. For, each new act of politicizing can itself create distinctions that (ironically) emanate from our preexisting locations in the same institutions whose norms of professionalism or expertise we wish to contest. Thus, even as the collective chose to agitate from the transnational space to rescue the jobs of the village-level NGO activists, it made Richa Nagar the primary person who could inhabit, converse, and translate in and from that space. But the collective had also learned that this contradiction did not necessarily make the transnational location more inauthentic and, therefore, guilty and the local spaces more authentic or innocent. Rather, the collective came to see the politics of knowledge production as deeply intertwined across local, national, and transnational scales. Rejecting authenticity as a political strategy or an intellectual stance, then, the collective became invested in translocal and transnational solidarities as a tool to reimagine and reconstitute the relations, conditions, and processes of knowledge production, as well as the purposes for which these reconstituted knowledges can be deployed.

Since June 2004, we have found ourselves confronting and challenging familiar attitudes and assumptions with respect to expertise, qualifications, and intellectual legitimacy—in publishing *Playing with Fire*; in negotiating the parameters of new projects with international organizations such as OXFAM and more alternative groups such as ASHA Trust (Lucknow); and in configuring Richa Singh's saathiship with AID and Sangtin's representation in NCERT. A key contradiction appears repeatedly. On the one hand, we witness an institutional desire to recognize the collective's accomplishments and to create space for sangtins as critics and community workers with a different kind of vision and caliber. On the other hand, the rules, practices, and cultures of professionalism in these institutions often make it difficult for them to accommodate some of the basic principles of our collaboration. Let us consider some examples that capture this tension.

Whereas Zubaan Press embraced all the authors as Sangtin Writers (and Sangtin Writers had a market in India by 2006 because of the controversy surrounding *Sangtin Yatra*), market considerations and cataloging systems made it difficult for the University of Minnesota Press to grant us formal authorship as nine sangtins: the collective had to be split into "Sangtin Writers" and "Richa

Nagar." Even the placement of Nagar's name after Sangtin Writers required negotiation before it was accepted by the U.S. publisher.

Both presses felt that the translation of *Sangtin Yatra* must be contextualized and its significance more clearly articulated in *Playing with Fire* for an audience that was more academic than the intended audience of the original book. The collective understood this point, but this requirement made Richa Nagar the only author who could write the framing chapters for a national and international readership. This resulted in deliberations about the tone and style through which the introduction and postscript could be used to resist the very idea of framing and authorizing. Once these two sections were drafted, every sentence was translated, discussed, and revised as necessary—until the entire text became an essential part of our journey. The contents of these two framing chapters fed directly into the new mission statement of Sangtin.[9]

Whereas academics interested in praxis and methodology frequently express a desire to understand the details of our collaboration, some find it difficult to accept collaboration or co-authorship as processes that cannot be contained or neatly outlined in ways that are replicable or verifiable. Further, well-intentioned members of academia and the NGO sector frequently ask why a collective whose eight members are far from fluent (or even comfortable with the idea of speaking or writing) in English claims authorship of *Playing with Fire*. In turn, the sangtins respond with two questions: Why is the collective not considered expert enough to make its own decisions about where, when, how, and through whom it wants to translate and circulate its narratives and critiques? And why are researchers and development experts who do not speak a word of Awadhi never asked the same question about documents they generate in the forms of dissertations, books, and reports to donors?

Finally, international and regional NGOs and solidarity groups that have approached us with the intention of assisting our journey often find themselves in a bind. First, their rules allow them to give grants only to "qualified" individuals (as principal investigators or project supervisors). Second, even if these supporters are willing to give us the space to redefine empowerment or violence on Sangtin's terms, their procedures often prevent the grassroots activists from claiming ownership of their own work and from sharing their critical reflections on that work in public fora so that their institutional critiques may circulate more broadly. Herein emerges yet another contradiction that haunts this project: whereas Richa Singh's resignation from the post of MS's district coordinator prompted NCERT and AID-MN to recognize the risks that she had taken for a collective battle and to honor her efforts as an individual, Sangtin's efforts to secure minimal funds from funding agencies in the name of the organization or its other volunteers (who seem less qualified on paper) have frequently met with resistance.

As the collective grapples with these tensions, we continue to face harder, more pressing questions surrounding the precariousness of livelihoods of sangtins. At a time when the term *foreign funds* continues to construct an opposition between imperial domination and national sovereignty in the context of left-leaning social movements, several organizations are developing political methods of building power through their own members as their "primary agents of possibility" (Armstrong 2004, 52). Even as Sangtin draws inspiration from these groups, it continues to experiment and struggle with its own context-specific challenges and limitations. Organizing *chikan* embroiderers and small-scale milk producers in Sitapur into cooperatives have been two such experiments. Although these initiatives have been difficult to sustain, they have enabled Sangtin to confront the critical question of how it might generate resources and energies for (a) improving the access, quality, and relevance of basic education available to the least privileged children, and (b) creating spaces for more collectives of women and men to emerge so they can envision self-empowerment through dialogue and devise strategies to fight political, economic, psychological, and physical violence. Our power to realize these simple dreams, however, hinges in crucial ways on our ability to continue pushing the borders of formal knowledge production, and expectations about who should reside within those borders.

Parallel Diary 1: Theory as Praxis

In terms of the politics of knowledge production, *Sangtin Yatra* underscores that knowledge is embodied in dialogue; each dialogue in a new setting imparts that knowledge a new language and meaning. Knowledge acquires multiple forms as it becomes part of new struggles generated by critique, conversation, and reflection. In this sense, the books *Sangtin Yatra* and *Playing with Fire*, the protest resignation by Richa Singh, the online petition, the newspaper articles, reviews, and commentaries on the books can all be seen as multiple forms of knowledge enabled by dialogues evolving in different sites touched by the sangtins' alliance. In this collective intellectual journey, theory is generated *as* praxis. That is, what matters is not just theory-as-product but rather the activity of making knowledge, especially as a medium for negotiating difference and power. Theorizing, then, is not only about what the members of an alliance are in a position to see or conceptualize—it is equally about what we are in a position to do in making knowledge—"namely, constitute ourselves as political actors in institutions and processes both near and far" (Nagar 2006c, 154).

Sangtin Yatra disrupts the notion of "the field over there" as a source of raw material for formal knowledge that is subsequently processed by the expert academic. Rather, as an ongoing journey, it repeatedly suggests that the field is everywhere, an idea that we expand on elsewhere (Sangtin Writers 2012,

Nagar and Singh et al. 2012). For quick examples in the context of the above controversy, one can think of at least four different sites that were impacted by sangtins' intervention in knowledge making. First, the attack from the director of MSUP led to critical conversations in what was then the women's studies department at the University of Minnesota about what constitutes ethical research, and about blurring the definitions of researcher and subjects of research, and of theory and praxis. Second, in the case of academic editing and publishing, sangtins' modes of self-presentation as well as the content of our analysis have frequently led to difficult conversations about authorship, participation, translation, and representation and the need for editors and publishers to interrogate their own tendency to reduce formally less-educated, rural people to ethnographic subjects and to inadvertently romanticize or exoticize them without being able to accept them as true intellectuals or authors. Such conversations happened around displaying authors' names and photos on the cover of *Playing with Fire*, demands to revise sangtins' words to fit the requirements of the presses, and how to address the queries of reviewers and copyeditors without falling prey to their problematic assumptions and stereotypes. A third field that became central to sangtins' journey was India's NCERT, where the intervention made by *Sangtin Yatra* resulted in Sangtin's participation in the process of restructuring the national school curriculum, and which led to a chapter of *Sangtin Yatra* being included in the Hindi textbook for the Central Board Secondary Examination (tenth grade). Last but not least, the arguments made in *Sangtin Yatra* and *Playing with Fire* sparked the interest of donor organizations, among them Oxfam, Association for India's Development, and Global Fund for Women, each of which entered into important conversations with members of Sangtin on the need to rethink a range of concepts and practices in the landscape of funded projects and activism, including violence against women, documentation of impact, skills and qualifications, and the very idea of a principal investigator.

In common parlance, the first two fields (women's/gender studies and academic publishing) are often associated with the realm of the northern academic establishment, and the last two (NCERT and donor organizations) are linked to "the ground." But sangtins' praxis allowed the concerns of the first two fields to become entangled with the other two. Subsequently, two members of the authors' collective, Surbala and Richa Singh visited the United States to participate with Richa Nagar in a series of academic, activist, and artistic forums with an explicit aim of looking at U.S. universities and organizations as their field sites.[10]

At the same time, a commitment to collaborative praxis translates into a longer, more difficult journey: the journey that involves living up to our own critique. With *Sangtin Yatra* and *Playing with Fire*, some critical issues began to crystallize for the movement that was emerging in the villages of Sitapur under the umbrella organization, Sangtin. To begin with, the movement could not imagine focusing solely on poor women. Overnight meetings led by sangtins in village after village revealed that access to irrigation waters, fair wages, livelihoods, and right to information were the key issues around which collective struggle needed to happen. Soon, Sangtin began to transition from a collective of nine women to become SKMS, an organization comprising mainly dalit peasants and laborers, approximately half of whom are men. This has periodically thrown up the most fundamental question—what is a *narivadi sangathan* (feminist organization)? Along with this growth came another basic question— what is SKMS's relationship with the state? Could SKMS remain oppositional to the state if its actions were engaging with and responding to the state's policies pertaining to rural development?

Even as the organization grapples with these questions, SKMS has been at the forefront of fighting difficult battles with the government for returning water in an irrigation channel, which had been denied to forty thousand small farmers for sixteen years. In a landmark victory in 2009, the organization also won unemployment compensation for 826 mazdoor families under NREGA after two and a half years of sustained agitation against the state. As the growing membership of SKMS grappled with the interbraided violence of unemployment, displacement, casteism, communalism, and heterosexism, it also became clear that the pasts and presents of untouchability, deprivation, and disabilities are not so easily erased and that in order to remain committed to being an antihierarchical organization, SKMS has to continuously find ways to make space for these pasts and presents to be understood, confronted, negotiated, and remade in the organization.

There are also other challenges. First, in the absence of any donors, how can SKMS sustain itself? Can SKMS survive without entering into a dependent relationship with the same capitalist market that it confronts for its everyday long-term survival? Another challenge has had to do with the negotiation of the relationship between authors of the book, *Sangtin Yatra*, and the authors of the movement that is unfolding everyday as well as the nature, role, and function of translocal and transnational alliances in the making and advancing of such a movement.

One of our saathis, Maya, whose struggle and tears inspired us to begin *Sangtin Yatra* in 2002 (see chapter 4), was brutally murdered in her village by her own family members in 2007.[11] Maya's murder had as much to do with her political activism as it had to do with the choices that she openly made about her personal life and intimacies. Maya was killed at a time when SKMS gained high visibility as a key people's organization in Uttar Pradesh that is challenging the developmentalist state. Her murder struck SKMS with the same basic question that we confronted in 2004—what is a feminist movement? And can

Photo 7. SKMS saathis take over Vikas Bhawan (District Development Office) to demand their rights under the National Rural Employment Guarantee Scheme. Sitapur, 2009. (Courtesy: Sangtin Archives)

Photo 8. Saathis prepare for the next phase of struggle as they fight for unemployment compensation under the National Rural Employment Guarantee Scheme. Sitapur, 2009. (Courtesy: Sangtin Archives)

Photo 9. Jawaabdehi rally of SKMS: Saathis demand accountability from the development officials. Sitapur, 2010. (Courtesy: Sangtin Archives)

we really afford not to focus on violence against women in an organization 90 percent of whose membership is dalit and 50 percent or more of whom are dalit women laborers?

Journeying through Questions: Possibilities and Contradictions of Collaboration

> The movement is a web of interconnected strands, of recurring themes and discernible patterns. Autonomy. Participation. Democracy. Diversity. The reinvention of power. The importance of creativity and subjectivity. Real and basic needs rather than ideology as the basis of political action. Access to the "commons"—whether water, public space, software, seeds, or the manufacture of medicines. And constant questioning and innovation, especially when the movement is the most self-satisfied or most despairing.
>
> For movement implies motion, journeying, change.
>
> —Notes from Nowhere, *We Are Everywhere*

आखिर ग्लोबल दुनिया है क्या?	What, after all, is this world that has gone global?
मुंशी पुलिया का सर्किल,	the roundabout of my neighborhood
सेठ की गाड़ी का पहिया,	the wheel of a rich man's car
कोल्हू का घेरा,	the circle treaded by the bullock in the *kolhu* that mashes the grain
गृहणी की रोटी या चकला,	a housewife's roti or *chakla*
साहिब की मेज पर रखा ग्लोब?	a globe placed on the officer's desk?
या हुक्मरानों का चेहरा,	Or is it the face of our rulers
ड्रोन हमले से उड़ते लाशों के चीथड़े,	pieces of corpses torn by drones
ध्वस्त होती इमारतें,	crushed buildings
तेल, पानी की जमीनों पर कब्ज़ा,	grabbing of land that bears oil and water
खुदकुशी करते किसान?	farmers committing suicide?

—Mukesh Bhargava, "Global Dunia"

संगतिन यात्रा पुस्तक आने के बाद कैसे चली हमारी यह यात्रा? कभी–कभी सोचती हूँ कि यदि ऋचा नागर इस लड़ाई में हमारे साथ न होती तो क्या बच पाता यह समूह? लड़ पाते हम इतनी लम्बी लड़ाई? हमें यह कभी नहीं लगा कि ऋचा नागर साथ नहीं होंगी, लेकिन सवाल यह है कि हम कहाँ और किस ताक़त के साथ बैठे हैं? ऋचा नागर के बिना भी लड़ाई चलती पर इतनी लम्बी नहीं चल पाती और समूह बिखर जाता। लेकिन उस सूरत में भी हम समझौता नहीं करते। दरअसल, बिखरने की क़ीमत पर भी *संगतिन यात्रा* में लिखी बातों से समझौता नहीं करना इस सामूहिक कार्य की एक बड़ी उपलब्धि है...

बराबरी के लिए काम कर रहे एन.जी.ओ. की दुनिया में पदों का बखूबी बँटवारा है––यह पद सिर्फ़ काम की ज़िम्मेदारियों के अनुसार तो क़तई नहीं होते। इनके साथ मानदेय हमेशा शामिल रहता है। किसका मानदेय अधिक है और किसका कम... और इसी के हिसाब से व्यक्तियों का मान घटता–बढ़ता है। क़ाग़ज़ पर मैं संगतिन की सदस्य हूँ और सुरबाला, सचिव। लेकिन क्या हम दोनों की स्थितियाँ बराबर हैं? सुरबाला और मैं जिन पदों को छोड़कर महिला समाख्या से निकले हैं उन पदों का फर्क़ ही हम दोनों में अन्तर पैदा कर देता है। जबकि सुरबाला ने अपनी मरज़ी से महिला समाख्या उस समय छोड़ी जब संगतिन महज़ एक नाम था, और मुझसे परिस्थितियों ने महिला समाख्या छुड़वाई। मुझे छोड़ने की कम तकलीफ़ हुई क्योंकि मेरा व्यक्तिगत जीवन बहुत प्रभावित नहीं हुआ। हाँ, मेरे पास पहले वाली सत्ता नहीं रही, और उस सत्ता की सुविधाओं और संसाधनों के बिना बदलाव के काम को जारी रखना हमारे लिए चुनौती बन गया।

मैंने जब महिला समाख्या छोड़ने का फैसला लिया, पूरा समूह मेरे साथ था। कुछ मित्रों ने कहा कि तुम छोड़ रही हो तो सबको छोड़ना चाहिए। पर मुझे मालूम था कि मैं अपनी रोज़ी–रोटी किसी तरह चला लूँगी। क्या अन्य संगतिनों की स्थिति ऐसी थी? एड–मिनिसोटा के साथियों ने साथीशिप तय करने से पहले मुझसे पूछा था कि मेरी ज़रूरत कितनी है। यानी सुरबाला को यदि यही साथीशिप मिलती, को उसकी ज़रूरत के हिसाब से ही मिलती।...

रात एक बजे से बैठी हूँ और इस समय साढ़े तीन बजा है। बिजली के जाने में थोड़ा समय है लेकिन अगर अभी चली गई तो जितना लिखा है वह भी न भेज सकूँगी। सीतापुर में लम्बे समय से बिजली लगभग दस से चौदह घन्टे नहीं रहती। इस छोटी–सी सुविधा से कितना फ़र्क पड़ता है यह यहाँ के गाँवों में काम करके मैं खूब देख पाई हूँ। मिश्रिख में सात दिन रात में लाइट रहती है और सात दिन दिन में – कई बार इसमें भी अनियमितता होती है। कई गाँव ऐसे हैं जहाँ महीनों लाइट नहीं रहती और ऐसे भी गाँव हैं जहाँ अभी भी बिजली नहीं पहुँची है। मिश्रिख, सीतापुर, लखनऊ और दिल्ली में बिजली की स्थिति मिलाने बैठो तो ज़मीन–आसमान का अन्तर है। बड़े शहरों में बैठे

साथी कई बार किसी काम को ई—मेल के माध्यम से तुरन्त भेजने को कहते हैं। लेकिन यहाँ बैठकर
स्थिति इतनी आसान नहीं होती। और अगर यही ज़िम्मेदारी सुरबाला या रामशीला पर आ जाये तो?
सुरबाला के गाँव में बिजली ही नहीं है और शीला के यहाँ अक्सर महीनों बिजली नहीं रहती। सीतापुर
में कम्प्यूटर की सुविधा के साथ रहना मुझे ख़ास तो बना ही देता है।

घुवीकरण के इस दौर में कहने को तो पूरा विश्व एक गाँव, एक बाज़ार बन रहा है। लेकिन कितनी
खाइयाँ हैं स्थितियों में, स्थितियों से पैदा होने वाली उन ज़रूरतों में जिनके हिसाब से अनुदान और
प्रोजेक्ट निर्धारित किये जाते हैं। जब कुछ लोग ख़ास सुविधाओं के साथ और बहुत सारे लोग बिना
सुविधाओं के बैठे हैं, फिर हम कैसे उम्मीद करते हैं कि दोनों—यानी, सुविधासहित और सुविधारहित
—बराबरी का काम और आपस में बराबरी का व्यवहार कर ले जायेंगे?

Every step of this journey thus far has carried enormous meanings for the
collective.[12] In different ways, every sangtin has poured her soul into it, risked
her honor for it. This probably could not have happened if we had not made a
commitment to confront at all times the uncomfortable differences among our
social and institutional locations, power, and access to resources. This awareness
of power differentials becomes especially palpable when we ask how our collaboration has continued after MSUP's angry attack on the livelihoods of seven
sangtins. Richa Singh bluntly asks whether such a long, hard battle could have
continued in the absence of not simply the commitment but also the power of
location and resources that Richa Nagar brought to the collective. She is confident that once the book was written and the risks taken, the battle would have
continued irrespective of Richa Nagar's involvement. She wonders, however, if
the collective would have been dismantled in the absence of the national and
transnational support that our journey was able to garner through networking
and solidarity building in which Richa Nagar's social, geographical, and institutional locations became major advantages for the collective. But while Richa
Singh can imagine the scattering of the collective in the face of threat to livelihoods, she cannot imagine that the sangtins could compromise the principles
articulated in *Sangtin Yatra*: This itself attests to the success of the yatra.

The world of NGOs, ostensibly committed to bringing about greater equality, is efficiently divided along the lines of positions. These positions are never
defined merely according to responsibilities. They are inevitably entangled with
honoraria amounts; the importance of NGO staff increases or diminishes on
the basis of who gets greater or lesser honorarium. On paper, Richa Singh is a
member of Sangtin and Surbala is the secretary, but does that make their situations approximately equal? The relative positions that each of them occupied
in MSS itself creates a distinction in their present circumstances. Surbala chose
to leave the security of an MS job at a time when Sangtin was merely a name,
whereas Richa Singh was forced to leave MS after *Sangtin Yatra* faced backlash
from MS officials. Richa Singh feels that her own personal life was not deeply
affected after she left MS. However, she did lose her official status and author-

ity, the absence of which resulted in the disappearance of many conveniences, facilities, and resources. And working in the absence of these became Sangtin's major challenge.

When Richa Singh decided to leave MS, the whole collective was behind her. Some supporters suggested in the spirit of solidarity and fair-mindedness that if Richa Singh was quitting, other members of the collective who were MS employees should also quit MS. But did the other sangtins have the same options of being able to acquire an alternative livelihood as Richa Singh did? No. And soon, AID-MN's saathiship for Richa Singh became a major supporter for the continuation of the dreams and stances we had taken in *Sangtin Yatra*. Yet, Richa Singh remembers that at the time her saathiship was being finalized, friends at AID-MN asked her what her "minimal financial needs" were. Richa Singh could not help asking: were Surbala to obtain the same saathiship, would her material circumstances automatically translate into her getting a lesser honorarium than Richa Singh?

On 20 June 2005, Richa Singh gets on the computer at 1 A.M. to write her thoughts in Hindi to send to Richa Nagar, who is responsible for putting it all together in the form of a chapter that we have been asked to contribute to an edited volume, *Colonial and Postcolonial Geographies of India*. At 3:30 A.M., Richa Singh realizes that she still has about an hour left before the electricity is cut off, but then worries that she will lose everything if the power is cut off early. For a long time now, Sitapur town has had daily outage ranging from ten to fourteen hours. Within the Sitapur district, Mishrikh development block receives electricity supply that alternates between daytime during one week and nighttime during the next, and even that supply is often irregular. There are villages in this district that do not get electricity for months in a row, and there are also villages where electricity has still not reached. If one starts comparing the hours of electricity supplied to Mishrikh, Sitapur, Lucknow, and Delhi, each comparison will yield a difference of night and day. Sometimes friends in big cities who want Sangtin's input on an important matter ask Richa Singh to take a look at something they shared on the Internet and then provide rapid feedback on behalf of Sangtin. But for Richa Singh, this desire of the more privileged well-wishers to include Sangtin in their deliberations raises serious questions. And what would happen if the same job were assigned to Surbala or Ramsheela? Surbala's village has no electricity, and Ramsheela's village gets it for a few hours over several months. In such a scenario, the very access that Richa Singh has to a computer in Sitapur town bestows privileges on her that problematically make her more special than the rest.

The globe has become a so-called village, an interconnected market. But how many gulfs keep yawning between our locations and between the needs created by those locations on the basis of which grants and projects are determined?

When a handful of people sit with very special facilities and scarce resources while the majority lose access to basic resources for survival, how do we expect that both the resource-rich and the resource-poor will come together in common institutional spaces to work and act as approximate equals?

On the surface, these questions seem no different from the ones with which we began our journey in 2002. But our yatra thus far has imparted them with deeper meanings. Although MS's backlash made us more confident than ever about the truth of our critique, it also showed what the price of articulating that critique could be. That the only source of livelihood of our most economically vulnerable sangtins could be snatched away as punishment for critical reflection and collaboration was a reality that shook us. In order to remain true to our commitment, however, the sangtins must continue identifying and challenging institutional norms and practices that exclude, diminish, or dominate them, or that maintain the status quo in the name of helping, empowering, or giving voice to the marginalized. The knots become tighter and harder for us as we gain access to some spaces and lose others by raising uncomfortable questions. We are committed to changing unequal distribution of privileges, resources, and power—whether it is hours of electricity, or the right to claim a truth as legitimate intellectuals, or the right to appear as authors on the cover of a book written in English. But we also have to be vigilant about what is at stake here. As we fight to claim intellectual authority and legitimacy for our insights; to redefine empowerment and violence on our own terms; and to engage in constructive criticism of the institutional spaces where we are hired, fired, or invited to work—we cannot afford to engage in critique that advances the careers or visibility of some in the collective while jeopardizing the access to livelihoods for others.

The primary objective of our journey has been to initiate and sustain difficult dialogues—among ourselves and with those institutions with which we become affiliated. Like Notes from Nowhere (2003) we, too, believe that it is only through these difficult dialogues that our journey can continue and move us forward. Through constant interrogation of the contradictions that remain within us, we want to steer away from simplistic claims about equality among us; but we also believe that if people sitting in unequal places will not come forward to build alliances then the gulfs between our intellectual and material struggles will continue to widen. The journey on which we have come thus far through trust, solidarity, and self-critique cannot stop at one or two critical experiments, one or two books, or one or two institutions. It is a dialogic process—a dialectical response—that can be sustained only through continuous movement and questioning.

Parallel Diary 2: Churnings of a Movement

Silence and Protest

Some children are constantly given opportunities to use their voices, and some find themselves in circumstances where they gradually start identifying their own notes. But there are many children whose voices are cruelly suffocated by society every time they try to express themselves. They learn to become silent—sometimes because of the schoolmaster's stick, sometimes by the slaps of the *malik*, sometimes by the thrashings from their Maa-Baap, and often by the insults hurled at their own families by others. And the little feet that start moving tentatively on the path of life begin to tremble at the very outset of the journey.

Those who feel most crushed by the dominant groups are frequently the same people who are dubbed *bevaqoof* and *nalayaq* by the mainstream. And these same definitions—like heavy *labadas*—become such unsheddable burdens for so many people in our villages that they do not get a chance to carve out new definitions for themselves. As the sangtins' journey moved forward, saathis began to understand the connections between their struggles; they began to understand how the suffocating of one's voice from childhood and the inability to carve out the definitions to undertake an analysis of one's own conditions take away the resources necessary for people to live a full life.

How deep are the relationships between the struggles of childhood, youth, and old age, and so tightly intertwined with our pasts, presents, and futures that one's childhood becomes synonymous with the history that is always present in one's current struggles. Perhaps it is because of the constant presence of our childhoods in our lives that the memories, desires, tears, and feelings dug from our pasts have become a potent medium for building relationships in the Sangathan. Through the language of childhood, struggle travels from one soul to another, from one person to another, from one world to another.

When saathis of the Sangathan sit down to reflect on our childhoods, we quiver with rage. How does one begin to describe the childhoods of our saathis, such as Banwari, whose roti was snatched away as punishment, sometimes for talking too much and sometimes for expressing a desire to play with the children of his *malik*'s family? Society thrashed him so hard that the waves that rose inside Banwari fell silent for years. He shut the doors of his heart and swore to himself that he would never open his mouth again. Saathis such as Banwari ask, "the country became independent, the drums of democracy have been continuously beaten, but how do we break the chains that have bound us?"

But when Banwari found the space of the Sangathan, his muffled voice started rising and blending with the voice of the Sangathan. Banwari says: "When I sit in the meetings of the Sangathan, I feel I have a place in this world. I feel valued. The fears that had locked my tongue for years are slipping behind."

It is through voices such as Banwari's that the intimate episodes and experiences of our lives find their grounds in the Sangathan. Somewhere or another in the innermost layers of all of our lives are experiences that we managed to recognize as injustice but were not able to create anything from that recognition. The merging of the silences and protests of saathis, such as Kailasha and Banwari, with the voice of the Sangathan allows all the saathis to learn how to take the recognition of injustice to its next destination. Without the notes attained through this recognition, the Sangathan could not have appreciated how deep a relationship exists between the following poem of Dhoomil (1999), the suffocated voices of childhood, and the silences that have the power to break other silences: The struggle to reclaim roti is not simply about who rolls or eats the roti. Nor is it merely about drawing attention to those in power who play with the roti; it is also about a silent violence of the powerful that can only be fought by enabling the silences of the deprived.

एक आदमी
रोटी बेलता है
एक आदमी रोटी खाता है
एक तीसरा आदमी भी है
जो न रोटी बेलता है, न रोटी खाता है
वह सिर्फ़ रोटी से खेलता है
मैं पूछता हूँ —
'यह तीसरा आदमी कौन है ?'
मेरे देश की संसद मौन है।

A man
rolls the roti
a man eats the roti
there is also a third man
who neither rolls nor eats the roti
he only plays with the roti
I ask
who is this third man?
the parliament of my country does not respond.

Murders, Silences, and Feminisms: Maya and Jinnati

Minneapolis, 24 November 2007. I have just hung up the phone after speaking with Richa Singh. Maya has been murdered. The same Maya, whose fearless voice always drowned the voices of others, has herself been silenced forever. The corpse of the same Maya, whose forceful presence I associate with the beginning of our journey as sangtins, was thrown to rot on top on the garbage by her murderers—to mock all those struggles that Maya lived with her each breath, each laugh, and each scream and threw an open challenge to her whole society.

Her heavy sobs shaking with terror and anger still echo in my ears—"All these people will kill me, just like they killed Jinnati."

And several of the women sitting around Maya in March 2002 had said almost in unison as they wiped the tears from Maya's eyes, "How can they kill you, Maya? It isn't that easy to lose or take someone's life. Aren't we with you?"

Five and a half years after that conversation, Maya was murdered in cold blood. Why? Because none of us could dare to live our most intimate relationships as Maya did? Because Maya did not allow any family, any husband, any job, any organization, or any ideology to govern her thoughts and life-style? Without ever uttering words such as "NGOization" or "feminism" from her mouth, Maya taught us most critical lessons that no one else could teach us—from her behavior, her relationships, her stubbornness, and her decisions. Yet no organization, no movement, no companion could stop this fearless Maya from being murdered. Isn't this a major defeat for us all?

—translated entry from Richa Nagar's diary

It was the year 2000. Five years before the birth of SKMS and more than a year before the beginning of *Sangtin Yatra*. In the Arthapur village of Kutubnagar in Mishrikh Block, a man killed his wife, Jinnati, by stabbing her body with a knife several times. The whisperings suggested that Jinnati was involved in an extramarital relationship with a young man from the village. Further murmurings revealed that Jinnati was a second wife, and her husband was many years older than herself. At the time of her death, Jinnati was the treasurer of the micro-credit program run in the Arthapur village by MSS. Outside a shop at a street corner in Kutubnagar, one of Jinnati's friends said to a companion, "What a tragedy that Jinnati's husband killed her so heartlessly."

Hearing these words, a man from Arthapur immediately declared, "What Jinnati's husband did was right. This is the best lesson for women such as Jinnati. If Jinnati were from my family, I would have gotten rid of her a long time ago." Most people called Jinnati characterless and saw her murder as inevitable.

Anyone's murder, anywhere, is a matter of profound pain and sadness. But Jinnati was not just anyone—she was involved in so many key discussions in MSS. No one doubted that she was emerging as a strong leader in her village. Yet, for the women who had plunged themselves into women's issues with Jinnati, her murder became a challenge. Far from expressing sadness or making efforts to bring her killer to justice, many women from Jinnati's own village and adjoining villages busied themselves with trying to prove the validity of Jinnati's murder. And yet, these same women knew of several men from Kutubnagar whose extramarital relationships were no secrets. At the time when people gathered to pay their last respects to Jinnati, it was not just the men who were absent. Even those women who were involved with Jinnati's own village-level micro-credit program did not step out of their homes.

The collective absence of women clarified the challenge that stood before MSS workers who opposed Jinnati's murder: making any public comment about Jinnati's death meant inviting bitter reaction against all those women who were becoming active on women's issues. The district-level administration of MSS understood full well that women who publicly opposed Jinnati's murder would be communally blacklisted as "characterless" women who "want to turn all the daughters and daughters-in-law in the area into Jinnatis." Even as hearts trembled with anger, they remained enveloped with the fear that no such word should slip out of any mouth that could become an excuse to push women back behind the closed doors of their homes. . . . At the same time, MSS leadership recognized its responsibility: "If we fail to question the society's definition of a good woman now, when would we take up this challenge? Isn't a silence over a foundational issue such as this one almost as big an injustice against Jinnati as her murder was?" In the end, MSS workers decided to organize a silent protest to raise this question in Sitapur.

In a tense environment, approximately three hundred women from Kutubnagar marched in the silent protest against Jinnati's murder. At the main intersection of Kutubnagar, they invited the men from the area to join in. Approximately a hundred men joined the *juloos* at that invitation, but left the march after covering barely half a kilometer. It was hard to tell how many of those men allowed themselves to open their hearts to the protest's message, but the *juloos* did bring an end to public discussions that had continuously proclaimed Jinnati as characterless. Later, Jinnati's husband was sentenced to life imprisonment.

How ironic that the cheerful and "big-mouthed" Maya, who remembered Jinnati's murder as she tearfully relayed the fear of her own end, was brutally murdered within a matter of a few years. Actively involved in both MSS and SKMS, Maya was admired and resented for her wild and daring ways. Maya disappeared from her village Narayanpur on the evening of 21 November 2007, and two days later her corpse was found on the village's garbage dump.

The main cause behind the murders of both Jinnati and Maya was that they had intimate relationships with men outside of wedlock. However, the quick pace at which Jinnati was accused of being immoral was something that did not repeat itself in Maya's case. In Jinnati's case, it also became a public fact that the perpetrator of her murder was her own husband, whereas in Maya's case, the identity of her killer remains a mystery. In the police network, one did hear stories about Maya's "illegitimate" relationships every now and then, but no "facts" were ever made public.

Together, MSS and SKMS organized a condolence meeting in Narayanpur on 26 November 2007. Besides prominent people such as Pradhanpati of Gramsabha Rannupur, more than one hundred saathis from nearby villages gathered to pay their respects to Maya. All these people also participated in the six-kilometer-long *padyatra* from Narayanpur to Kutubnagar that was held immediately after the gathering. The meeting and *padyatra* made it clear that no matter how many people taunted Maya for her *hekadi*, men from the Sangathan remember Maya's every gesture with fondness and respect. Shivram recalls how Maya often put her hand on his shoulder and said, "Why, Shivram, you say what we should do next." Shivram's voice gets choked with tears as he remembers that *sahaj* style of Maya. No matter how tired Maya might have been of the pangs of poverty, the chains of our society could not touch her soul, her ways of embracing life. That is precisely why society could not tolerate Maya's forceful laughter and honestly lived relationships while she was alive.

Along with this painful recognition, however, we faced a powerful truth that made the tears shed after Maya's death very different from the suffocated screams that followed Jinnati's murder. When Jinnati was killed, MSS activists had to strategize about how to help people understand that the very attempt to justify her murder was criminal, while also making sure that village-level volunteers who opposed Jinnati's murder were not branded as loose or immoral.

The scene in Narayanpur village on 26 November 2007 was intimately reminiscent of, yet in complete contrast with, what was seen in Arthapur eight years earlier. Whereas not even one man had stepped up to publicly condole Jinnati, several hundred men were present along with SKMS's women saathis to extend their respects to Maya. The manner in which people discussed the frightening meanings of Maya's murder was something that could never have happened after Jinnati was killed. These differences forced the saathis to ask ourselves several questions: Even if a lot remains to be changed, what kind of transformation has already taken place that allowed our men saathis to publicly weep as they remembered Maya? What has changed as a result of the Sangathan's work that allowed our men saathis to declare angrily that the accused must be punished? Why is it that this time, instead of lowering their voices at the intersection in Kutubnagar, saathis such as Ram Avtar and Bhainu could scream with rage in their tear-filled voices: "An injustice like this against women cannot be tolerated!"

If Ram Avtar and Bhainu had not been saathis of SKMS, would they have been able to gather the courage to shame their community in this way? Perhaps not. But before we raise our hands to pat our own backs for this accomplishment, larger questions scream at the saathis and make our hands numb. What is the price that the saathis must pay for this project of social transformation that we have embraced? Has Maya been forced to pay that price with her own life? If this is true, why is it so? As these questions torment us, we are also faced with the questions that our critics often pose before SKMS.

For example, one question that has been posed on several occasions is whether the political journey that began with the book *Sangtin Yatra* was sidetracked by the making of SKMS. Did the collective critique through which the sangtins had sharpened their feminist thought lose its edge as the group transformed into an organization of laborers and peasants? This question acquires even more urgency in the context of Maya's murder. In departing from a sole focus on women's issues and creating an organization of peasants and workers, has the Sangathan committed a strategic or ideological mistake that has resulted in our paying the price with the murder of a courageous companion such as Maya?

Whomever joined the journey of sangtins saw a couple of simple dreams somewhere along the way: the dream of a society where one does not have to be humiliated because they are materially poor, dalit, or landless, or because they pull a rickshaw or *thelia*. A dream of a society where memories of one's childhood do not automatically bring tears to one's eyes. A dream that turns humiliations of childhood and difficulties of life into energy that radiates hope.

In these simple dreams of living a life with respect, the sangtins could not see anything that should have been confined only to poor women. Nor did the sangtins, in connecting this dream with all the exploited workers and peasants of our villages, feel for a moment that we were leaving women behind. Are women not peasants? Are they not laborers? If the mere mention of a peasant or laborer evokes the image of a man's face in our minds, by what words should we define such feminist thought?

At the same time, a bitter truth has prominently informed the Sangathan's struggle: the everyday humiliation and tortures suffered by women transform themselves far too easily into the murders of Mayas and Jinnatis. The everydayness of humiliation suffered by our men saathis, by contrast, does not place them at the risk of murder. The mockery of a woman's existence that happens in our homes and communities in the name of "respect" and "protection," and the tireless efforts to crush her dreams and render her desires invisible are, after all, the everyday killings that become the stepping-stones to gruesome murders of living, dreaming, and fighting women such as Jinnati and Maya. A fearless woman is battered inside her home so that she cannot advance her struggle with confidence. A woman saathi returns home from a victorious rally on NREGS, only to be cursed in a public place by a husband or relative who wants to establish his or her power over the woman before the world—"Look! she is under our control. No matter how strong a leader she might become outside the home, deep inside we can destroy her soul in whatever way we choose." The Mayas who collide with multiple systems of domination are grave threats because the courage of their ideas and the force of their determination place in the circle of suspicion all their "saviors"—from the district administration, the NGOs, the Pradhans, and the police to their husbands, lovers, and family members.

It is only by advancing these bitter truths in the Sangathan that we have learned the complexities of struggles that insist on identifying and finding their own notes in the midst of the terrifying possibility of being silenced forever. And it is these same truths that have enabled the saathis to see the violence inflicted by hunger as deeply connected with the violence inflicted by murder. If struggle against both forms of violence is intertwined and inevitable, then the Sangathan must also confront the risks and sacrifices that come with these necessary choices: for Kailasha, that risk translates into giving up her day's food, and for Maya it becomes the loss of her life. The difference in the magnitude of the two sacrifices shrinks with the recognition that both sacrifices are borne of a simple hope that the Sangathan enables—the hope for a dignified and fulfilling life. In a context where premature crushing of life is hardly any news, saathis such as Kailasha and Maya pay the cost of this hope with their bodies.

"No Entry Signal!"

After the rally of 23 August 2006, the gaze of political forces on the active saathis had become more vigilant. The same people who previously dismissed the sangtins as women working on women's issues were now feeling threatened by SKMS's growing visibility. The economic equations that had emerged in the game of development were feeling the sangtins' burden. The information about when the saathis were planning which activities in which villages were now being assembled actively outside the Sangathan. In these circumstances, the three women who were working full-time as organizers—Richa Singh, Surbala, and Reena—felt an urgent need to remain in continuous contact with the movement's membership. The long queues at public call booths made it difficult to discuss highly politicized and volatile matters with the members. Finally, Reena had a landline installed and Surbala arranged for a mobile phone. Having access to the phone made it far easier for them to do the planning associated with the Sangathan's activities. In the midst of all this, Sarvesh of Sabelia village said to Surbala one day:

"Didi, Can you help me buy a phone, too?"

"Why don't you purchase some wheat to feed the family instead? The winter nights are cold and you don't even have a *razai*. Why don't you get a *razai* from your earnings? What will come from getting a phone?" Surbala lectured Sarvesh.

Then Sarvesh went to Richa Singh with the same request. Her response was similar: "Sarvesh, I would not advise you to get a phone."

Sarvesh went and purchased a phone himself.

When Surbala saw Sarvesh with a phone, she complained—"Sarvesh, we tried to make you understand why you shouldn't waste money on a phone. But you didn't listen!"

Sarvesh said—"When you purchased a phone, did I ever try to tell you to not get one? That your expenses will increase because of the phone? Then why did you tell me not to get a phone? Isn't that what everyone else says? That 'when you poor folks get some money you lose sight of what your *real* need is. All you do is spend your money on wasteful things such as radios and phones.' When you told me the same thing, I was incensed. So I just went and purchased a phone."

When Surbala first heard Sarvesh's words, she was livid, but soon her anger turned into an intense restlessness. Why did Sarvesh interpret her advice in this way? After several days, Surbala discussed this issue in a meeting with other saathis and confronted the truth of what Sarvesh said. Can she or Richa or any other saathi truly assess what Sarvesh can or cannot do with the wages of his sweat? Can they determine what is or is not his need? Is it not true that despite their best intentions, those who organize and lead movements end up pointing their fingers at Sarvesh's *tabqa* and their ideas about his *tabqa* lead many to presume and define things for that *tabqa*? Why? Just because they have tried to stand with them or extended a little bit of support in their fight for their roti? Sarvesh's *tabqa* is the one that supports our movements precisely like our thumb blends with our hand to reinforce it into a powerful fist. And even after reinforcing the fist, it never preaches at anyone. Then why is it that Surbala assumed that she knew what Sarvesh's need was?

Today, Surbala does not mind Sarvesh's purchasing of the phone or his harsh directness with her. In fact, she sees these as "no-entry" signals. No-entry signals that remind her that she has no right or ability to decide how Sarvesh's life should carry on, what his needs are, or what would give him happiness. Remembering this incident, Surbala wrote in her diary—"After this incident, my relationship with Sarvesh has deepened. Now when the people of our villages return with a radio in their hands after pulling the cycle rickshaws in Lucknow, I do not flinch. I still wrestle with the questions—'Why did they purchase this radio? Wasn't their need something else?' But I don't dare to think that I am even in a position to understand the answers."

Sarvesh, like others in SKMS, pushes us to confront the reality that the Sangathan's collective struggle for recognition of injustice is impossible without a recognition of the limits imposed by each saathi's own privileges and perspectives . . . our own inability to fully know any saathi's feelings, desires, actions, or reasoning. It is this politics of recognition that gives all the saathis of the Sangathan the tools to measure the sacrifices of Kailasha and Maya, and to derive courage and inspiration from them.

The stories of Banwari, Sarvesh, Maya, and Jinnati challenge their audiences—wherever they might be located—to reconsider the questions surrounding silence, power, and context, as well as the centrality of desire in shaping the politics of struggle, solidarity, alliance, and representation.[13] In writing the journeys of saathis such as Banwari, the movement asks a question: how has SKMS's work enabled these saathis to speak with conviction and authority? But this question is undergirded by another question: in which environments and circumstances do people assert their power to speak with confidence? The movement commits itself to providing precisely such an environment so that saathis can claim their first occasions for interaction and participation in a setting that is radically different from the worlds that have denied them dignity for most of their lives. Worlds in which their speech, their passions, their analyses remained unarticulated or unheard. In making this commitment, the movement recognizes that those who are silent are often those who are most critical and suspicious—even if unconsciously or implicitly—about language. The movement appreciates that, far from being a neutral medium, language is always shaped by power and operates in particular environments to entrench and normalize hierarchical relations around caste, class, gender, and geography.[14]

At the same time, the stories poignantly indicate the ways in which desire and pleasure are read as excessive when expressed by the disenfranchised and the poor, by people who are expected to fight for their daily survival and sustenance in the forms of livelihoods and "basic needs." Although Maya's and Jinnati's fates cannot easily be compared with Banwari's or Sarvesh's, and their desires are enmeshed in quite different structures and configurations of power, each one of their stories is about how the very expression of desire for pleasure or indulgence—whether expressed through extramarital affairs or through an "unnecessary" desire for cricket or a cellphone—becomes a transgression of their auqat or "rightful place." In explicitly articulating or remembering their desire for pleasure—and in politicizing that pleasure as their right—Banwari, Sarvesh, Maya, and Jinnati resist the dominant perceptions about the rightful place of the marginalized and about what they should or should not be entitled to. Their insistence actively redefines the notion of "the political." While the previous chapters of *Muddying the Waters* chiefly engaged with modes of acting and being that are self-consciously political—whether in the academy or "on the ground"—the stories of Banwari, Sarvesh, Maya, and Jinnati introduce a different modality of the political, one that pushes us to reconsider who and what is read as an agent of knowledge production, and how. Such rethinking requires a redefinition of the notion of the political itself, a theme to which I return in the last chapter as four truths of storytelling and coauthorship in alliance work.

6. Four Truths of Storytelling and Coauthorship in Feminist Alliance Work

Purva Naresh's play *Ok, Tata, Bye-Bye* provides a good starting point for this discussion of storytelling and coauthorship in feminist alliance work. In *Ok, Tata, Bye-Bye*, Naresh (2012) fictionalizes her own struggles as a documentary filmmaker, specifically in relation to a project that she carried out in an impoverished community alongside a highway between Rajasthan and Madhya Pradesh. This community depended for its survival on truckers who stopped in their village for food, petrol, and sex. Girls born in the village were taught that they were not to be married, for they were born for sex work and to become breadwinners for their families. The play revolves around the attempts of "Pooja," an Indian documentary filmmaker who arrives from the United Kingdom with her British partner and British funding, to make a film on the lives of these sex workers through the oral narratives of two young women, Seema and Roopa. Pooja believes that if she can record Seema's and Roopa's stories as sex workers, she would then be able to raise support from NGOs in Britain to intervene in, and save these young women from, their awful fate.

Of these two potential storytellers, Roopa, who has had some primary schooling, seems to have internalized the same narrative of her own victimhood that drives Pooja's project—and Roopa is more than happy to provide the story that Pooja wants her audience to hear. In fact, Roopa happily provides a fake story that reinforces all of Pooja's assumptions because she is aware that providing that story may open new doors of opportunity for Roopa. Seema, on the contrary, has never been to school and passionately embraces everything her life offers her. She fiercely rejects Pooja's assumption that she is a victim of terrible circumstances, and continuously pushes Pooja to acknowledge all the ways in which Pooja—despite her privileged class position, expensive movie camera, and ideas about women's emancipation—is also chained by oppressions parallel to Seema's own.

The events of the play can be interpreted in several ways, but for the purposes of this chapter, it is helpful to focus on Seema's and Roopa's very different responses to Pooja's overtures. Seema refuses to be Pooja's coauthor unless Pooja is willing to be interrogated and judged by Seema in the same way as Pooja wants to interrogate and judge her. In so doing, Seema explicitly confronts the power geometry that connects elite knowledge producers to their subaltern counterparts.[1] Roopa, by contrast, plays the same power geometry—the putative superiority of Pooja's feminism and the relatively immense resources that underwrite it—to her own ends by signing up to be a participant and coauthor in Pooja's project.

On the one hand, Roopa's formal schooling allows Pooja to hear and understand her. On the other hand, it is Seema's unschooled presence that challenges Pooja and that claims an authority in the narrative that cannot be expressed through formal coauthorship. Together, the two responses highlight the complexities of subaltern agency and the ways in which the formulations of radical desire (including a desire for coauthorship) might be unruly, ill-tempered, incomplete, conformist, and/or seemingly contradictory, and refuse to align with hopes of dialectical resolution on some "pure" theoretical terms. At the same time, Roopa and Seema push their audiences to interrogate their own assumptions about marginality, oppression, liberation, and charity in the same way as they challenge Pooja's; and the three women's struggles with collaborative storytelling effectively convey the messiness of representation in alliance work.

As I watched the play, I noticed the parallels between the concerns about representation, experience, and knowledge making that drove the drama of this particular case, and ongoing debates about the ways in which dominant forms of academic engagement (including but not only limited to feminist research) serve to reinforce the persistent hierarchy of knowledge producers and knowledges. When the structure of knowledge production largely disallows research subjects from interrogating, evaluating, or dislodging the knowledge produced by the academic expert, the status of academic researcher as the "true intellectual thinker" remains undisturbed, along with the hierarchies that elevate theory, research, and academic knowledge production to a higher plane than method, community-based dialogues, and nonconventional academic writing. This hierarchization categorizes as "methodology," or "activism," or "atheoretical" most efforts that seek to destabilize or advance academic frameworks on the basis of dialogues outside academia (Nagar and Swarr 2010). Piya Chatterjee elaborates further on this problem when she argues that "critiques which frontally challenge the terms of hegemonic knowledges, and are grounded in critical or radical praxis (in language, stances and modalities of expression) are often dismissed as unsophisticated, untheoretical and 'too activist.' . . . Even with the important feminist questions raised about the intimate relationships between epistemology and power, formal scholarly evaluation is often wary and dismissive of research that is open about its commitments and investments to radical and progressive critique and social change" Chatterjee (2011, 2). In effect, then, we have a perpetuation of recurring problems in academic knowledge production: knowledges that dominate and languages that exclude to reinforce what Berenice A. Carroll has called "the class system of the intellect":

> The class system of the intellect parallels in intellectual life the class system in the realm of so-called "productive" labor and capital. It uses claims of "originality" and associated terms ("innovation," "creativity," etc.) to rationalize and justify claims to property in ideas and lines of inheritance, preserving for small groups . . . both intellectual hegemony and control of a variety of rewards and privileges. . . . The system operates in substantial measure on various forms of appropriation and exploitation of the material and physical labor of those relegated to lower classes, including predecessors erased from memory and history. Academic ranks and hierarchies are situated in this system . . . but should not be confused with the more general class system of the intellect, which extends beyond academia. (Carroll 1990, 138)

Several feminist scholars have highlighted the epistemic violence enacted by this "system of the intellect" and reflected on the ways in which it can be interrupted. Sharmila Rege's critique of mainstream sociology in the Indian context can be applied to mainstream social sciences more broadly: "Women, dalits, adivasis, may be included as substantive research areas of sociology and in optional courses but this inclusion keeps the cognitive structures of the discipline relatively intact from the challenges posed by dalit or feminist knowledges. Thus 'good sociology' continues to be defined in terms of the binaries of objectivism/subjectivism, social/political, social world/knower, experience/knowledge, tradition/modernity and theoretical brahman/empirical shudra" (Rege 2010, 90). Rege challenges this approach through one that is based on the Phule-Ambedkarite principle of "Educate, Organize, Agitate." Rather than being a sequence of progressive steps or actions (e.g., educate → organize → agitate) this mode of engagement can be imagined as a nonlinear, continuously evolving, co-constitutive dialogue where education becomes inseparable from organizing struggles over recognition and redistribution for social transformation. In this multidirectional pedagogy, all the participants are teachers and learners and "the possibilities and constraints on agency as it intersects with social formation cannot be predefined" (Rege 2010, 95).

In *Ghostly Matters*, Avery Gordon makes similar points about subjugated knowledges and subjectivity when she defines haunting as that "domain of turmoil and trouble . . . when the cracks and rigging are exposed, when the people who are meant to be invisible show up without any sign of leaving"

(Gordon 2008, xvi). Gordon turns haunting into a methodology that inter-braids the individual, the social, and the political in order to grapple with the social-subjective matter to "richly, conjure, describe, narrate, and explain the leins, the costs, the forfeits, and the losses of modern systems of abusive power" (Gordon 2008, xvii). This methodology resists the assumed distinctions between subject and object of knowledge, between fact and fiction, between presence and absence, between past and present, between present and future, between knowing and not knowing. In seeking to learn from "that which is marginalized, trivialized, denied, disqualified, taxed, and aggrieved," this approach commits itself to "redistributing respect, authority, and the right to representability or generalizability—the right to theorize"—a right that Gordon argues "entails the capacity to be something other than a local knowledge governed or interpreted by a putative superior" (Gordon 2008, xviii).

A radical rethinking of how we can (re)make knowledges and redistribute the "right to theorize" requires a serious engagement with geography. As Gillian Hart notes, "Any strategy to mobilize . . . must be firmly grounded in particular configurations of material and cultural conditions, and engage directly with specific local histories and translocal connections, as well as with meanings, memories, and the making and remaking of political subjects" (Hart 2002, 313). These meanings and memories are inseparable from what Katherine McKittrick calls the "language and concreteness of geography—with its overlapping physical, metaphorical, theoretical, and experiential contours . . . as they overlap with subjectivities, imaginations, and stories" (McKittrick 2006, xiii). Thus, theories, poems, plays, and narratives that have been erased, dismissed, or rendered invisible can "disclose" new spaces and places, giving birth to poetics of landscape that can creatively "influence and undermine existing spatial arrangements" (McKittrick 2006, xxiii). Coauthoring stories opens up rich possibilities for such creative intervention, especially in alliance work where academic knowledges intersect with knowledges that are produced in and through struggles in sites that are not bound to the academy (see, e.g., Bondi et al. 2002, Mountz et al. 2003, Benson and Nagar 2006, Community Economies Collective and Gibson 2009, Gibson-Graham and Roelvink 2011, Pratt 2012).

If one recognizes all theorizing as an exercise in storytelling, then it is also possible that the epistemic violence of existing paradigms and frameworks can be resisted, mitigated, or confronted by telling stories differently. Clare Hemmings observes that the tales that feminist theorists tell intersect with wider institutionalizations of gendered meanings, and therefore, it matters *how* feminists tell their stories (Hemmings 2011). She writes:

> For example, stories that frame gender equality as a uniquely Western import, as a way to measure or enforce economic and democratic development, reso-

nate disconcertingly well with feminists stories that place "feminism" as a radical knowledge project firmly in the Western past. When feminists celebrate the move beyond unity or identity, when they lament the demise of a feminist political agenda, or when they propose a return to a feminist vision from the past, they construct a political grammar. . . . Feminist theorists need to pay attention to the *amenability* of our own stories, narrative constructs, and grammatical forms to discursive uses of gender and feminism we might otherwise wish to disentangle ourselves from if history is not simply to repeat itself. (Hemmings 2011, 1–2)

However, paying attention to our storytelling is no easy undertaking. Here again, Hemmings reminds us that as narrations about the past, stories are motivated by the positions that the tellers occupy—or wish to occupy—in the present. Yet, a corrective approach will try to erase the conditions of its own construction, particularly if it purports to give us the final word (Hemmings 2011, 13–14).

Struggling with coauthorship can be a potent way to grapple with challenges of storytelling. It can allow coauthors from varied locations to draw upon and scrutinize their co-evolving and even conflicting experiences, truths, and selves while exploring how these interconnect with expert knowledges produced in the professional realms. Far from seeking perfect resolutions, such an exercise must confront the fact that "power is never really external to dialogue, participation and experience" (Rege 2010, 97), and it must open up spaces to examine the complexities of organizing and struggle in relation to subjectivity, a topic that has received inadequate attention. As Elisabeth Armstrong notes:

> Recent feminist theories usually accord struggle an honorable mention. However, their primary focus on the subject and subjectivity ignores the integral relation- ship between organization and struggle; what works in feminism, how it works, and what feminism support[s] . . . [In discussing only] the feminist subject and feminist subjectivity [w]e have lost explicit articulations about vital questions of representation in organization, [and] also of leadership and interconnection with other political movements. . . . We have lost the opportunity to [debate feminism as] an ongoing process of resistance and assertion. (Armstrong 2002, 92)

Coauthoring stories in and through feminist alliance work makes it possible to mobilize experience and memory work in ways that connect questions of feminist subject and subjectivity with those of representation in organization, leadership, and movement politics. While nostalgia, observes Armstrong, recon- structs or reinterprets a self-contained past for itself, memory work—including that in the form of diaries, stories, and testimonios—seeks to imagine new sets of beginnings (Armstrong 2002, 111). This, in part, is the reason why Zapatismo embraces memory work as "the methodology of the inverted periscope":

> One can never ascertain a belief in or vision of the future by looking at a situa- tion from the position of "neutrality" provided for you by the existing relations

of power . . . such methods allow you to see the field only from the perspective of those who rule at any given moment. In contrast, if one learns to harness the power of the periscope . . . by placing it deep below the earth, below even the very bottom of society, one finds that there are struggles and memories of struggles that allow us to identify not "what is," but more importantly "what will be." By harnessing the transformative capacity of social movement, as well as the memories of past struggles that drive it, the Zapatistas are able to identify the future and act on it today. (El Kilombo Intergaláctico 2007, 9)

In the context of alliance work, coauthoring stories offers a creative space to mobilize memories in "a polyvocal framework attuned to a complex politics of difference; a process- versus product-based approach [to knowledge production, and] an explicit pedagogical rhetoric that encourages readers to become potential allies" (Connolly-Shaffer 2012, 171–72). As a self-reflexive critical practice, this kind of coauthorship cannot be conceptualized as a text produced by two or more sovereign persons. Rather, such coauthorship can only be imagined as an ongoing dialogue among continuously co-evolving multiple selves that may frequently contradict—yet continue to grow without obliterating—one another. Stories emerging from these dialogues can interrupt the forms of epistemic violence identified by Gordon and Rege and trouble what Jacqui Alexander calls "inherited boundaries of geography, nation, episteme, and identity" so that they can be replaced by frameworks that underscore ongoing "reciprocal investments we must make to cross over into a metaphysics of interdependence" (Alexander 2005, 6).

I now turn to my second story—one that unfolds in multiple stages and sites— and use it as an entry point to articulate what I call four truths about coauthoring tales. I use the term "truth" here in order to acknowledge the importance of knowledges that rely on experience, memory work, and truth claims. Through these truths, I reflect on the labor process, assumptions, possibilities, and risks associated with coauthorship as a tool for mobilizing intellectual spaces in which stories from multiple locations in an alliance can speak with one another.

Unfolding Stories and Stages

In the San Francisco meetings of the Association of American Geographers (AAG) in 2007, Geraldine Pratt organized an "Authors Meet Critics" panel for *Playing with Fire/Sangtin Yatra*. Sangtin saw Gerry Pratt's invitation to the 2007 AAG as an opportunity to advance our alliance work, and two of the eight activist coauthors, Surbala and Richa Singh, traveled from Sitapur to San Francisco to attend this panel.

Surbala's and Richa Singh's five-week-long trip to the United States was marked by difficult conversations and painful reflections on subjects and languages of—and hierarchies in—knowledge making as well as efforts to rethink the dominant meanings of fieldwork in academia and in the "women's empowerment" sector of the development establishment. Surbala, Richa Singh, and I kept diaries during those five weeks of traveling through academic and activist spaces in Minnesota, California, and New York, and these reflections laid the foundation of our second book in Hindi, *Ek Aur Neemsaar*, which was published in January 2012 in India (Nagar and Singh et al. 2012). *Ek Aur Neemsaar* is a diary of the making of SKMS in the aftermath of the debates triggered by *Sangtin Yatra*. With this quick backdrop, I first share a translated section of *Ek Aur Neemsaar* that begins with an excerpt from Surbala's diary and then shifts to third-person narration. I then describe an event that followed the reading of this excerpt in Sitapur.

> We were headed to Syracuse. As soon as I walked through the security check, the machine shrieked in the same way that it had done in New Delhi and Amsterdam. The culprits were my bangles and anklets. . . . The anklets came off, but the glass bangles with iron rims were impossible to take off—they had been on my wrists for nineteen years. I passed the check point after the usual drama, but for the rest of the trip I kept worrying, "How often will I have to deal with this? These bangles will draw me in the circle of suspicion each time we travel somewhere."
>
> The bangles became a barrier in my way . . . I recalled in that instant how once a gender trainer from the city interrogated us in Mahila Samakhya for putting sindur in our hair.[2] Sindur, she claimed, was symbolic of patriarchy. In some branches of Mahila Samakhya village-level workers were prevented from putting on sindur. But in Sitapur, we refused to comply with this expectation because we believed that it was a form of ideological exploitation. Sindur and bangles give us tremendous respect in the places we come from. So why should we give these up simply because they are deemed unfeminist by our gender trainers?
>
> —from Surbala's U.S. diary, April 2007

In Syracuse, Surbala cut her iron-rimmed bangles after nineteen years and left the pieces in the hotel's trash. Someone who was a witness to all this could argue, perhaps, that it was easy for Surbala to get rid of her bangles because she was in a place where her bangles carried no meaning. But for Surbala, whose identity as a woman was intertwined with these bangles for almost two decades of her marriage, it was a huge mental struggle to convince herself that the removal of bangles was critical for her to make the rest of her path smoother. If someone had pressured her to remove her bangles and anklets because these would cause problems along the way, Surbala would have considered such a pressure as "ideological exploitation."[3] As Surbala points out, "Arriving at the conviction that those bangles had to be cut and discarded had to be my own journey. In pretty much the same way as a butterfly must find its own strength to break its cocoon. Only then, will the butterfly be strong enough to reach its full flight" (Surbala's U.S. diary, April 2007). In other words, unwanted assistance in breaking its "cocoon" can be a curse for the butterfly.

Those who swear by the label "feminism," as well as those who trash it, are often guilty of equating feminism with an already cooked recipe of ideas and positions. Many of these people assume that feminist practices can be widely found among educated, urban, salaried women and that these women are capable of empowering another category of women who are dalit, exploited, and subordinated. What are the issues of these supposedly subordinated women? How must they be empowered? How should they form their relationships with their lovers, husbands, mothers-in-law, sons, and daughters? The solutions associated with these questions often sit in canned forms on all the so-called feminist shelves. Expert feminists will not be able to listen to our movements unless they are prepared to throw out these canned assumptions en masse and restock their shelves with a new approach to feminism. Our companion Kamala from Khanpur Village finds it imperative to resist the language of those women's NGOs that repeatedly tell her to prove her credentials as an "empowered" woman: "If you are truly empowered, go fight your man for your half of the bread!" Kamala retorts: "Which half of my roti should I fight for when my family's access to any roti at all is gravely endangered? Fighting for half a roti is meaningless for me in the absence of a struggle for the whole roti."

The original Hindi version of the above excerpt, along with two other passages, was read at the book launch of *Ek Aur Neemsaar* in Sitapur on 5 January 2012. On a cold, foggy day, the event was attended by 250 people, approximately half of whom were members of SKMS and another half were residents of Sitapur, with a handful of activists and public intellectuals visiting from Lucknow. At the end of the event, Aparna (alias), a feminist theater activist and consultant from Lucknow who knew Surbala well from past training exercises and meetings of MSS, immediately sought out Surbala and asked sarcastically: "So Surbalaji, when are you going to break your bangles again?"

Surbala was hurt by the way in which Aparna used their past intimacy to pose this question, which mocked the critique of mainstream feminism and NGOized empowerment projects that Surbala and other sangtins have tirelessly articulated. But she replied in a level tone: "Why should I break my bangles twice? I will do something else that will surprise you." As Surbala recounted this incident to her coworkers in SKMS, she noted how the demands of her family and her work had kept her away from her writing, and how this encounter reminded her of her own ability to powerfully articulate critiques of mainstream feminist assumptions and platforms.

In their everyday confrontations with mainstream discourses of development and empowerment, Surbala and other saathis of the movement "write," theorize, and rethink power in profoundly complex ways. In so doing, they create knowledge that cannot be easily captured by available vocabularies and frameworks. Surbala's reply to Aparna indicates this alternative vocabulary, yet the exchange also triggered in Surbala a restlessness and guilt (for not writing) that suggest a deep contradiction. Surbala's recognition of her own ability to write in ink (even as her circumstances prevent her from doing so), makes it impossible for her to not be attracted to the possibility of translating her knowledge into a language that can be understood by the likes of Aparna. One could argue that Surbala's sense of guilt (re)legitimizes and reinforces the elevated status of formal writing that most of her fellow saathis cannot claim or participate in. Surbala's desire to engage through writing is inseparable from the manner in which formal knowledge production affects the conditions under which she and her saathis live. Yet, the collective struggle of SKMS is one where that which can be written in ink must necessarily converse with that which cannot be written in ink. And Surbala understands this in poignant ways.

This story helps me articulate four interrelated and interdependent truths about coauthoring tales through alliance work. Although my discussion builds on previously referenced conversations in feminisms, these truths relate to a wide range of collaborative efforts that seek to enact horizontal forms of solidarity in achieving transformation.

Four Truths about Coauthoring Tales in Feminist Alliance Work

> Money is a minor part of what we call "transformative work." It
> is the power of collective social experience and feeling, which
> actually turns naked hills into lush greenery.
> —Rajendra Singh, activist

In his chair's address at the book launch of *Ek Aur Neemsaar*, Arun Trivedi, the director of Hindi Sabha in Sitapur, described the book as "a true story of the churnings of sangtins' soul and the making of their movement" (Trivedi 2012).[4] He elaborated on the nature of this truth:

> This tale connects us with the social truth of our unfolding present. This truth is one that is lived intimately by the poor in our villages and one that is revealed to them as they experience and struggle with [state violence in the name of development]. This is not to say that this book simply narrates or describes; essentially, in presenting the picture of a happening condition, the book goes further than a truth that has been seen, felt and experienced, to give a literary character to a truth of doing. Here, Radha's words [from *Sangtin Yatra* that are revisited in *Ek Aur Neemsaar*] are profoundly moving; the passage [recalling her words] states: "There is a huge difference in bearing a deep sorrow or humiliation on the one hand, and feeling it on the other." Essentially, this book is constituted by the struggles of those who have borne these experiences. (Trivedi 2012)

I quote from Trivedi's speech because of the delicate manner in which his emphasis on the "truth of doing" and "social truth" links praxis with experience while simultaneously connecting both of these to authorship, representation, and political struggle. It is in the same spirit that I deploy and claim some "truths" here—to highlight the nature, significance, and unfolding of those knowledges that can be *enabled* and *authored* only through a collective commitment to recognize the mutually inseparable nature of doing, feeling, representing, theorizing, and dreaming in alliance work. To summarize loosely, the first truth underscores an always-evolving praxis of translation that is guided by love. The second emphasizes a shared politics, while the third highlights the necessity of staging truths in alliance work. The fourth truth returns us to the theme of radical vulnerability in alliance work.

The First Truth

The meanings of Surbala's encounter with Aparna will most likely be lost unless the story is embedded in the ten-year journey of an alliance from the writing of *Sangtin Yatra* to its translation and circulation as *Playing with Fire* and from there to the making of *Ek Aur Neemsaar* and its launch in Sitapur. The process of making knowledge about a single event is often informed by complex journeys, translations, and relationships in an alliance, and this process can itself inspire ever-evolving agendas and visions while refusing compartmentalization of research from pedagogy, of academic from activist labor, of theorizing from organizing. In this expansive and syncretic understanding of coauthorship as alliance work that moves through and across different contexts and spaces, coauthorship does not merely include the work of writing but the ways that writing is informed—and coauthored—by all the processes and events undertaken by those in an alliance. Committed alliance work is about building multifaceted relationships through trust; it is about how we engage difference, disagreements, mistakes, and dissonance—or, the "wounds and fissures" that mark the collective "we" (Nagar 2006a, xxxiv–xxxv). This is a process where the possibility of becoming a "community"—with all its strengths and shortcomings—is only realizable through a commitment to becoming radically vulnerable together. The labor of carrying out this commitment, this love, is never purely intellectual or political; it consumes the mind, the muscles, the tissues, and the bones. Tinsely, Chatterjea, Gibney, and Wilcox articulate the demands of this labor with reference to their work in Ananya Dance Theatre:

> we were literally working with water; we, northern-living brown women were figuratively working with fluidity. this is a woman of color dance troupe, and central to its vision are artistic excellence, political awareness and community, and creating these across lines of race, ethnicity, and sexuality to perform meaningfully post-colonially. if i brought my stumbling ankles back day after day it was because

this pan-brown fluidity was not only inspiring but necessary, absolutely necessary to being whole and present here in this place northern europeans violently robbed first from the dakota, then the ojibwe, and that they imagine as "their" own land (not water). . . . but to work with this figurative fluidity is also hard. what does our work of bridging colors, religions, races, sexualities mean? what does it mean to imagine being "minorities" together? . . . figurative fluidity is hard, and i know this as materially as i know the heaviness of a bucket of water. . . . but the solution to this unevenness can't be eliminating fluidity, can't be throwing over attempts to organize in multicolored, multigendered ways in favor of organizing . . . around a single identity. much as i and my co-dancers might long for a dry, smooth stage some days, as if that were possible with all our sweat. no. the solution can only be no solution, can only be maintaining tension between what rushes us together and what flows us apart, returning endlessly to negotiate this balancing act and then re-negotiate it and re-negotiate it again. as rinaldo walcott . . . puts it: "what is demanded is a rethinking of community that might allow for different ways of cohering into some form of recognizable political entity. put another way, we must confront singularities without the willed effort to make them cohere into oneness; we must struggle to make a community of singularities . . ." singularities that roil and clash and teem with life like the spaces where currents meet: because jumping in here you know it will hurt and you know it will be hard but it will be movement, this, putting pressure on water means movement. (Tinsely et al. 2010, 162–64)

If alliance work can be imagined as dance choreography, then coauthorship in alliance work is precisely about building singularities that roil and clash and teem with life. And whether expressed in words or in motion, coauthorship in alliance work is about a continuous and creative tension between the original and the translated so that the definitions and forms of what counts as "original" and what counts as "translated" are themselves in motion. This leads me to my first truth:

Coauthored stories are continuously evolving in and through all the sites of struggle that are part of the alliance. These coauthored tales of alliances are constituted by people who build multifaceted bonds through dreams, dissonance, affect, and trust, and who make and sustain movements through everyday relationships, emotional investments, and creative skills. Translations enabled by these bonds lie at the heart of these coauthored tales: What emerges from and gets debated and articulated in one location gets translated for another location into another language, and the critiques and insights emerging in all the locations inform the revisions and refining of ideas, positions, strategies, and arguments. In these always evolving translations, the solution can only be no solution. For, reaching a solution means the end of fluidity—the end of that which roils, clashes, and throbs with life.

The Second Truth

In a 2008 essay, Ruth Wilson Gilmore tells us about places that have experienced the abandonment characteristic of contemporary capitalist and neoliberal state reorganization. She draws attention to the resourcefulness of people in these locales who—despite the daily violence of environmental degradation, racism, underemployment, overwork, shrinking social wages, and the disappearance of whole ways of life *and* of those who lived them—refuse to give up hope (Gilmore 2008, 32). If identities change in and through action and struggle, asks Gilmore, what sort of political-economic and cultural projects can highlight the structural and lived relationships between marginal people and marginal lands in both urban and rural contexts and inspire residents in these locales to explore ways in which they can "scale up their activism from intensely localized struggles to something less atomized and therefore possessed of a significant capacity for self-determination" and "life-affirming social change" (Gilmore 2008, 31)? She proposes a *syncretic* approach to research and activism that offers provisional resolutions to contradictions and challenges by engaging problems, theories, and questions in terms of "their stretch, resonance, and resilience." Similar to Rege's vision of Phule-Ambedkarite feminist pedagogy, Gilmore (2008, 37–38) envisions such syncretic practices as having the ability to garner unpredictable energies through collective action to reach further than the immediate object without bypassing its particularity (stretch); support and model nonhierarchical collective action without necessarily adhering to already existing architectures of sense making (resonance); and enable questions to be malleable rather than brittle, so that the project can remain connected with its purpose, even as it encounters and engages the unexpected (resilience). This brings me to the second truth:

If politically engaged scholarship begins with a politics of recognition and intentionally grapples with the ways that such scholarship can help to produce the new realities that it is fighting for, then coauthoring stories is one way of working across sociopolitical, cultural, and institutional locations, languages, and histories to do this grappling. In so doing, such stories can forge generative connections across struggles while remaining grounded in their soil. Although trust is essential to enable any coauthored knowledge or storytelling, trustful relationships—in the absence of intentional grappling with specific political questions and shared political agenda—do not translate automatically into alliance work.

The Third Truth

The next truth revolves around the theme of representation. Everybody represents somebody in politically engaged alliance work. This means that an individualistic conception of leadership and representation—that is, the idea that movements can only be represented by leaders who speak on behalf of the rank and file and that knowledge created by a movement can only be authorized by a person who makes it intelligible through one's written words or access to publicity—must be complicated by those who want to conceptualize and enact collaborative movements and alliances across borders.

If movement making and knowledge making are fluid and always evolving, then the task of representation cannot conclude. When a movement such as SKMS explicitly recognizes that everybody who participates in a struggle must be forever attentive to their task as a representer, such recognition also challenges those who are "grounded" primarily in the academy to constantly rethink the relationship between authorship of words and authorship of struggles. For example, I might represent Surbala in this chapter while Surbala might represent her encounters with U.S.-based academics and activists in conversations that she participates in on various activist platforms. Similarly, she might represent SKMS's saathis such as Tama and Manohar in a confrontation with the chief development officer (CDO) of Sitapur; Tama might represent the CDO in a song that he sings at a rally; and we all might represent SKMS in multiple fora. In all these instances, each one of us is required to make tough decisions about which stories, experiences, vulnerabilities, or disagreements we can politicize and circulate; and which and whose complicities with violence we can share, when, why, how, and for whom.

As a movement that wants to be leaderless, SKMS is continuously trying to evolve practices that resist the idea of a single identifiable leader or representer of the saathis' struggle in any given context. For instance, if there is a protest at the district development headquarters, a well-established practice of SKMS is that nobody keeps the microphone in their own hands for more than five minutes, so that it keeps moving from one person to another. And when the district development officer asks the Sangathan to send a representative to his office for negotiations, the saathis decline: "No one person can represent the movement. You come out of your office and talk to all of us, because all of us are representatives of the movement." Thus, the movement strives to keep alive its commitment that everybody who is engaged in the struggle must also reflect on her or his task as a representer. In so doing, it pushes us to rethink the dominant meanings of author and authorship.

After winning the battle against the director of MSUP (see chapter 5), the six authors of *Sangtin Yatra* who were still employed by MS not only continued their jobs there, they also received promotions and significant raises.[5] The demands on their energy as well as their personal circumstances led them to decide that they could no longer participate in the movement-building work of SKMS. However, two years later, when SKMS began to earn social and political recognition in Sitapur, these six authors expressed an interest in becoming full-time members of SKMS. If they quit their jobs in MS and became a part of SKMS, they asked, would SKMS give them honoraria similar to what they were making in MS? As founders of Sangtin who wrote *Sangtin Yatra*, the six women felt that they should always have a space in SKMS, and that such space should be accompanied by monetary compensation. But the stance of five thousand or so members of SKMS at that time was that since SKMS had no donor funds, every saathi should volunteer at least six months of their full-time labor to movement building. After that, the movement would try to provide some monetary compensation to those members with whatever resources it had. In other words, there was no privileged place for the authors of the book *Sangtin Yatra* because several thousand others had become authors of the everyday struggles that were unfolding in the villages of Sitapur.

The publication of *Playing with Fire* may have been critical at the time when the authors of *Sangtin Yatra* were attacked by the director of MSUP; beyond that, however, *Playing with Fire* did not carry much meaning for a vast majority of the members of the movement evolving in Sitapur. The meanings that the controversy around *Sangtin Yatra* acquired were important for mobilizing people initially, but in some ways, the written word ceased to be relevant as soon as the struggle for irrigation water started. There is a strong tendency in academia to reduce the meanings of coauthorship and coauthored texts to the printed word. In order to imagine collaborations as alliances that might enable critical transformation in multiple sites of knowledge making, however, we must ponder how coauthorship is about the varied dimensions of a struggle, not all of which can one attempt to capture through the written word. It also requires us to be attentive to how different members of a movement theorize their own responsibility as coauthors and representers of a struggle in different contexts.

Sometimes this representation involves difficult choices that may not meet the approval of audiences in all the sites where the stories of sangtins' journeys may be traveling. For example, the absence of Richa Singh's and my own autobiographical narratives in the book *Sangtin Yatra* raised a question for some academic readers about whether this choice inadvertently reinforced something similar to a sawaran-dalit dichotomy where the two "more-privileged" Richas became the representers of the seven "less-privileged" diary writers, Anupamlata, Ramsheela, Reshma, Shashibala, Shashi, Surbala, and Vibha. When graduate students in feminist studies at Minnesota posed a similar question in 2007 to Surbala, Richa Singh, and me, Richa Singh and I accepted this as a valid critique, even though the incorporation of our stories would have made it a different kind of book. Surbala however, regarded the critique as disrespectful attitude of elite readers toward the collective's decision to not include the diaries of the two Richas. She stated that the repeated posing of—as well as the assumptions associated with—this critique were similar to the attitude of the bank officers in the villages of Sitapur who tell poor women that they cannot open a bank account in their own name unless they can prove their trustworthiness by presenting a bank passbook issued in the name of their husbands. Surbala said, "Why do the seven diary writers need the stories of Richa Singh and Richa Nagar to authorize our own stories? Why can't the collective's decision to present only seven stories in the book be respected as *a collective decision*?"

There is much that can be said about this last example. For the present purpose, however, I would like to suggest that the meanings of struggles that shape collective writing cannot be fully apparent to its readers in multiple locations, nor can the implications of that writing be predicted by the writers in advance. On the one hand, the discursive, political, and strategic requirements of the kind of alliance work that SKMS represents make it necessary for the authors to maintain some control over their intellectual, theoretical, and creative coproduction. On the other hand, the meanings and effects of SKMS's coproduction are always unfolding. In the same way that there is an intimate back and forth between the authoring of the words and the authoring of the struggles, alliance work also demands a continuous decentering and recentering of the writers, the readers, the actors, and the spectators in a delicate dance where theory, story, and strategy are deeply entangled, mutually co-constitutive, and thoroughly inseparable. Furthermore, that which is written—and that which remains unwritten—hold different meanings for, and give different kinds of power to, differently situated members of an alliance at different times. Alliance-based coauthorship derives its radical potential from its ability to mobilize spaces for both legitimized and hitherto erased (or invisible) critiques to speak with one another, so that they can evolve into more nuanced critical interventions in multiple sites. A multisited dialogue that is grounded in a political struggle should allow people from each of those sites to be aware of how their circumstances and strategies are articulating with those in other sites, and what that articulation is enabling or stifling in each site. Thus, my third truth is as follows:

Since coauthored tales in alliance work selectively mobilize experience for particular political ends, the labor of the writer, translator, and academic hinges on how s/he reduces and expands stories and silences in relation to context and audience. In this sense, all activism can be likened to political theater, and those responsible for the labor of writing must continuously make ethical decisions about the relationship between the conversations happening in the backstage and the content that is to be presented on the front stage based on the political terrain of a given context and audience (Shank and Nagar 2013). This labor of back and front staging is as much about making political choices (e.g., which stories should be circulated for whom) as it is about making theoretical choices about how to tell—and how not to tell—the stories that are necessary to share. Because of this selective mobilization of experience and frontstaging and backstaging of politi-

cal conversations, the possibilities, potentialities, and labors of coauthorship are always in process. The written text alone is too limited to apprehend the complex intersections among feminist subject, subjectivity, and organizing; or the work that is enabled by the authors' engagements with difference at particular histori- cal and political moments. The written text is also unable to adequately capture the resonances of these engagements in the multiple sites where alliance-based knowledges and arguments are interpreted, consumed, contested, or reshaped into other knowledges.

The Fourth Truth

If structures of oppression and subordination are legitimized through profes- sions, that is, cults of expertise that have the power to create knowledge and to selectively empower or devalue knowledges, then the kind of coauthoring I am arguing for asks that alliance workers simultaneously trouble this picture in multiple sites. It demands interventions through which academic knowledges and vocabularies can be troubled by knowledges emerging from sites that are systematically excluded, illegitimized, or rendered invisible in the dominant class system of the intellect—interventions that push predefined assumptions and boundaries of what is legitimized as important knowledge.

To a certain extent, each member of an alliance has to ethically navigate her responsibility as an independent critic and as a member of a collective; but this necessary negotiation between the "I" and the "we" can often become more delicate and demanding for the academic, especially if the academic has the primary responsibility of narrating and translating the alliance's struggles for audiences located in very different worlds. Rigor in this work, then, demands delicate negotiations between the "I" and the "we," which in turn require ongo- ing reciprocities and investments rooted in trust and in shared commitments that may themselves undergo continuous revision.

At the same time, this kind of alliance work requires each member of the collective to be skeptical of the increasing professionalization of our political and intellectual labor. For example, many feminists have critiqued the ways in which the professionalization of feminism through the academy, NGO circles, the media, and mainstream politics aids the translation of our intellectual and political stances into marketable commodities that give us name, rewards, and celebrity. As a transformative program, then, the concept and practice of coau- thorship can only be meaningful if people coming together from these different locations commit themselves to addressing these processes and their effects. If imagined and enacted in this way, coauthorship can help us to complicate multiple "fields" in relation to one another through what Susan Sánchez-Casal and Amie A. Macdonald refer to as "communities of meaning" or "knowledge making communities" (Sánchez-Casal and Macdonald 2002).

If the responsibility to represent in alliance work is an ongoing one, two questions for feminists engaged in this work are: First, how do we imagine and enact a thorough, fluid, and multisited methodology of accountability that allows us to theorize complex intersections of location and power, as well as their attendant contradictions, without seeking easy resolutions? Second, how might such a methodology articulate the accountability of the academic to the nonacademic collaborators, the accountability of the activist to the people whom s/he represents, and the accountability of both the academic and the activist to one another and to the struggles they claim to stand for?

These questions have affinities with what Naomi Scheman calls an "epistemology of trustworthiness" in the context of a crisis generated by the question of why the knowledge claims that come from inside of universities ought to be credible to those outside of—and too often alienated from—them (Scheman 2011). For Scheman, this epistemology refers to "the conditions under which it is rational to accept what others say about matters that concern you. Those conditions, require on the one hand that the institutions within which the relevant inquiry takes place are trustworthy . . . something that . . . calls for demonstrated commitments to social justice; and on the other hand that modes of inquiry involve respectful engagement with the diverse communities that are knowledgeable about the objects of that inquiry and dependent on or likely to be affected by the results of it" (Scheman 2012, 3). Rather than center these questions solely on the university, however, a methodology of accountability demands radical vulnerability. This requires all the coauthors to inspect how each of their locations might enable the conditions under which an epistemology of trustworthiness can be sustained, and what kind of intellectual and political labor might be needed to address the factors that stifle it. This brings me to my fourth truth:

As a multisited cross-border feminist engagement with questions of power, privilege, and representation, coauthorship in alliance work demands that all the authors question their own complicities with the violence of colonial histories and geographies and with capitalist relations of power, as well as their own embeddedness and investments in and relationships with institutional reward structures, markets, and celebrity cults. This questioning must be a part of an always evolving methodology of accountability that pushes each member of the alliance, individually and as part of a collective, to analyze our shifting intersectional locations and contradictions; and to confront the ways in which the institutions and organizations supporting our critical work might be themselves complicit with the forms of violence we might be opposing.

In other words, coauthoring stories in alliance work demands radical vulnerability from those who inhabit different communities of meaning, whether academia, activism, or elsewhere. If feminist alliance work is to realize its transformative

possibilities, collaborators must recognize each other as coauthors joined in rela-
tions of affect, trust, imagination, and critique, ever open to interrogation by their
collaborators, and willing to forego the putative superiority of their protocols of
understanding and sites of knowledge making. Far from weakening every differen-
tially located coauthor in the alliance, a praxis of representation and translation
that is guided by radical vulnerability gives each coauthor—and the alliance as a
whole—more courage to take risks and to continue dreaming and struggling on.

As reflections from an ongoing journey, the truths I have articulated above
are not meant to serve as final conclusions, but as points to recenter otherwise
marginalized conversations about which or whose knowledge counts, and how.
When academic truths gain their rigor through conceptual and methodological disciplining and reductionism, it is easy to declare such truths universally
replicable and verifiable. The wild, complex, irreducible contexts of lives, struggles, and relationships are often treated as irrelevant or actively shoved into the
background in the process of producing such truth claims. The truths or tales
produced through radical vulnerability and love, however, derive their richness
and nuances by actively embracing the challenges posed by such contextual
complexities. Essentially, these truths are a plea to not give up hope in the beauty,
power, and possibilities of alliance work, a point made by Tinsely, Chatterjea,
Gibney, and Wilcox: "We cannot afford to give up hope. Is that specific to the
experience of marginalization? Possibly. . . . All our projects are about hope
ultimately. . . . What enables us to dance? To dance, really? There is so much
to remind us we are dancing on other people's blood. It takes work to be able
to create that beauty as a healing force and to enjoy creating it. Building that
community and ensemble is about finding a way to let hope materialize into
energy" (Tinsely et al. 2010, 164).

It is in the spirit of continuing to find ways to let hope translate into energy
that I revisit the arguments made in this chapter through a scene of a play coauthored with members of SKMS.

Coauthoring Intersectionality and Alliance:
Aag Lagi Hai Jangal Ma

In the sweltering heat of August 2010, Bitoli and Kusuma left their villages in
Pisawan block of Sitapur District to undertake a three-hour trip to the town of
Sitapur. There, they were joined by ten more saathis of SKMS: Meena, Jamuna,
Radhapyari, Roshanlal, Manohar, Ramkishore, Sri Kishan, Anil, Surendra, and
Tama, as well as additional supporters, including Kamal, Shivam, Rajendra,
Richa Singh, and me. The women and men saathis were of different ages and
personalities and came from different villages. Some of them had been active

in SKMS for several years, while others were just beginning to get acquainted with the Sangathan's work. However, these differences were soon absorbed by an all-consuming process of remembering and retelling, of enacting and creating as we all came under one roof to work together for the next five days and nights, setting aside our preoccupations and worries, our farms and homes, and our families, parents, and children. From this process evolved SKMS's street play in Hindi and Awadhi, *Aag Lagi Hai Jangal Ma* (*The Forest Is Burning*), under the direction of Tarun Kumar (Sangtin Kisaan Mazdoor Sangathan 2011, Nagar 2013). *Aag Lagi Hai* fiercely resists a ghettoization of issues based on gender, caste, or minimum employment through an analysis of multiple forms of violence at scales ranging from the body (hunger, domestic violence, disappearing livelihoods) to the earth (disappearing forests, ever-rising mansions, pathways obstructed by polythene, overconsumption by the rich), and by embedding itself in an epistemology and framework in which the meanings of "politics" can only emerge cautiously *through struggle*.

Here I offer the prologue and the last scene of *Aag Lagi Hai* in translation, as these theorize and enact alliance through coauthorship. As each actor announces her/his own perspective, concern, or truth, s/he contributes to a fuller collective truth of the struggle that could not be realized without the process of coauthorship. The play ends with a song about a bird and an elephant and their relationship to a fire that is turning the forest into ashes. The bird symbolizes those who are relatively powerless, the elephant denotes those in more comfortable locations who are not immediately threatened by the fire, and the fire itself stands for the havoc of displacement, drought, and death caused by destructive development. Importantly, however, SKMS does not conceptualize the positions of the bird and the elephant as fixed. The same person who is a bird (and trying to extinguish the fire from a position of relative marginality) in one context may become an elephant (and fan the flames or join its trunk with the bird's beak) in another. The scene—and particularly this song—not only attests to the collective's commitment to cocreate through intersectional analyses, but also recognizes the strength that resides in acknowledging mutual vulnerability, resonating strongly with Jacqui Alexander's call to cross over into a metaphysics of interdependence (Alexander 2005).

In identifying the sociopolitical processes, practices, interests, and dependencies through which state corruption comes to inhabit and thrive in the rural development machinery, and in naming the co-constitutive relationships between the mansions of the rich and the hunger of the poor, and between the legal and the illegal, *Aag Lagi Hai* offers a commentary on the manner in which the development apparatus of the neoliberal state actively underdevelops the poor people and places in order to make the wealthy more prosperous. Particularly noteworthy is the power of the recurring line in the third scene:

कहब त लाग जाई धक्क से!
If I speak my truth, you will feel a stabbing pain!

The repeated utterance of this line—borrowed from a song sung by SKMS's member Rambeti interbraids multiple truths of the movement. In so doing, these words underscore intersectional knowledge as the core of the collective and vividly capture the resistance of SKMS saathis to the imposed categories and expertise that ensure the reproduction of the systems that serve to stifle them. These systems include the differing yet connected structures that ghettoize gender-based issues, reproduce caste politics, and repeat patterns of violence in the realm of the intimate. The movement struggles with and against the narratives (re)produced by these interconnections. The recurring line reinforces the play's engagement with knowledge production as a struggle against silences—not simply against the silences that suppress stories of hunger, poverty, and violence, and not merely against the silences that reside inside and outside the machines of development in the offices or houses of the elected representatives and salaried officials, but also against the silences that result from the absence of an analysis of those things that can never be fully known, felt, or accessed by those who live and play their power. Officials may know their projects and files, but their positions may never allow them to see or feel how corruption does not lie merely in the hands of one particular official or scheme, nor the ways in which the development of some operates through the underdevelopment of others on a systemic level. Indeed, their locations may entirely prevent them from apprehending, imagining, or analyzing the bitter truths that make the fates of the elephant and the bird inseparable.[6]

The power of the line "कहब त लाग जाई धक्क से! *If I speak my truth, you will feel a stabbing pain!*" emanates from the politics of silences and assumptions that are forced upon those who must at once absorb the system and reproduce it—with their own bodies and with their children's bodies—while their voices and stories remain necessarily absent from the narratives of the nation, democratic state, and development programs such as NREGS and Indira Awaas Yojana (Indira Housing Scheme). Saathis disrupt power by highlighting the ways in which we categorize, name, and understand the moving pieces that shape the structures of family, village, and state—both separately and in conversation with one another. Each moving piece brings its own suffering, but the collective truth that emerges from the suffering caused by all the pieces is far greater than what the officials or the elite can know or bear. Each utterance of the line "कहब त लाग जाई धक्क से! *If I speak my truth, you will feel a stabbing pain!*" reinforces the complex relationship between what is lived and what can be known: you do not know what I know, the lines can be read to say, but I spare you the knowledge of that truth because you will not be able to bear the pain of that brutal truth. Yet the truth emerges from the violence that you help to inflict upon me every day.

Because there is no singular system of power to fight or fix, the play is not simply oppositional to power. Rather, it upholds the need for creativity and strategic collaboration with the state authorities in the saathis' everyday encounters with the development machinery so that they can claim precisely those rights and entitlements that are invoked in the name of the poor in order to justify and legitimize the existence of a democratic state. In other words, *Aag Lagi Hai* offers a vision in which radical protest and intersectional critique do not entirely erase the possibilities of cooperation and alliance across difference and where the hope for solidarity is always present so that the elephant may unite with the bird to prevent the jungle from burning down.

At the same time, *Aag Lagi Hai* does not abandon the movement's responsibility to provide its own self-critique. The success and growth of SKMS in the realm of district development offices has been paralleled by painful conflicts in the homes of saathis, posing a continuous challenge in the lives of women who have embraced the movement. This reality cannot be blamed on the state's schemes and machinations and represents other "schemes" that also serve to replicate the structures of domination and subordination. The play grapples with this question as one of gendered violence, while being careful to not minimize or glamorize it, or to turn it into a spectacle. Ultimately, the play is cautious not to celebrate SKMS's own achievements; in building connections across spaces and issues, it recognizes its own limits, absences, and gaps, as well as the fact that the journey has barely begun.

Prologue to the Play

Tama leads the saathis with his song:

> जब दिल की कोठरिया साफ नहीं तब गंगा नहाये से का होई?
> मन की गाड़ी, ज्ञान का इन्जन, ड्राइवर कहाये से क्या होई?
> एक्सीडेन्ट जब हुई गवा, तो हारन दबाये से का होई?
> जब दिल की कोठरिया साफ नहीं तब गंगा नहाये से का होई?
>
> ख्यात गयो खरिहान गयो, पीछे पछताये का होई?
> जब ख्यात चिरैया चुनि गई तब डण्डा हलाये से का होई?
> जब दिल की कोठरिया साफ नहीं तब गंगा नहाये से का होई?
>
> पंच बने, परधान बने, सी.डी.ओ. कहाये से का होई?
> जब सारा पैसा खाय गये, तब कलम चलाये से का होई?
> जब दिल की कोठरिया साफ नहीं तब गंगा नहाये से का होई?
>
> बी.डी.ओ. बने, डी.डी.ओ. बने, फिर डी.एम. कहाये से का होई?
> जब जनता आफिस आय गई, तब कलम चलाये से का होई?
> जब दिल की कोठरिया साफ नहीं तब गंगा नहाये से का होई?

When the heart is filthy, what will come from taking a dip in the Ganga?
Heart is the car, knowledge is the engine; what's the point of being called the driver?
When the accident has already happened, what's the point of pressing the horn?
When the heart is filthy, what will come from taking a dip in the Ganga?

The field is gone, the farm is gone, why regret the loss now?
The birds have already fed on the crop, why swing the baton now?
When the heart is filthy, what will come from taking a dip in the Ganga?

You may become a Panch or a Pradhan, you may be called a CDO.
When you have eaten all the money, what's the point of wasting ink now?
When the heart is filthy, what will come from taking a dip in the Ganga?

You may be a BDO, you may be a DDO, or you could be the DM.
What's the point of issuing new orders when the protesting people are at your door?
When the heart is filthy, what will come from taking a dip in the Ganga?

Scene 3

Meena: [asks the audience] Can deflating one officer truly end state corruption?

Sri Kishan: *Arey*, how will this corruption end? Don't we know how deep its roots are and how widely their tentacles are spread?
With a beat of the *dholak*, all recite the following line:
कहब त लाग जाई धक्क से!
If I speak my truth, you will feel a stabbing pain!

Roshan: Look at the state of our schools—whether it's the midday meal, or whether it's the state of education.

Kusuma: The porridge that comes to the Anganwadis[7] is sold away for pennies. The porridge that is given for the children of the poor is actually eaten by the animals of the rich.

Jamuna: And what can I say about the government hospitals? Sometimes it's the doctor who is missing, and at others it's the medicines.
कहब त लाग जाई धक्क से!
If I speak my truth, you will feel a stabbing pain!

Surendra: Thousands of liters of water are pumped in and out of swimming pools in the cities. In the Gomtinagars of Lucknow and the Vasant Kunjs of Delhi, electricity is supplied round the clock. If we can get access to all that electricity and water, we can produce loads after loads of wheat and rice.

Anil: So many of us don't even have a tiny farm. In the registers of the government, the entitlement is in our name, but the real control is in someone else's hands.

Manohar: It's not as if the fields of those who control their own lands are
   blooming, anyway. The mazdoors and kisaans suffer beatings of the stick
   in order to get access to a little bit of fertilizer!
Ramkishore: How can we ever get the fertilizer? We don't even have the
   Kisaan Bahi.
   कहब त लाग जाई धक्क से!
   If I speak my truth, you will feel a stabbing pain!
Tama: The salaries of the central government folks have increased. The legislators and the members of the parliament give themselves raises every other
   day. But how much has our daily wage increased in proportion to theirs?
   Roshan sings with a beat on the *dholak*:
   मँहगाई हमका मारै डारे सुनो गरीबन भइया!
   Inflation is killing me, listen my companions in poverty!
Roshan: [with another beat on the *dholak*] What can I say? For two years
   now, I have not tasted *arhar dal*. Tomatoes are forty rupees per kilo. What
   can we get in the wages of a hundred rupees a day? If you and I won't die
   of disease and hunger, then who will?
Sri Kishan: Have you encountered a single *dhaba* in Piswan or Sitapur where
   our children are not seen washing the dishes?
   कहब त लाग जाई धक्क से!
   If I speak my truth, you will feel a stabbing pain!
Tama: Our well-wishers at the top may or may not increase our wages, but
   they certainly make sure that there are plenty of shops at every intersection to supply us with gutka, bidi, and liquor.
Ramkishore: If the hungry worker drinks the government's liquor, the government is happy and its liquor becomes legal. But if we make our own
   liquor, the police raids our homes!
   कहब त लाग जाई धक्क से!
   If I speak my truth, you will feel a stabbing pain!
Manohar: All of this agony makes sense only if we can save this earth of ours.
   Hardly a downpour happens and every town, every city seems to be on
   the brink of flooding. And why wouldn't it flood? These enormous roads
   and mansions have swallowed our trees and forests.
Meena: Wherever you look, polythene and plastic are obstructing our paths.
   The *kumhars* in our villages are dead.
   कहब त लाग जाई धक्क से!
   If I speak my truth, you will feel a stabbing pain!
Bitoli: *Arey*, all these tears and complaints of ours have gone on for decades.
   No matter which government comes or goes, the poor continue to be
   subjected to the same old games. Policies and programs are run in our
   names; research and analyses are conducted in our names, but it's the

Photo 10. Bitoli poses a question to the audience of *Aag Lagi Hai Jangal Ma*. Mishrikh Tehsil Office, 2013. (Photo: Tarun Kumar)

mansions of the rich that become taller. And it's not as if these owners of big mansions who live on our sweat and blood reside only in Mishrikh and Pisawan—they are spread all over the world. Whether it's Lucknow or Delhi, whether it's Israel or America!

Anil: Tell me one more thing. The drama that we saw in the home of Kamala and Ramautar—which grand scheme did that drama belong to? Don't think that such dramas happen only in our huts. In the big mansions, there are even bigger dramas between women and men.

Radhapyari: *Baap re baap*. This is not a drama. This is a fire. A massive fire that will engulf us all.

The whole group sings with Manohar and Tama:

आग लगी है जंगल मां
चिड़िया आग बुझाय रही
हाथी खड़ा तमाशा देखे
हाथी खड़ा तमाशा देखे
यत्ती बात समझ ना पावे
चिड़िया आग बुझाय रही

जंगल जरी तो ओहू ना बचिहे
अपना गर्व देखाय रहे
लेकर चिड़िया चोंच में पानी
जंगल आग बुझाय रही।
हाथी अगर न आग बुझाई
चिड़िया के संग जरि–मरि जाई।

There is a fire in the jungle, the bird is extinguishing the fire.
The elephant looks on. He just looks on.
The elephant does not understand, it's the bird who is extinguishing the fire.
When the jungle burns, he will burn, too. But he is preoccupied with his own pride.
Filling water in her little beak, the bird carries on fighting the fire.
If the elephant does not join in, he will also burn with the bird.

These songs, these fragments of *Aag Lagi Hai Jangal Ma*, are among the last words that I offer in *Muddying the Waters*. Like all other translated fragments and journeys that make this book, my attempt to translate these fragments—however inadequately—is entangled with small hopes. A hope that you, the reader, will be moved by them so that the spirit of *Aag Lagi Hai Jangal Ma* can reverberate more broadly in everyday struggles with molding, consuming, and sharing knowledge and truths. A hope that these fragmented translations can inspire us to embrace the risk of continuously decentering ourselves and of making ourselves radically vulnerable—as writers and readers, as teachers and learners, as artists and alliance workers, as members of our families and communities, as knowledge makers. A hope that the boatperson will have a reason to want to save the pundit's life. A hope that we can appreciate the co-constitutiveness and conviviality of theories, stories, and strategies, as well as the love and radical vulnerability that make this imagination possible.

Notes

Introducing *Muddying the Waters*

1. The affective turn in feminist and queer studies, and the humanities in general, has stressed the need to address the impasse or political fatigue of poststructuralist theory by studying the relationships of the emotions and of the sensorial and the embodied to the social and political. These conversations, however, have remained largely segregated from dialogues around ethics and methodologies of alliance work and around questions of solidarity and responsibility in border crossings.

2. For a thought-provoking discussion on the need to retain a commitment to scholarly objectivity, see Kamala Visweswaran 2011.

3. Situated solidarities also have affinities with the work of scholars such as Anjali Arondekar (2009), Lauren Berlant (2011), and Elizabeth Povinelli (2006), who theorize the complex relationships between self and other and underscore the need to formulate more context-specific politics of emotion, collaboration, and responsibility.

4. For an elaboration of Carole Boyce Davies's discussion of critical relationality, see her chapter, "Negotiating Theories or 'Going a Piece of the Way with Them.'"

5. I am grateful to Elakshi Kumar, who first used the term "academic memoir" to describe this project, which I found useful in giving *Muddying the Waters* its final shape.

6. Sangtin Kisaan Mazdoor Sangathan (SKMS, also referred to at times in this book as "Sangathan" or movement) can be translated as Sangtin Peasants and Laborers Organization. SKMS currently works in Mishrikh, Pisawan, and Reusa development blocks of Sitapur District in the Indian state of Uttar Pradesh. The struggles of approximately six thousand members of SKMS, spread in seventy villages of the district, have focused on issues of access to livelihood and fair payment; access to irrigation waters; caste-, class-, and gender-based violence; and on linking processes of intellectual empowerment and disempowerment with those that constitute socioeconomic and political empowerment and disempowerment. More than half of SKMS's members are women, and over 95 percent are dalit.

7. Desiree Lewis's incisive comments on sangtins' diary have helped me to articulate my points here and in the next paragraph.

8. Deborah Gould defines affect as the "body's ongoing and relatively amorphous inventory-taking of coming into contact and interacting with the world" (Gould 2009, 23). It includes the bodily, sensory, inarticulate, and non-conscious experience that may escape us and our languages, "but is nevertheless in play, generated through interaction with the world, and affecting our embodied beings and subsequent actions." Attending to the affective, then, is a way to preserve a space for human political action and inaction that may be "nonconscious, noncognitive, nonlinguistic, noncoherent, nonrational, and unpredetermined" (23). While privileging affect runs the danger of obscuring and leaving unresolved democratic commitments to the principle of participation by all affected interests (see Barnett 2008), I agree with Pratt that "feelings or affect are not at odds with, and need not replace, nuanced thought or critical democratic politics" (Pratt 2012, xxx).

9. Dia Da Costa, "The Good Women of Chharanagar," under review for inclusion in *Budhan Theatre*, edited by Dakxin Bajrange and Ganesh Devy (Baroda: Purva Prakashan).

10. This has parallels with Stuart Hall's elaboration of a Marxism without guarantees. Hall reminds us of how ideological categories are developed and generated out of given materials and transformed according to their own laws of development and evolution, and also of the necessary openness of historical development to practice and struggle. Arguing for a need to acknowledge the real indeterminacy of the political, Hall states: "Understanding 'determinacy' in terms of setting of limits, the establishment of parameters, the defining of the space of operations, the concrete conditions of existence, the 'givenness' of social practices, rather than in terms of the absolute predictability of particular outcomes, is the only basis of a 'marxism without final guarantees.' It establishes the open horizon of marxist theorizing—determinacy without guaranteed closures. . . . Certainty stimulates orthodoxy, the frozen rituals and intonation of already witnessed truth. . . . It represents the end of the process of theorizing, of the development and refinement of new concepts and explanations which, alone, is the sign of a living body of thought, capable still of engaging and grasping something of the truth about new historical realities" (Hall 1996, 45).

Chapter 1. Translated Fragments, Fragmented Translations

The epigraph to this chapter is by Katyayani, a poet and activist based in Uttar Pradesh. This poem appears in her *Footpath Par Kursi*.

1. Tarun Kumar and I wrote "Theater of Hopes" at the invitation of Mary Thomas and Christian Abrahamsson for *Environment and Planning D: Society and Space*. A freelance actor, director, and writer, Tarun Kumar is based in Mumbai and frequently works with SKMS. "Theater of Hopes" was inspired by Tarun Kumar's diary in Hindi, where he reflected on the theater workshops that he and I organized in Sitapur and Minneapolis in 2007 and 2008.

2. Several of the "fragments" that appear in this column were originally shared with Piya Chatterjee in the two long letters that I wrote to her between December 2010 and June 2011.

3. The faculty matters and promotion and tenure files mentioned in this paragraph are associated with the responsibilities that I was carrying out at that time in my capacity as associate dean for faculty in the College of Liberal Arts at the University of Minnesota.

4. Adrienne Rich, "North American Time," 1983. The complete poem can be found at http://macaulay.cuny.edu/eportfolios/smonte10/files/2010/08/North-American-Time .pdf, accessed 8 March 2014.

5. Gayatri Chakravorty Spivak 2000b, 370.

6. Babli is my sister's nickname.

7. I wrote the original Hindi poem in response to a poem that Bhashwati wrote and shared with me in 2003. I initially translated it into English in 2012. In September 2013, Elakshi Kumar revised the translation.

8. My poem, "Dar es Salaam ke Naam" was translated into English by Raza Mir and published as "For Dar es Salaam" in *South Asian Magazine for Action and Reflection* (winter/spring 2001): 19.

9. My joint family included my paternal grandparents and Baba; my paternal uncle and his wife and son; and my parents and siblings.

10. The term *bhangi* is casteist. At the same time, it specifies the continuing dehumanization to which members of this caste are subjected. It is to mark this specificity, and to show the subtle and non-subtle ways in which this casteism and untouchability endure, that I use this label here.

11. *Mochi*, like *bhangi*, is a casteist term; see previous note.

12. This was an interview that this collective of scholar activists conducted with me in February 2011 for *Kültür ve Siyasette Feminist Yaklaşımlar* (Feminist Approaches in Culture and Politics, www.feministyaklasimlar.org), an online e-journal published quarterly in Turkey since October 2006.

13. In fall 2012, for example, a teacher from a New York high school invited me to a Skype meeting with her twelfth-grade English literature students, who were preparing to visit West Bengal later in the academic year. The teacher had assigned *Playing with Fire* so that the students could understand "gender issues in India." Throughout the session, the teacher and the students remained preoccupied with such topics as untouchability, female infanticide, and oppression of rural Indian women. Far from engaging with the ways in which the sangtins complicated these topics in conjunction with the violence of NGOization as well as the role played by educated experts who think they know rural women's issues in the global south, the group insisted on deploying the dominant discourse on violated Indian women and how NGOs can help in their so-called emancipation.

14. Lini Wollenburg, David Edmunds, and Chesha Wettasinha, 2013, invitation letter to Rambeti to attend a workshop, Climate Change, Innovation and Gender, in Phnom Penh, Cambodia, 28 April-1 May 2013. Issued by Prolinnova and Climate Change, Agriculture and Food Security, 3 January.

Chapter 2. Dar es Salaam

1. Social places are constituted and reconstituted in a space that is formed by the coexistence of social interrelations and interactions at all geographical scales. A place,

then, is made out of a particular set of social relations interacting at a particular location (Massey 1992a, 1992b).

2. While life stories took anywhere between five hours to several days to record, shorter interviews usually lasted less than three hours.

3. *Reflexivity* refers to the capacity of the self to reflect upon itself as well as on the underlying systems that create it (Prell 1989, 251). Intersubjectivity can be defined as the shared perceptions and conceptions of the world held by interacting groups of people (Johnston et al. 1986, 236).

4. My use of "Hindi/Urdu" seeks to complicate the artificially created divide between Hindi and Urdu.

5. Interview with Farida (alias), Dar es Salaam, 7 October 1992.

6. Personal communication, 4 June 1993.

7. These faculty members included Professors Louis Mbughuni, Patricia Mbughuni, Marjorie Mbilinyi, Zubeida Tumbo, Issa Shivji, Suleiman Sumra, Muhsin Alidina, Adolpho Mascarenhas, Ophelia Mascarenhas, and Abdul Sheriff.

8. The shift from "I" to "she" is deliberate on the part of the author. Gloria Anzaldúa's (1987) work provides powerful tools to wrestle with this excerpt from Abbas (1993) and several other passages that I share in the original chapter of my dissertation, from which this sidebar is extracted.

9. Interviews with Shana Bajaj, 4 November 1992; Muhsin Alidina, 17 February 1993; Damji Rathod, 15 October 1992; Jasu Damji, 16 November 1992; Parin Jaffer, 27 January 1993; Vadan Majithia, 24 September 1992; Roshan Bai, 30 July 1993; Francis Fernandes, 10 December 1992.

10. Farida interview, 22 October 1992.

11. Nargis interview, 27 January 1993.

12. Farida interview, 22 October 1992.

13. Maria Pereira interview, 15 November 1992.

14. Immanuel interview, 1 July 1993.

15. Sujata Jaffer interview, 25 November 1992.

16. Damji Rathod interview, 23 January 1993.

17. Jasu Damji interview, 16 November 1992.

18. Sarla Rathod interview, 9 October 1992.

19. Julie Mohammed interview, 13 November 1992.

20. Ibid.

21. Muhsin Alidina interview, 15 January 1993.

22. Ibid. These concerns of the community leaders were expressed in *Federation Samachar* 25, no. 3 (July 1991): 23; Tabligh Report, in *Khoja Shia Ithna Asheri Jamaat, Dar es Salaam: Biennial Report, 1988–89*, 13.

23. Alidina interview, 15 January 1993.

24. The frequency with which Bollywood actors and singers are invited to Dar es Salaam can be gauged from the concerts that were held there between April and July 1993. In March, two Indian film stars, Govinda and Ayesha Zulka, were invited to Dar es Salaam for Eid celebrations. A private group called the Papla Trust organized concerts of pop-music singers from India and of ghazals and geets in April (*Daily News*, 6 April

1993), while another group invited several singers from India to perform all over Tanzania (*Daily News*, 26 April 1993). A Qawwali singer was invited from India in April and May (*Daily News*, 8 May 1993). Hindi movie stars from Bombay were invited to perform in the Best Dancing Stars Nite in the Diamond Jubilee Hall in June (*Daily News*, 16 June 1993). Another group of dancers and film singers was invited to perform at the Starlight Cinema for a week in July (*Daily News*, 21 July 1993). The popular English weekly, *The Express*, featured a permanent information plus gossip column on Hindi films, film stars, singers, and musicians to keep its readers informed of the latest developments in Bollywood.

25. Alidina interview, 15 January 1993.

26. Ibid.

27. Mohamedali Meghji, cited here, was president of the Supreme Council of the Federation of the Khoja Shia Ithna Asheri Jamaats of Africa.

28. Razia Tejani interview, 25 September 1992.

29. Ibid.; Razia JanMohamed interview, 27 September 1992.

30. *Federation Samachar* 24, no. 1 (September 1989): 29.

31. Muhsin Alidna interview, 15 January 1993.

32. Faizal interview, 4 October 1992.

Chapter 3. Reflexivity, Positionality, and Languages of Collaboration in Feminist Fieldwork

1. We recognize the problematic nature of homogenizing dichotomies such as western-nonwestern, first world–third world, and north-south. Here, we use these terms to refer to an unequal structure of knowledge production—rooted in post/colonial hierarchies—in which scholars based in resource-rich institutions of the north (wherever that north might be geographically located) continue to dominate the contexts in which knowledge about southern peoples and places is produced, circulated, consumed, and critiqued.

2. The second epigraph to this section is from H-NET's call for papers for "Acts of Knowledge: Collaborative Epistemologies and Economies of Thought," 5 November 1997.

3. For a discussion of discursive geographies, see Pratt (1999).

4. The original edition of *Sangtin Yatra* was self-published by Sangtin and went out of print within eight months. A revised edition was published by Rajkamal Prakashan, with the authors identifying as Sangtin Lekhak Samooh (2012).

Chapter 4. Representation, Accountability, and Collaborative Border Crossings

1. The two movements Dreze refers to are the Mazdoor Kisaan Shakti Sangathan and Akal Sangharsh Samiti.

2. Although I have interacted with activists and workers in nongovernmental organizations from various parts of South Asia, my most sustained work has been with NGO workers and activists in Uttar Pradesh.

3. Interview with Farah Ali (alias), Lucknow, 27 March 2002. Most of the names of people and places associated with Farah's life have been changed in the analysis I present here.

4. Ibid.

5. The U.S. Immigration and Naturalization Service (INS) has since been replaced by Immigration and Customs Enforcement (ICE).

6. *Chamars* are officially classified as a scheduled (formerly, "untouchable") caste, while *yadavs* are classified as members of the OBC or other backward castes. Hari (alias) belongs to the *yadav* caste. Maya is a *chamar*, and Kishan (alias), also a *chamar*, is Maya's husband's brother.

7. Notes from Mahasangh meeting, Mahila Samakhya program in Sitapur, 25 March 2002.

8. These women were seen as "founders" in the sense that they signed the registration papers for the organization, Sangtin, which had not yet undertaken any activities, but which was there to step in after Mahila Samakhya phased out from Sitapur.

9. The activities include writing, sharing, and collective reflection on journal entries over a period of several months, followed by recording, transcription, and editing, and interpretation of life-historical interviews of each member. For more details on how this process eventually unfolded, see my introduction in *Playing with Fire* (Nagar 2006a).

10. The English translation of this poem, titled "Chuppi" (silence or muteness) in Hindi, first undertaken by me in 2002, was revised by Elakshi Kumar in 2013. I thank Elakshi for this revision.

Chapter 5. Traveling and Crossing, Dreaming and Becoming

1. This chapter incorporates notes in Hindi that Richa Singh drafted in June 2005 for a coauthored chapter with Richa Nagar (Singh and Nagar 2006).

2. For many women living in Sitapur, the *mayaka* and *sasural* tend to be in separate villages, towns, or districts.

3. For detailed discussion of the collective process, see introduction and chapter 1 of *Playing with Fire* (Nagar 2006a, Sangtin Writers 2006).

4. For a discussion of inequalities in status, salaries, skills, and circuits of influence, their strategic deployments, and how these were negotiated within the collective, see Sangtin Writers (2006). An ongoing struggle with such power differentials has been a critical part of this journey.

5. This and the following translated excerpt from *Sangtin Yatra* appear in chapter 6 of *Playing with Fire* (Sangtin Writers 2006).

6. Since Surbala had already left MSS in 2000 to build Sangtin, she did not receive this communication.

7. Director of MSUP, letter 31 May 2004.

8. Gender trainers can be described as consultants, usually from urban centers, who are hired by NGOs to provide "gender training," in this case to rural women, who are educating or "sensitizing" others in their communities about gender issues (see also note about gender trainer in chapter 6).

9. Sangtin's new mission statement of 2006 stated: "Founded in 1998 by a group of local women in the Sitapur district in Uttar Pradesh, the organization, Sangtin, works for the sociopolitical and intellectual empowerment of rural women, youth and children and of the communities in which they are embedded.... [The] book *Sangtin Yatra* constituted a critical part of Sangtin's growth. *Sangtin Yatra* was fired by a desire to imagine how the organization Sangtin could become a true *sangtin* ... for the most marginalized women of Sitapur. Sangtin is committed to enhancing the ability of ... least powerful individuals and groups to challenge and change—in their favor—existing power relationships that place them in subordinate economic, social and political positions. At the same time, *Sangtin Yatra* has also inspired a vision that aims to empower the local communities intellectually by questioning the very idea of who is on the margins. ... Rather than thinking of marginalized communities as people who need to be connected with the mainstream, Sangtin wants to work towards getting rid of the structures that create the margins in the first place."

10. The introduction and chapter 6 contain details about what this emotional and intellectual labor entailed and about some of the insights that emerged from it.

11. Maya, who was active in the Mahila Samkhya Program, never participated in any writing activities of Sangtin Writers or of Sangtin Kisaan Mazdoor Sanagthan. However, her active participation in the movement building work from the very beginning made her inseparable from the journey of Sangtin.

12. Quoted in the second epigraph above, Mukesh Bhargava has worked closely with members of SKMS since the mid-1990s. This epigraph is from a longer poem, "Global Dunia," that Bhargava first wrote in the mid-1990s and later expanded in 2003 during the second U.S. invasion of Iraq.

13. Elakshi Kumar's incisive remarks have helped me to articulate my points in this chapter about desire, knowledge, and the meanings of the political.

14. Desiree Lewis's insightful comments on an earlier version of this chapter have helped me refine my ideas about language and power in SKMS's vision and work.

Chapter 6. Four Truths of Storytelling and Coauthorship in Feminist Alliance Work

1. For an elaboration on "power geometry," see Doreen Massey (1993).

2. "Gender trainer" here refers to a feminist expert or consultant. These trainers were often hired from women's organizations in the urban centers to provide "gender training" to women who were mobilizing other women in rural areas. The assumption guiding this practice is obvious: that rural women do not have a theory of gender to interpret the politics of gendered difference and have to be, therefore, schooled in this theory through consciousness-raising.

3. In the above diary excerpt, Surbala's reference to the removal of sindur and bangles as ideological exploitation is not simply a comment on the problem of hierarchization of knowledges and practices. She is also providing a critique of the imposition of certain kinds of ideological work (in this case by gender trainers) on subalternized others.

4. I translated this passage from a written version of Arun Trivedi's speech, cited by *Dainik Jagran* (Hindi Daily, Sitapur, 6 January 2012, 9). The epigraph above by Rajendra Singh is from a speech given at a meeting hosted in Washington, D.C., by the Maryland chapter of AID, 3 June 2004.

5. Recall that Richa Singh resigned from MS in protest of her transfer from Sitapur in 2004 and that Surbala had left her position in MS in 2000.

6. Discussions with Sofia Shank have helped me to refine my discussion of *Aag Lagi Hai Jangal Ma* here and elsewhere.

7. Anganwadi refers to a government-sponsored child-care and mother-care center. The Anganwadis were started by the Indian government in 1975 as part of the Integrated Child Development Services program to combat child hunger and malnutrition.

Glossary

aangan: courtyard
AID: Association for India's Development
AID-MN: Minnesota chapter of AID
auqat: rightful place
Awadhi: the language of Awadh, predominantly spoken in the rural areas of central
    and eastern Uttar Pradesh, including the districts of Bahraich, Barabanki, Faizabad,
    Gonda, Hardoi, Lakheempur, Lucknow, Raibareli, Sitapur, Sultanpur, and Unnao
Baa: my father's mother
BDO: block development officer
bevaqoof: idiot
Bhaiyya: brother
bidi: hand-rolled cigarette
bindi: dot worn on the forehead
cha bagan: tea plantation
chandlo: same as bindi
chautara: mixed, impure, or half-caste in common parlance
chhoti bahu: younger daughter-in-law
communal: pertaining to religious affiliation
Dadaji: my father's father
dala-dala: small bus
dalit: name embraced by members of scheduled castes in India
Dar: Dar es Salaam
dharna: sit-in, protest
dhaba: small roadside restaurant
dholak: drum
dupatta: long, wide scarf
ghoonghat: head and face cover
gutka: a mild stimulant made from betel nut and tobacco

hekadi: arrogance
jawaabdehi: accountability
juloos: procession
kem chho?: how are you?
kisaan: farmer
Kisaan Bahi: administrative land record that determines a peasant household's access
    to fertilizer
kumhar: potter
kunba: extended family
labada: cloak
langar: community kitchen where anyone can eat for free
leyi: homemade glue
Maa-Baap: parents
maatam: mourning, refers here to mourning during the month of Moharram
madrassa: school where pupils learn about Islam
majlis: refers here to a religious gathering
malik: boss, employer, owner
maraham: healing ointment
mazdoor: laborer
mayaka: natal home
mehfil: refers here to a religious gathering
MS: Mahila Samakhya, a national level program for the empowerment of women
MSS: Mahila Samakhya, Sitapur (district level branch of MS)
MSUP: Mahila Samakhya Uttar Pradesh (state headquarters of MS)
Muhindi: "Asian"
Mzungu: "European"
nahar: distributary channel
nalayaq: useless
Nani: my mother's mother
NGO: nongovernment organization
NREGA/NREGS: India's National Rural Employment Guarantee Act, which authorized
    India's National Rural Employment Guarantee Scheme
padyatra: march
Pradhan: elected head of the village council
rangmanch: theater
razai: quilt
saathi: companion, member of SKMS
saathiship: fellowship for activists given by AID
sahaj: easygoing
Sangathan: organization, refers here to SKMS
sangtin: Awadhi word for a woman who shares solidarity, reciprocity, and close com-
    panionship with another woman or with a group of women

Sangtin: the organization registered by sangtins in Sitapur, out of which SKMS emerged

sangtin yatra: the journey of sangtins, which began as a journey of nine women in Sitapur district in 2002 and evolved into SKMS

Sangtin Yatra: the title of a book in Hindi published in 2004 (Anupamlata et al., 2004); in the 2012 revised edition, the authors are identified as Sangtin Lekhak Samooh

sasural: conjugal home

sawarn: upper caste

Shi'i: Shia, Shitte

sindur: vermillion

SKMS: Sangtin Kisaan Mazdoor Sangathan (Sangtin peasants and laborers organization)

tabqa: class

tempo: small eight-seat bus

thelia: a manually pulled wooden cart used to haul goods and people

Wahindi: "Asians"

Waswahili: "Africans"

yatra: journey

References

Abbas, Nuzhat. 1993. "Post-colonialism, Migrancy and the Female Subject: A Story about Subject Construction." Paper presented at the Minnesota Midwestern Literature Association Conference, Minneapolis, November.

Abu-Lughod, Lila. 2001. "Orientalism and Middle East Feminist Studies." *Feminist Studies* 27 (1): 101–13.

———. 1998. "Introduction: Feminist Longings and Postcolonial Conditions." In *Remaking Women: Feminism and Modernity in the Middle East*, edited by Lila Abu-Lughod, 3–31. Princeton, N.J.: Princeton University Press.

———. 1993. *Writing Women's Worlds: Bedouin Stories*. Berkeley: University of California Press.

Ahmed, Sara. 2000. *Strange Encounters: Embodied Others in Post Coloniality*. London and New York: Routledge.

Alatas, Syed Farid. 2001. "The Study of the Social Sciences in Developing Societies: Towards an Adequate Conceptualization of Relevance." *Current Sociology* 49 (2): 1–19.

Alcoff, Linda Martín. 2011. "An Epistemology for the Next Revolution." *Transmodernity: Journal of Peripheral Cultural Production of the Luso-Hispanic World* (fall): 67–78.

Alexander, M. Jacqui. 2005. *Pedagogies of Crossing: Meditations on Feminism, Sexual Politics, Memory, and the Sacred*. Durham, N.C.: Duke University Press.

———, and Chandra Talpade Mohanty. 2010. "Cartographies of Knowledge and Power: Transnational Feminism as Radical Praxis." In Swarr and Nagar, *Critical Transnational Feminist Praxis*, 23–45.

Anupamlata, Ramsheela, Reshma Ansari, Vibha Bajpayee, Shashibala, Shashi Vaishya, Surbala, Richa Singh, and Richa Nagar. 2004. *Sangtin Yatra: Saat Zindgiyon Mein Lipta Nari Vimarsh*. Sitapur: Sangtin.

Anzaldúa, Gloria. 1987. *Borderlands/La Frontera: The New Mestiza*. San Francisco: Aunt Lute Books.

Appadurai, Arjun. 1988. "Introduction: Place and Voice in Anthropological Theory." *Cultural Anthropology* 3 (1): 16–20.

Armstrong, Elisabeth. 2004. "Globalization from Below: AIDWA, Foreign Funding, and Rendering Anti-Violence Campaigns." *Journal of Developing Societies* 20 (1–2): 39–55.

———. 2002. *The Retreat from Organization: U.S. Feminism Reconceptualized.* Albany: State University of New York Press.

Arondekar, Anjali. 2009. *For the Record: On Sexuality and the Colonial Archive in India.* Durham, N.C.: Duke University Press.

Barnett, Clive. 2008. "Political Affects in Public Space: Normative Blind-Spots in Non-Representational Ontologies." *Transactions of the Institute of British Geographers* 33: 186–200.

Beauvoir, Simone de. 1973. *The Second Sex.* New York: Vintage Press.

Behar, Ruth. 1993. *Translated Woman.* Boston: Beacon Press.

Bender, Thomas. 1998. "Scholarship, Local Life, and the Necessity of Worldliness." In *The Urban University and its Identity*, edited by Herman Van Der Wusten, 17–28. Boston: Kluwer Academic.

———. 1993. "The Cultures of Intellectual Life: The City and the Professions." In *Intellect and Public Life: Essays on the Social History of Academic Intellectuals in the United States*, edited by Thomas Bender, 3–15. Baltimore, Md.: Johns Hopkins University Press.

Bennett, Jane. 2008. "Editorial: Researching for Life: Paradigms and Power." *Feminist Africa* 11: 1–12.

Benson, Koni, and Richa Nagar. 2006. "Collaboration as Resistance? Reconsidering the Processes, Products, and Possibilities of Feminist Oral History and Ethnography." *Gender, Place and Culture* 13 (5): 581–92.

Berlant, Lauren. 2011. *Cruel Optimism.* Durham, N.C.: Duke University Press.

Bhargava, Mukesh. 2003. "Global Dunia." Unpublished poem received from author, 10 November 2013.

Bondi, Liz, et al. 2002. *Subjectivities, Knowledges, and Feminist Geographies: The Subjects and Ethics of Social Research.* Lanham, Md.: Rowman and Littlefield.

Butler, Judith. 1990. *Gender Trouble: Feminism and the Subversion of Identity.* New York: Routledge.

———. 1987. "Variations on Sex and Gender: Beauvoir, Witting, and Foucault." In *Feminism as Critique: Essays on the Politics of Gender in Late Capitalist Societies*, edited by Seyla Benhabib and Drucilla Cornell, 128–42. Minneapolis: University of Minnesota Press.

Callaway, Helen. 1992. "Ethnography and Experience: Gender Implications in Fieldwork and Texts." In *Anthropology and Autobiography*, edited by Judith Okley and Helen Callaway, 29–49. New York: Routledge.

Carroll, Berenice A. 1990. "The Politics of Originality: Women and the Class System of the Intellect." *Journal of Women's History* 2 (2): 136–63.

Chambers, Iain. 1994. *Migrancy, Culture, Identity.* London and New York: Routledge.

Chari, Sharad, and Henrike Donner. 2010. "Ethnographies of Activism: A Critical Introduction." *Cultural Dynamics* 22 (2): 75–85.

Chatterjee, Piya. 2011. "Dissident Feminisms." Book proposal submitted to the University of Illinois Press.

————. 2009. "Transforming Pedagogies: Imagining Internationalist/Feminist/Antiracist Literacies." In Sudbury and Okazawa-Ray, *Activist Scholarship*, 131–48.

Community Economies Collective and Katherine Gibson. 2009. "Building Community-based Social Enterprises in the Philippines: Diverse Development Pathways." In *The Social Economy: International Perspectives on Economic Solidarity*, edited by Ash Amin, 116–38. London: Zed Books.

Connolly-Shaffer, Patricia K. 2012. "Staging Cross-Border (Reading) Alliances: Feminist Polyvocal Testimonials at Work." PhD diss., University of Minnesota.

Da Costa, Dia. Under review. "The Good Women of Chharanager." In *Budhan Theatre*, edited by Dakxin Bajrange and Ganesh Devy, Baroda: Purva Prakashan.

Davies, Carole Boyce. 1994. *Black Women, Writing, and Identity: Migrations of the Subject.* New York: Routledge.

Dean, Jodi. 1998. "Feminist Solidarity, Reflective Solidarity." *Women and Politics* 18 (4): 1–26.

————. 1995. *Solidarity of Strangers: Feminism after Identity Politics.* Berkeley: University of California Press.

De Vault, Marjorie. 1999. *Liberating Method: Feminism and Social Research.* Philadelphia: Temple University Press.

Dhoomil. 1999. "Roti aur Sansad." In *Kal Sunana Mujhe*. New Delhi: Vani Prakashan.

di Leonardo, Micaela, and Roger N. Lancaster. 1997. "Introduction: Embodied Meanings, Carnal Practices." In *The Gender/Sexuality Reader: Culture, History, Political Economy*, edited by Roger N. Lancaster and Micaela di Leonardo, 1–10. New York: Routledge.

Dreze, Jean. 2002. "On Research and Action." *Economic and Political Weekly* 37 (9): 817–19.

Dutta, Aniruddha. 2013. "Globalizing through the Vernacular: Gender/Sexual Transnationalism and the Making of Sexual Minorities in Eastern India." PhD diss., University of Minnesota.

El Kilombo Intergaláctico. 2007. *Beyond Resistance Everything: An Interview with Subcomandante Insurgente Marcos.* Durham, N.C.: PaperBoat Press.

Faust, David, and Richa Nagar. 2001. "Politics of Development in Postcolonial India: English Medium Education and Social Fracturing." *Economic and Political Weekly* 36 (30): 2878–83.

Federation Samachar. English-language periodical of the World Federation of Khoja Shia Ithna-Asheri Muslim Communities. Dar es Salaam.

Frisch, M. 1990. *A Shared Authority: Essays on the Craft and Meaning of Oral and Public History.* Albany: State University of New York Press.

Geiger, Susan. 1997a. "Exploring Feminist Epistemologies and Methodologies through the Life-Histories of TANU Women." Paper presented at the Feminist Studies Colloquium, University of Minnesota, Twin Cities, April.

————. 1997b. *TANU Women: Gender and Culture in the Making of Tanganyikan Nationalism, 1955–1965.* Portsmouth, N.H.: Heinemann.

————. 1990. "What's So Feminist about Women's Oral History?" *Journal of Women's History* 2 (1): 169–82.

————. 1986. "Women's Life Histories: Method and Content." *Signs* 11 (21): 334–51.

Gibson-Graham, J. K., and Gerda Roelvink. 2011. "The Nitty Gritty of Creating Alternative Economies." *Social Alternatives* 30 (1): 29–33.

Gilmore, Ruth Wilson. 2008. "Forgotten Places and the Seeds of Grassroots Planning." In *Engaging Contradictions: Theory, Politics, and Methods of Activist Scholarship*, edited by Charles R. Hale, 31–61. Berkeley: Global, Area, and International Archive, University of California Press.

Gordon, Avery F. 2008. *Ghostly Matters: Haunting and the Sociological Imagination.* Minneapolis: University of Minnesota Press.

Gould, Deborah B. 2009. *Moving Politics: Emotion and ACT UP's Fight against AIDS.* Chicago and London: Chicago University Press.

Hall, Stuart. 1996. "The Problem of Ideology: Marxism Without Guarantees." In *Stuart Hall: Critical Dialogues in Cultural Studies*, edited by David Morley and Kuan-Hsing Chen, 25–46. New York: Routledge.

———. 1988. "The Toad in the Garden: Thatcherism Among the Theorists." In *Marxism and the Interpretation of Culture*, edited by Cary Nelson and Lawrence Grossberg, 35–73. Urbana: University of Illinois Press.

Hart, Gillian. 2002. *Disabling Globalization: Places of Power in Post-apartheid South Africa.* Berkeley: University of California Press.

Hemmings, Clare. 2011. *Why Stories Matter: The Political Grammar of Feminist Theory.* Durham, N.C.: Duke University Press.

Hertz, Rosanna. 1997. "Introduction: Reflexivity and Voice." In *Reflexivity and Voice*, edited by Rosanna Hertz, vii-xviii. Thousand Oaks, Calif.: Sage Publications.

Hulme, David, and Michael Edwards. 1997. "NGOs, States, and Donors: An Overview." In *NGOs, States, and Donors: Too Close For Comfort?*, edited by David Hulme and Michael Edwards, 3–22. London: Macmillan Press in association with Save the Children.

Jacka, Tamara. 1994. "Countering Voices: An Approach to Asian and Feminist Studies in the 1990s." *Women's Studies International Forum* 17 (6): 663–72.

John, Mary E. 1996. "Dalit Women in Western Ethnography." *Economic and Political Weekly* 31 (8): 463–64.

Johnston, Ron J., et al. 1986. *The Dictionary of Human Geography.* Oxford: Blackwell.

Kamat, Sangeeta. 2002. *Development Hegemony: NGOs and the State in India.* New Delhi: Oxford University Press.

Katyayani. 2006. *Footpath Par Kursi: Katyayani ki Kavitayen.* Lucknow: Parikalpana Prakashan.

Katz, Cindi. 2001. "On the Grounds of Globalization: A Topography for Feminist Political Engagement." *Signs* 26: 1213–34.

———. 1994. "Playing the Field." *Professional Geographer* 46 (1): 54–66.

Kawash, Samira. 1996. "The Autobiography of an Ex-Coloured Man: (Passing for) Black Passing for White." In *Passing and the Fictions of Identity*, edited by Elaine K. Ginsberg, 59–74. Durham, N.C.: Duke University Press.

Khoja Shia Ithna Asheri Jamaat. 1989 Dar es Salaam: Biennial Reports.

Khalfan, Mohammed. 1989. "Gujarati: A Common Language." *Federation Samachar* 24, no. 1.

Kumar, Krishna. 2004a. "Striyon ke Shabd." *Jan Satta* (Hindi daily, New Delhi), 11 July, 2.

———. 2004b. "Village Voices: Positive Trends in Education in UP." *Times of India* (English daily, New Delhi), 6 August. Downloaded 7 Aug 2004 from http://timesofindia.indiatimes.com/articleshow/804426.cms.

Kushawarti, Bandhu. 2004. "Saat Zindgiyon Mein Lipta Nari Vimarsh." *Aakhir Kab Tak* (Hindi monthly, Lucknow) (March): 25–26.

Lang, Sabine. 2000. "The NGO-ization of Feminism: Institutionalization and Institution Building within the German Women's Movement." In *Global Feminisms since 1945*, edited by Bonnie Smith, 290–304. New York: Routledge.

Larner, Wendy. 1995. "Theorising 'Difference' in Aotearoa/New Zealand." *Gender, Place and Culture* 2 (2): 177–90.

Lazreg, Marnia. 2002. "Development: Feminist Theory's Cul-de-sac." In *Feminist Post-Development Thought: Rethinking Modernity, Postcolonialism and Representation*, edited by Kriemild Saunders, 123–45. London: Zed Books.

Lowe, Lisa. 1991. "Heterogeneity, Hybridity, Multiplicity." *Diaspora* 1 (1): 24–44.

Mama, Amina. 2009. "Challenging Patriarchal Pedagogies by Strengthening Feminist Intellectual Work in African Universities." In Sudbury and Okazawa-Ray, *Activist Scholarship*, 55–72.

Marcus, G. E. 1992. "Commentary: 'More (Critically) Reflexive than Thou': The Current Identity Politics of Representation." *Environment and Planning D: Society and Space* 10: 489–93.

Massey, Doreen. 1993. "Power-Geometry and a Progressive Sense of Place." In *Mapping the Futures: Local Cultures, Global Change*, edited by J. Bird, B. Curtis, T. Putnam, G. Robertson, and L. Tickner, 59–69. London: Routledge.

———. 1992a. "A Place Called Home?" *New Formations* 17: 3–15.

———. 1992b. "Politics and Space/Time." *New Left Review* 196: 65–84.

Mbilinyi, Marjorie. 1989. "'I'd Have Been a Man': Politics and the Labor Process in Producing Personal Narratives." In Personal Narratives Group, *Interpreting Women's Lives*, 204–27.

McKittrick, Katherine. 2006. *Demonic Grounds: Black Women and the Cartographies of Struggle*. Minneapolis: University of Minnesota Press.

Meghji, Mohamedali. 1968. Preface. *The Elements of Islamic Studies*. 1st ed. Dar es Salaam: Bilal Muslim Mission of Tanzania.

Messer-Davidow, Ellen. 2002a. *Disciplining Feminism: From Social Activism to Academic Discourse*. Durham, N.C.: Duke University Press.

———. 2002b. "Feminist Studies and Social Activism." Paper presented at the Feminist Studies Colloquium Series, Department of Women's Studies, University of Minnesota, Minneapolis, 30 September.

Mignolo, Walter. 2000. *Local Histories/Global Designs: Coloniality, Subaltern Knowledges, and Border Thinking*. Princeton, N.J.: Princeton University Press.

Mirza, Sarah, and Margaret Strobel, eds. 1989. *Three Swahili Women: Life Histories from Mombasa, Kenya*. Bloomington: Indiana University Press.

Mohanty, Chandra Talpade. 2003. *Feminism without Borders: Decolonizing Theory, Practicing Solidarity*. Durham, N.C.: Duke University Press.

Mountz, Alison, Ines M. Miyares, Richard Wright, and Adrian J. Bailey. 2003. "Methodologically Becoming: Power, Knowledge and Team Research." *Gender, Place and Culture* 10 (1): 29–46.

Mwakitwange, Wilfrem R. 1993. "Indigenisation Is for Survival." *Business Times* (English daily), 15 January.

Nagar, Richa. 2013. Translation of and commentary on SKMS's play. "*Aag Lagi Hai Jangal Ma* (*The Jungle Is Burning*): Confronting State Corruption and Rural (Under) Development through Feminist Theatre." In *Gender, Space and Resistance: Women's Theatre in India*, edited by Anita Singh, 569–88. New Delhi: DK Printworld.

———. 2006a. "Introduction: Playing with Fire: A Collective Journey across Borders." In Sangtin Writers, *Playing with Fire*, xxi-xlvii.

———. 2006b. "Local and Global." In *Approaches to Human Geography*, edited by Stuart Aitken and Gill Valentine, 211–17. Thousand Oaks, Calif., and London: Sage.

———. 2006c. "Postscript: NGOs, Global Feminisms, and Collaborative Bordercross-ings." In Sangtin Writers, *Playing with Fire*, 132–55.

———. 2002. "Footloose Researchers, 'Traveling' Theories and the Politics of Transna-tional Feminist Praxis." *Gender, Place and Culture* 9 (2): 179–86.

———. 2000. "*Mujhe Jawab Do* (Answer Me!): Women's Grassroots Activism and Social Spaces in Chitrakoot (India)." *Gender, Place and Culture* 7 (4): 341–62.

———. 1997. "Exploring Methodological Borderlands through Oral Narratives." In *Thresholds in Feminist Geography*, edited by J. P. Jones III, H. J. Nast, and S. M. Rob-erts, 203–24. Lanham, Md.: Rowman & Littlefield.

———. 1995. "Making and Breaking Boundaries: Identity Politics among South Asians in Postcolonial Dar es Salaam." PhD diss., University of Minnesota.

Nagar, Richa, and Amanda Lock Swarr. 2010. "Theorizing Transnational Feminist Praxis." In Swarr and Nagar, *Critical Transnational Feminist Praxis*, 1–20.

———. 2004. "Organizing from the Margins: Grappling with 'Empowerment' in India and South Africa." In *A Companion to Feminist Geography*, edited by Lise Nelson and Joni Seagar, 291–304. Malden, Mass., and Oxford: Blackwell.

Nagar, Richa, and Richa Singh, with Surbala Vaish and Reena Pande. 2012. *Ek Aur Neemsaar: Sangtin Atmamanthan aur Andolan*. New Delhi: Rajkamal Prakashan.

Nagar, Richa, and Saraswati Raju. 2003. "Women, NGOs, and the Contradictions of Empowerment and Disempowerment: A Conversation." *Antipode* 35 (1): 1–13.

Naresh, Purva. 2012. *Ok, Tata, Bye-Bye*. Staged in Prithvi Theater, Mumbai, as part of Rage's Writer's Bloc-3, 15 January 2012, under the direction of Rabijita Gogoi.

Nast, Heidi. 1994. "Opening Remarks to 'Women in the Field,'" *Professional Geographer* 46 (1): 54–66.

Ngaiza, Magdalene, and Bertha Koda, eds. 1991. *The Unsung Heroines*. Dar es Salaam: Women's Research and Documentation Project.

Ngũgĩ wa Thiong'o. 1994. "The Language of African Literature." In *Colonial Discourse and Postcolonial Theory: A Reader*, edited by Patrick Williams and Laura Chrisman, 435–55. New York: Columbia University Press.

Nnaemeka, Obioma. 2004. "Nego-Feminism: Theorizing, Practicing and Pruning Africa's Way." *Signs* 29 (2): 357–85.

Notes from Nowhere, ed. 2003. *We Are Everywhere: The Irresistible Rise of Global Anti-capitalism.* London and New York: Verso.

Ong, Aihwa. 1995. "Women Out of China: Traveling Tales and Traveling Theories in Postcolonial Feminism." In *Women Writing Culture*, edited by Ruth Behar and Deborah Gordon, 350–72. Berkeley: University of California Press.

Ortner, Sherry B. 1995. "Resistance and the Problem of Ethnographic Refusal." *Society for Comparative Study of Society and History* 37 (1): 173–93.

Patai, Daphne. 1994. "Sick and Tired of Scholars' Nouveau Solipsism." *Chronicle of Higher Education* 40 (25): A52.

———. 1991. "U.S. Academics and Third World Women: Is Ethical Research Possible?" In *Women's Words: The Feminist Practice of Oral History*, edited by Sherna Berger Gluck and Daphne Patai, 137–53. New York: Routledge.

Peake, Linda, and D. Alissa Trotz. 2001. "Feminism and Feminist Issues in the South." In *The Companion to Development Studies*, edited by Vandana Desai and Robert B. Potter, 334–37. London: Arnold.

———. 1999. *Gender, Ethnicity and Place: Women and Identities in Guyana.* New York: Routledge.

Peake, Linda, and Audrey Kobayashi. 2002. "Policies and Practices for an Antiracist Geography at the Millennium." *Professional Geographer* 54 (1): 50–61.

Personal Narratives Group, ed. 1989. *Interpreting Women's Lives: Feminist Theory and Personal Narratives.* Bloomington: Indiana University Press.

Popular Memory Group. 1982. "Popular Memory: Theory, Politics, Method." In *Making Histories*, edited by Richard Johnson et al., 205–52. London: Hutchinson, in association with the Centre for Contemporary Cultural Studies, University of Birmingham.

Povinelli, Elizabeth A. 2006. *The Empire of Love: Toward a Theory of Intimacy, Genealogy, and Carnality.* Durham, N.C.: Duke University Press.

Pratt, Geraldine. 2012. *Families Apart: Migrant Mothers and the Conflicts of Labor and Love.* Minneapolis: University of Minnesota Press.

———. 2004. *Working Feminism.* Philadelphia: Temple University Press.

———. 2000. "Research Performances." *Environment and Planning D: Society and Space* 18: 639–51.

———. 1999. "From Registered Nurse to Registered Nanny: Discursive Geographies of Filipina Domestic Workers in Vancouver, BC." *Economic Geography* 75: 215–36.

———, and Victoria Rosner. 2012. "Introduction: The Global and the Intimate." In *The Global and the Intimate: Feminism in Our Time*, edited by Geraldine Pratt and Victoria Rosner, 1–27. New York: Columbia University Press.

Prell, Riv-Ellen. 1989. "The Double Frame of Life History in the Work of Barbara Myerhoff." In Personal Narratives Group, *Interpreting Women's Lives*, 241–58.

Pushpa, Maitreyi. 2004. "Baden Laanghti Striyan." *Rashtriya Sahara* (Hindi daily, New Delhi), 20 March, 9.

Radcliffe, S. A. 1994. "(Representing) Post-colonial Women: Authority, Difference and Feminisms." *Area* 26 (1): 25–32.

Raju, Saraswati. 2002. "We Are Different, But Can We Talk?" *Gender, Place and Culture* 9 (2): 173–77.

Red Thread. 2000. *Women Researching Women: Report on the methodology employed by Red Thread for surveys on domestic violence and women's reproductive and sexual health in Guyana as well as the results of these surveys.* Conducted by Red Thread Women's Development Programme, Georgetown, Guyana, in conjunction with Dr. Linda Peake, York University, Toronto.

Rege, Sharmila. 2010. "Education as Trutiya Ratna: Towards Phule-Ambedkarite Feminist Pedagogical Practice." *Economic and Political Weekly* 45 (44–45): 88–98.

Rosaldo, Renato. 1989. *Culture and Truth: The Remaking of Social Analysis.* Boston: Beacon Press.

Rose, Gillian. 1997. "Situating Knowledges: Positionality, Reflexivities and Other Tactics." *Progress in Human Geography* 21 (3): 305–20.

Roy, Arundhati. 2004. "Tide? Or Ivory Snow? Public Power in the Age of Empire." Speech, American Sociological Association Annual Meeting, San Francisco, 16 August. http://www.democracynow.org/2004/8/23/public_power_in_the_age_of, accessed 14 March 2014.

Sabea, Hanan. 2008. "Transnational What? Encounters and Reflections on Questions of Methodology." *Feminist Africa* 11 (December): 13–27.

Said, Edward W. 2002. "Opponents, Audiences, Constituencies and Communities." In *Reflections on Exile and Other Essays*, edited by Edward W. Said, 118–47. Cambridge, Mass.: Harvard University Press.

Sánchez-Casal, Susan, and Amie A. Macdonald. 2002. "Feminist Reflections on the Pedagogical Relevance of Identity." In *Twenty-First Century Feminist Classrooms: Pedagogies of Identity and Difference*, edited by Amie A. Macdonald and Susan Sánchez-Casal, 1–28. New York: Palgrave Macmillan.

Sandoval, Chela. 2000. *Methodology of the Oppressed.* Minneapolis: University of Minnesota Press.

Sangtin Kisaan Mazdoor Sangathan. 2011. *Aag Lagi Hai Jangal Maa (The Jungle Is Burning).* Street play in Awadhi and Hindi. *Hamara Safar* 6 (1).

Sangtin Lekhak Samooh (Anupamlata, Ramsheela, Reshma Ansari, Richa Nagar, Richa Singh, Shashibala, Shashi Vaishya, Surbala, and Vibha Bajpayee). 2012. *Sangtin Yatra: Saat Zindgiyon Mein Lipta Nari Vimarsh.* Rev. ed. New Delhi: Rajkamal Prakashan.

Sangtin Writers [and Richa Nagar]. 2006. *Playing with Fire: Feminist Thought and Activism through Seven Lives in India.* New Delhi: Zubaan Books and Minneapolis: University of Minnesota Press.

Scheman, Naomi. 2012. "Thinking Like a University: Toward Models of Sustainable Inquiry." Proposal for the Imagine Fund Arts, Design, and Humanities Chair, University of Minnesota.

———. 2011. *Shifting Ground: Knowledge and Reality, Transgression and Trustworthiness.* Oxford: Oxford University Press.

Scott, Joan W. 1991. "The Evidence of Experience." *Critical Inquiry* 17 (4): 773–97.

———. 1986. "Gender: A Useful Category of Historical Analysis." *American Historical Review* 91 (5): 1053–75.

Shank, Sofia, and Richa Nagar. 2013. "Retelling Stories, Resisting Dichotomies: Staging Identity, Marginalization and Activism in Minneapolis and Sitapur." In *Rethinking*

Feminist Interventions into the Urban, edited by Linda Peake and Martina Rieker, 90–107. Oxford: Routledge.

Sharpe, Jenny, and Gayatri Chakravorty Spivak. 2003. "A Conversation with Gayatri Chakravorty Spivak: Politics and the Imagination." *Signs* 28 (2): 609–24.

Sheriff, Ali H. 1991. "Language Perplexity in the West." *Federation Samachar* 26, no. 1 (November).

Shohat, Ella. 1996. "Notes on the Postcolonial." In *Contemporary Postcolonial Theory: A Reader*, edited by Padmini Mongia, 321–34. London: Arnold.

Singh, Richa, and Richa Nagar. 2006. "In the Aftermath of Critique: The Journey after *Sangtin Yatra*." In *Colonial and Postcolonial Geographies of India*, edited by Saraswati Raju, Satish Kumar, and Stuart Corbridge, 298–319. London: Sage.

Somers, Margaret. 1992. "Narrativity, Narrative Identity and Social Action." *Social Science History* 16 (4): 591–630.

Spivak, Gayatri Chakravorty. 2000a. "Discussion: An Afterword on the New Subaltern." In *Subaltern Studies XI: Community, Gender, and Violence*, edited by Partha Chatterjee and Pradeep Jeganthan, 305–34. Delhi: Permanent Black and New Delhi: Ravi Dayal Publishers,.

———. 2000b. "The Politics of Translation." In *The Translation Studies Reader*, 2nd ed., edited by Lawrence Venuti, 369–88. New York and London: Routledge.

———. 1994. "Responsibility." *Boundary 2* 21 (3): 19–64.

———. 1988. "Can the Subaltern Speak?" In *Marxism and the Interpretation of Culture*, edited by Cary Nelson and Lawrence Grossberg, 271–313. Urbana: University of Illinois Press.

Srivastava, Shikha. 2004. "Likhna, Aurat ki Zindagi!" *Hindustan, Adaab Lucknow* (Hindi daily, Lucknow), 1 April, 1.

Staeheli, Lynn, and Richa Nagar. 2002. "Feminists Talking across Worlds." *Gender, Place and Culture* 9 (2): 167–72.

Sudbury, Julia, and Margo Okazawa-Rey, eds. 2009a. *Activist Scholarship: Anti-racism, Feminism, and Social Change*. Boulder, Colo.: Paradigm Publishers.

———. 2009b. "Introduction: Activist Scholarship and the Neoliberal University after 9/11." In Sudbury and Okazawa-Ray, *Activist Scholarship*, 1–14.

Swarr, Amanda L., and Richa Nagar, eds. 2010. *Critical Transnational Feminist Praxis*. Albany: State University of New York Press.

———. 2004. "Dismantling Assumptions: Interrogating 'Lesbian' Struggles for Identity and Survival in India and South Africa." *Signs* 29 (2): 491–516.

Thompson, John. 1991. "Editor's Introduction." In *Pierre Bourdieu: Language and Symbolic Power*, edited by John Thompson, 1–31. Cambridge, Mass.: Harvard University Press.

Tinsely, Omise'eke Natasha, Ananya Chatterjea, Hui Niu Wilcox, and Shannon Gibney. 2010. "So Much to Remind Us We Are Dancing on Other People's Blood: Moving Toward Artistic Excellence, Moving from Silence to Speech, Moving in Water, with Ananya Dance Theatre." In Swarr and Nagar, *Critical Transnational Feminist Praxis*, 147–65.

Trivedi, Arun. 2012. "Ek Aur Neemsaar." Speech, Maya Chaudhari Memorial Event and book launch of *Ek Aur Neemsaar*, Sitapur, 5 January.

Verma, Lal Bahadur. 2004. "Tootte Pinjare, Naye Asman." *Vagarth* (Hindi monthly, Kolkata), November, 24–26.

Visweswaran, Kamala. 2011. "Conclusion: Fragile Facts on Scholarship and Activism." *Cultural Dynamics* 23 (1): 73–79.

———. 1994. *Fictions of Feminist Ethnography.* Minneapolis: University of Minnesota Press.

Watts, Michael J. 1992. "Space for Everything." *Cultural Anthropology* 7 (1): 115–29.

Williams, Patrick, and Laura Chrisman. 1994. "Introduction: Theorising Post-coloniality: Discourse and Identity." In *Colonial Discourse and Postcolonial Theory: A Reader*, edited by Patrick Williams and Laura Chrisman, 373–75. New York: Columbia University Press.

Wolf, Diane L. 1997. "Situating Feminist Dilemmas in Fieldwork." In *Feminist Dilemmas in Fieldwork*, edited by Diane L. Wolf, 1–55. Boulder, Colo.: Westview.

Index

All India Muslim Personal Law Board,
   113, 114
Altınay, Ayşe Gül, 44–45
Aminzade, Ron, 31
Ananya Dance Theatre, 167–168
anecdotes, 2, 13, 22
Anganwadis, 190n7
Ansari, Reshma, 102, 126, 129, 133, 171
anti-disciplinary feminist scholarship, 89
Anupamlata, 102, 116, 126, 129, 133, 171
Aotearoa/New Zealand, 88
Appadurai, Arjun, 86
Armstrong, Elisabeth, 162
Asians, 31, 33, 35, 50, 69, 100; attitudes to-
   ward Africans, 63–64; identity among,
   65–66; identity politics in postcolonial
   Tanzania, 52–53; and language in Dar
   es Salaam, 51, 58; normative and racial-
   ized categories, 54, 83; segregation of,
   55–56, 71–76; sex workers, 68; stereo-
   typing of, 61–62, 65. *See also* Dar es
   Salaam; South Asian communities in
   Dar es Salaam, Tanzania
Aslan, Özlem, 42
Association for India's Development
   (AID-MN), 136, 137, 139, 141, 147
Association of American Geographers
   (AAG), 163
Ateşle Oynamak, 45
authenticity, 9, 10, 12, 14, 83, 93–95, 138
authorship, 96–97, 120–121; and autho-
   rizing, 172; claims, 139; of struggles,
   170–172
autobiography, 15, 102, 117, 171
Avadh College, 27
Awadhi, 21, 26, 27, 137, 139, 176

Baba, 25, 30–34, 185n9
Babri Masjid, 33
backlash, 35, 102, 129–130, 136–137, 146,
   148
backstaging of political conversations,
   172–173
Bajpayee, Vibha, 102, 116, 126, 129, 133, 171
Behar, Ruth, 55
Bender, Thomas, 100
Beyond Resistance Everything, 1

Bhargava, Mukesh, 145, 189n12
Bhartiya Janata Party, 33
Boatman and the Pundit, The, 6–7, 182
body/bodies, 13, 15, 17, 38, 40–43, 64–66,
   119, 184n8; mobility and, 47; and violence, 116, 131, 155
Bora, Aksu, 44–45
border crossings, 5–6, 8–12, 18–20,
   107; collaboration and, 101, 107–108,
   111–115, 120–123; as geographies of
   engagement, 120–121; interrogating
   "relevance" with, 105–108; from partial
   knowledges to collaborative, 108–110;
   producing a methodology to *speak
   with* the Sangtin Collective, 115–118;
   as responsibility in the context of an
   encounter, 110–115; with situated solidarities, 85–89; through and beyond
   Sangtin Yatra, 125–129; in translation,
   111–118, 121–123; transnational border
   crossings as dialogues, 108
borders, 18–20, 108; academia-activism,
   2; alliances and coauthorship across,
   21, 22, 36, 125–140, 170, 174; collabora-
   tion/ collaborative journeys across,
   38, 98, 101, 107, 108; geographical,
   sociopolitical, cultural, linguistic and
   institutional, 15, 18, 20, 22, 37, 90, 100;
   north-south, 15; resonance across, 20;
   telling stories across, 26, 47; translations across, 15
Boulder, 34
Bundeli: activists, 95; women, 91
Bundelkhand, 91, 97

Cape Town, South Africa, 22, 46–49
Carroll, Berenice A., 160
castes/ casteism, 102, 103, 127, 130, 132,
   136, 142; intersections with race and
   language in Dar es Salaam, 71–76; Mahila Samakhya program and, 116–117;
   and racial otherness, 8–10; scheduled
   castes, 116; untouchability and, 28, 41,
   43, 117, 131–132, 142, 185n10, 185n13
categories: normative, 54; problematizing, 2–3, 37, 52–57, 65, 83–84, 94, 108
Chambers, Iain, 70

"Reflexivity, Positionality, and Identity in Feminist Fieldwork: Beyond the Impasse," 36
"Reflexivity, Positionality, and Languages of Collaboration in Feminist Fieldwork," 17–19
Rege, Sharmila, 160, 163, 169
relationality, 5, 35, 51, 55, 80, 84; critical, 5
relationships, 15, 17, 20, 52, 58, 60; collaborative, 107, 115; in Dar es Salaam, 51; ethical, 82; family, 31, 111; identity and, 53; power in fieldwork, 85, 93; social, 66–70; social boundaries and, 55
relevance, 12, 35, 43, 80, 85, 93, 105–108
religion, 15, 33, 52, 73, 79, 84, 111; NGO activism and, 102, 131, 132; politicized, 120; problematizing categories of, 54; social boundaries and, 55, 56; stereotyping and, 61, 71
representation, 169–173; claims about, 94; crisis of, 82; injunction to represent, 110; messiness of, 159; question of, 20; self-representation and self-determination, 120; task of, 170
"Representation, Accountability, and Collaborative Border Crossings: Moving Beyond Positionality," 18–19
researcher: as object of study, 16
research performances, 108–109
research praxis, 55–56. *See also* feminist research
responsibility, 1–6, 15, 19, 46, 87, 89, 95, 110, 152, 171, 173, 178, 183n1; and representation, 47, 115; and *Sangtin Yatra*, 126; and translation, 45
"Responsibility," 1
Rich, Adrienne, 25–26
right to information, 7
right to theorize, 161
risks, 14, 23, 38, 42, 46, 139; of coauthorship, 163; economic and social, 103, 155; political, 89; of solidarities, 2
Rose, Gillian, 84, 108
Rushdie, Salman, 30, 35
Russian, 28, 49

Sabea, Hanan, 11
Said, Edward W., 98, 135

Sánchez-Casal, Susan, 173
Sandoval, Chela, 5
Sangtin Kisaan Mazdoor Sangathan (SKMS), 7, 9–10, 15, 21, 27, 124, 175–176; *Aag Lagi Hai*, 176–182; climate change and, 46–47; collective struggles and, 38–39; focus of, 142–144, 189n9; membership, 183n6; representation by, 170–171; response to murders, 151–155; scribe of, 42–43; script on, 27; segregation between men and women in, 10–11
Sangtin, 189n9; women's collective, 18
sangtins, 7; Collective, 110; producing a methodology to "speak with" the, 115–118
Sangtin Samooh, 18
Sangtin Writers, 6–7, 9, 44–45, 138; critique, coauthorship, and translations in journey with, 101–104
Sangtin Yatra, 7, 9, 10, 16, 20–21, 28, 45, 125, 189n9; Association of American Geographers meeting and, 163–164; backlash against, 129–130, 136, 141; border crossings through and beyond, 125–129; changing focus of, 142; collective struggles, 38; collective work and, 102–103; knowledge as dialogue and, 140–141; origins, 126; praise for, 133–134; representation and, 171; specifying and translating the politics of knowledge production, 129–138; struggle for survival, 138–140; support for, 134–136, 139; theory as praxis in, 140–144
Sarvesh, 155–156
sawarn: 9, 28, 48; -dalit dichotomy, 171
Scheman, Naomi, 3, 174
Scholarship: activist, 2–6; as journey, 51
segregation: caste, 8–9, 43; gender, 10–11, 97; racial, 71–6, 91
self-reflexivity, 17–18, 37, 39, 84, 90
sexual practices, 33, 62, 82, 100
Seychellois, 75
Shalala, Donna, 105
Shank, Sofia, 13
sharing as translation, 46
Shashibala, 102, 126, 129, 133, 171

Richa Nagar is a professor of gender, women, and sexuality studies at the University of Minnesota and co-author of *Playing with Fire: Feminist Thought and Activism through Seven Lives in India.*

Dissident Feminisms

The University of Illinois Press
is a founding member of the
Association of American University Presses.

———————————————————
 ·

University of Illinois Press
1325 South Oak Street
Champaign, IL 61820-6903
www.press.uillinois.edu